D1453221

Josie Underwood's Civil War Diary

Josie Underwood's Civil War Diary

✥ ✥

Edited by Nancy Disher Baird

✥ ✥

Foreword by Catherine Coke Shick

THE UNIVERSITY PRESS OF KENTUCKY

Copyright © 2009 by Nancy Disher Baird and Catherine Coke Shick

Scholarly publisher for the Commonwealth,
serving Bellarmine University, Berea College, Centre College of Kentucky, Eastern
Kentucky University, The Filson Historical Society, Georgetown College, Kentucky
Historical Society, Kentucky State University, Morehead State University, Murray
State University, Northern Kentucky University, Transylvania University, University
of Kentucky, University of Louisville, and Western Kentucky University.
All rights reserved.

Editorial and Sales Offices: The University Press of Kentucky
663 South Limestone Street, Lexington, Kentucky 40508-4008
www.kentuckypress.com

13 12 11 10 09   5 4 3 2 1

Library of Congress Cataloging-in-Publication Data

Underwood, Josie, 1840-1923.
  Josie Underwood's Civil War diary / edited by Nancy Disher Baird ; foreword by
Catherine Coke Shick.
     p. cm.
  Includes bibliographical references and index.
  ISBN 978-0-8131-2531-2 (hardcover : alk. paper)
  1. Underwood, Josie, 1840–1923—Diaries. 2. Women—Kentucky—Bowling
Green—Diaries. 3. Unionists (United States Civil War)—Kentucky—Bowling
Green—Diaries. 4. Bowling Green (Ky.)—History, Military—19th century.
5. Bowling Green (Ky.)—Social life and customs—19th century. 6. Bowling
Green (Ky.)—Biography. 7. Kentucky—History—Civil War, 1861–1865—Personal
narratives. 8. United States—History—Civil War, 1861–1865—Personal narratives.
I. Baird, Nancy Disher. II. Title.
  F459.B7U53 2009
  976.9'7403092—dc22   2008049856

This book is printed on acid-free recycled paper meeting
the requirements of the American National Standard
for Permanence in Paper for Printed Library Materials.

Manufactured in the United States of America.

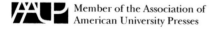

Member of the Association of
American University Presses

For
William Gaston Coke Jr.
Lowell H. Harrison
and
Linda and Howard Surface

Many, many thanks!

CONTENTS

Illustrations follow page 98

FOREWORD

During the 1960s, I was raised at McCutchen Meadows, a dairy farm just outside of Auburn, Kentucky, which is approximately fifteen miles west of Bowling Green. The farm was a land grant awarded to my great great great great grandfather, John McCutchen, for his service during the War of Independence, when he was a private in Colonel John Gibson's company of the 9th Virginia Regiment and fought at the Battle of King's Mountain in October 1780. I grew up in this place steeped in history, and consequently, I've always been interested in the stories of our extended family. My immediate family relocated to Nashville, Tennessee, in 1966, and in the late 1970s I went away to school. My grandfather William Gaston Coke continued to work the dairy farm until his death. Unfortunately, at that time my father decided that maintaining it was too burdensome, and the farm was sold at auction in 1980. Although the Kentucky home of my childhood was no longer in our family, and although I lived and worked elsewhere for many years, my heart and my thoughts were never far from south central Kentucky. Several years ago, I was living in Los Angeles when my son was born. That event rekindled my interest in the histories of my and my husband's families, and I began to work on genealogies of both.

My aunt Esther Coke knew of my interest in the many branches of my family and decided to send me a copy of

Josie's diary from the Underwood side of my ancestry. It captured my imagination immediately. I was thrilled to read an impassioned first-person account of youthful experiences during the early part of the Civil War, written by a member of my distant family. Her voice was clear, her personality strong, and her chronicle vivid. The immediacy of her writing affected me and drew me into her world. The detail with which she expressed herself made me visualize her surroundings, made me hear the passionate and divergent beliefs of her family and friends, and made me empathize with the personal pains of war and loss. I was struck by the love that she felt for members of her family with whom she completely disagreed and the sincerity of her dueling emotions as events unfolded. It was a Civil War diary like none I had ever read before.

At the time, I believed it was important for the diary to be published for two reasons. One, I hoped that others would have a similar experience in reading the work. And two, I thought that as an historical document, this diary about life in south central Kentucky during the Civil War was unique.

With my husband's assistance, we attempted to trace the long, mysterious journey the diary must have taken over the years. What we knew was that a manually typed, Xeroxed copy of the diary arrived at Christ Episcopal Church in Bowling Green in 1976; it had been sent from the dead letter division of the Atlanta post office. It was sent to Christ Church because there was a copy of Josie Underwood Nazro's marriage certificate with the diary. She had married Charles A. Nazro in the church on the 26th of October 1870. Christ Episcopal Church subsequently turned it over to Western Kentucky University because there was a large Underwood collection in their Kentucky Library Manuscript Division. That leg of the journey was indeed unusual, but the larger questions of who typed the diary, where it was sent from, and how it arrived at the dead letter division of the Atlanta post office continue to remain a mystery. There was also the not insignificant issue of the legal ownership of the diary.

As I discussed these issues with my aunt and my father, they revealed that they had been searching for the original handwritten diary off and on for some years. They had searched in other parts of the country where family members had relocated, from New York to California, but the original was never found.

With this information, my husband and I decided that to protect the integrity of the diary we needed to establish ownership of the copyright. Ownership of the copyright is the necessary prerequisite to obtaining the right to publish. If we could not establish the ownership of the copyright, the diary would fall into the public domain, allowing anyone the right to publish all or any part of the diary for their own purposes. We thought it was important that the diary not be altered or disembodied, but that it should be read and appreciated as written, with only contextual, historical information added for clarity. In order to do this, we knew we had to determine the chain of events that the diary took after the death of Josie.

In her last will and testament, entered into the court record in Warren County, Kentucky, in the July 1924 term, Josie Underwood Nazro names her granddaughter, Joanna, as recipient of the diary. Joanna in turn, bequeathed her entire estate to her husband, Joseph Mullen, when she died in September 1963. In 1974, Joseph Mullen left the residue and remainder of his estate, which included the diary, split evenly between Rice University and the Sloan-Kettering Institute for Cancer Research.

We contacted both institutions. Sloan-Kettering had no material objects from Joseph Mullen's estate, and renounced any rights it may have had to the diary. Rice University did have material objects from the estate, and graciously assigned to me its rights in the diary. With this documentation, I obtained ownership of the copyright, and prevented the diary from falling into the public domain.

When my husband, son, and I relocated to Nashville in 2000, I was aware that Nancy Baird was interested in publishing the diary with her commentary, and that she had some interest from the University Press of Kentucky in her doing so. For a variety of reasons we could not effectively collaborate, as we were unable to communicate directly to discuss her research and writing. I continued my work on the diary and worked on a variety of other projects, and time passed. Around mid-2006, I was contacted by Western Kentucky University's attorney, and discussions began as to the possibilities and problems with moving forward toward publication. After much review and revision, I am satisfied that the completed work allows Josie's voice to be heard clearly, with all the passion and empathy that she possessed.

I appreciate the determination and commitment of both Nancy Baird and the University Press of Kentucky in bringing the Josie Underwood diary to the public. I strongly believe that it constitutes a valuable contribution to the study of the early years of the Civil War in south central Kentucky.

Catherine Coke Shick

PREFACE

Mystery surrounds the Civil War diary kept by Josie Underwood. On her death in 1923 the diarist left the two-volume journal to her eighteen-year-old granddaughter, Joanna, then living in Texas. Joanna later married a widower, interior decorator Joseph Mullen; the couple, who remained childless, lived most of their married years in New York. Joanna died in 1963, and shortly thereafter Joseph gave a monetary gift to the Hammond Museum in North Salem, New York, to honor her memory. His gift did not include any correspondence, diaries, or other historical materials. Joseph died in 1974, and those who settled his estate found no personal papers of any kind related to the Civil War.

Meanwhile, in the late 1940s, descendants of the Underwood family in Bowling Green gave a large collection of family papers to the Kentucky Library (Special Collections) at Western Kentucky University. The gift included an account kept by the diarist's father, Warner Underwood, during his 1830s trip to Texas, a typescript of a brief diary he wrote during the 1850s, his 1862 passport, the diary Josie's brother penned in Scotland, and a few postwar family letters. The largest portion of the collection consists of correspondence and other items from the family of Josie's uncle, Joseph Underwood, including about 360 letters written between 1849 and 1853 during his term in the U.S. Senate. The collection contained only one letter from the Civil War era.

In 1976, the Rev. Howard Surface, rector of Christ Episcopal Church in Bowling Green, received from the dead letter office in Atlanta a 167-page photocopy of a typescript of Josie's journals, sent to him because a copy of her marriage certificate was attached. Assuming that a member of the library faculty had mailed it, he brought the package to the Kentucky Library. Its receipt reminded one of the librarians of a rumor that when the large Underwood Collection came to the library nearly three decades earlier, someone decided not to include the Civil War diary. Passions and hatreds generated by the war and its aftermath still lingered and in some cases were quite strong in the community. Concern apparently existed that descendants of those criticized by Josie's sharp pen as "contemptible," or "a traitor," or other unflattering labels might be offended. (Three grandsons of Josie's friend Lizzie Wright held prominent positions in town, and their family-conscious aunt was a member of the library staff.) However, a thorough check of the correspondence file between the donors and librarians (all deceased by the 1970s) found no mention of a Civil War diary. Furthermore, years of concerted efforts by the library staff and members of the Underwood family, many of whom had heard of the famed diary but had never seen it, have located neither the original handwritten diary nor the original typescript.

What was the fate of the original diary? Why was it typed? Perhaps it had deteriorated so badly as to be nearly illegible. Or maybe Josie's handwriting was difficult to read, for her postwar script challenges its readers. Did someone attempt to create a more readable, typed copy and then destroy the original? What happened to the original typed copy? Who mailed the copy that the dead letter office forwarded? To whom had it been sent? Despite considerable detective work, no answers have surfaced.

The editor and others have carefully considered the authenticity of the diary. Could it be a fake, written by someone well versed in Civil War history? Anything is possible. However, the diary's author possessed an intimate familiarity with the Underwood family, considerable knowledge about local folks, and a personal connection to the events that occurred between December 1860 and September 1862—details that would be difficult (but not impossible) for another to know. In addition, Josie wrote about some of the events of the Civil War in Bowling Green's *Daily News* a few years before her death. Her published overview of the Civil War did not echo the diary's wording or include family information, but it did give a two-thousand-word account of the town's experiences during the Confederate occupation and the arrival in Bowling Green of Union forces—events described in the journal that Josie willed to her granddaughter. In addition, several decades before the diary came to the library, descendants of Josie's siblings had heard about it. History is filled with mysteries. The diary of Josie Underwood is one of them.

In preparing the diary for publication, all events mentioned it its pages have been checked against the large collection of Civil War letters, diaries, official records, and other primary materials available to researchers in the Kentucky Library. All appear to be historically accurate, yet some may have been added after the event. Did Josie elaborate the details of a few incidents years later? The story of the surrender of the Baton Rouge Arsenal, for example, is discussed several days before it happened, and other accounts of the surrender do not mention her aunt's majestic, eye-catching retreat. Josie also told of B. F. Terry's death nearly three months before he died and reported several other events long after they happened. Can these discrepancies be explained by slow communications and details being added months later?

Without her original journals, it is impossible to determine what was added or if and where the transcriber mistyped dates or names. Nevertheless, the writing style of the diary—the run-on sentences and use of affectations, appellations, and abundant dashes—is similar to the several surviving letters Josie wrote during the postwar period. The typescript also includes one handwritten page that may have been photocopied from the original diary; the script matches letters penned by Josie in the 1880s.

The diary was copied with a manual typewriter. Apparently the typist was unfamiliar with the names of the immediate family members and members of the community and, perhaps unable to read Josie's handwriting, constantly misspelled them. For example, the name of Josie's brother-in-law Benjamin Grider is mistyped "Girder" throughout the diary. Likewise, her cousin Marius Henry is Marions. Norton is mistyped Morton, Loving appears as Loring, Magoffin is typed McGoffin, Rousseau is Reasseau, and so on. It is doubtful that Josie, an area resident, or a student of the Civil War would have made these errors.

For the reader's ease, the editor has assumed that the misspelled names and obvious typographical errors are the fault of the transcriber and has corrected them. However, the abundance of dashes, so characteristic of the era and of the diarist's writing style, remain. The editor has also divided the diary into chapters and provided each with a brief introductory paragraph. Beyond these few changes and the movement of a couple poems to an endnote, the typescript diary is presented in its entirety.

Josie identified most members of her family when she mentioned them—sister Jupe, cousin Jane Todd, and Uncle Gus Henry, etc. First names have been supplied, when known, for those she merely mentioned as Mrs., Mr., or by military rank. A brief "Who's Who" has been included as an appendix to help with the identification of family members, area residents, and others who play an important role in the diary. Unfortunately, many persons could not be identified.

For his interest in and encouragement of this project and his endeavors to solve the mystery of the missing original diary, I am deeply indebted to William Gaston Coke Jr., Josie's ever-so-great nephew and the grandson of her brother Henry. Bill visited and canvassed distant relatives in his quest to locate or learn about the handwritten journals. Unfortunately, none seemed to have knowledge of them or possessed a copy in any form.

I also appreciate Dr. Lowell H. Harrison's interest and suggestions concerning how to introduce this fascinating diary. Dr. Harrison has been a loyal mentor and advisor as well as a special friend to me and to hundreds of other students of history during his lengthy teaching and writing career. From all of us, many thanks!

History professors Carol Crowe Carraco, Helen Bartter Crocker, Thomas H. Appleton Jr., Glenn W. LaFantasie, and Charles P. Roland also deserve bouquets for reading the manuscript and making suggestions that improved it. Catherine Coke Shick has my gratitude for her support and for providing family genealogical information. This monograph, like most published endeavors, results from the encouragement, support, advice, and expertise of family, friends, colleagues, editors, designers, marketing experts, and a variety of other "bookmakers" whose talents and hard work are essential to producing a good volume. To all, many thanks!

The typescript of Josie Underwood's diary, a gift from the postal service, is housed in the Kentucky Library at Western Kentucky University, and for three decades it has fascinated students of history. Most Civil War diaries chronicle military activities and the hardships of army life. Josie's journal documents the trials experienced by a town and its civilians caught in the war's wake. Despite the diary's mysterious provenance, it is a vivid account of Kentucky's traumatic times when, to paraphrase Josie, the Philistines were upon us.

☙ *INTRODUCTION* ❧

THE PHILISTINES ARE UPON US

Today I was mad enough to knock a little upstart of an
officer down. He came up to me with a smirk and said,
"Miss Underwood—I heard of the incident at the depot
[she had purchased food for hungry Confederate POWs]
. . . and *as a friend* I would advise you to be careful of
giving aid and comfort to Rebels." I replied in a flash—
"When I wish advice I will seek it of *my friends*. Pardon
me for not thanking you for yours." Aid and comfort to
rebels indeed—poor hungry prisoners.

—June 22, 1862

The 1860–1862 diary of Kentucky Unionist Johanna Louisa
(Josie) Underwood provides a unique and intimate look at
the emotional question of secession and the trauma visited
on a family, community, and state torn asunder by civil war.
Well-read, observant, knowledgeable, and outspoken, Josie
often wrote acerbic comments that painted with great clarity
the frustrations, deprivations, and heartaches of a conflict
pitting brother against brother and father against son. She
related the hardships suffered by civilians during occupation, first by the Confederate Army and then by the Union,

and the risks taken by those who spoke out against either. She even hinted at the bitterness that would linger beyond the war years. The initial invaders of her peaceful town in south central Kentucky, Josie labeled "Philistines." Most civilians would soon view whoever camped in the area as unwelcome trespassers and comrades of Goliath.

Little is known about Josie Underwood except what appears in her journal. Born in November 1840 and raised in Bowling Green, she probably received most of her early education at one of the town's private schools and spent at least one session at an academy in the District of Columbia, as had one of her sisters and a couple of cousins. She completed her formal schooling in the spring of 1860 at the Russellville Female Institute, an academy of local note. One of her teachers praised her as an "ideal pupil" who possessed an "ardor to learn."[1]

Fresh from the classroom, in many ways Josie was a typical southern belle for whom life promised to be a grand affair. Intelligent, well-educated, and apparently attractive (unfortunately, there are no known pictures of her), this vivacious daughter of a locally important family attracted a host of young gentlemen who escorted her to parties, dances, and the theater. She received flattering proposals and might have married any one of a number of prominent Southern gallants. However, current events rather than romance ruled the interests of the twenty-year-old. Young ladies of her day were not supposed to clutter their minds with politics or take part in heated discussions about what many considered a man's sphere. But Josie did. She tried to abide by society's rules and exhibit proper decorum, yet the political environment and the realities of the times directed her life, as well as that of her family.

Josie lived with her parents, Lucy and Warner Lewis Underwood, and younger siblings on a large farm on the northeastern fringe of Bowling Green, Kentucky, a river port of about 2,500 residents and the seat of Warren County (population 17,300). Founded in the last days of the eighteenth century, the community had become an important commercial center to which area farmers brought their goods, especially hams, tobacco, and corn, to ship by river and rail to distant markets on the Ohio and Mississippi rivers. By the eve of the Civil War the prosperous town was the largest between Louisville, Kentucky, and Nashville, Tennessee. Its residents could brag of a couple of fine private schools, several attractive hotels and churches, many employment opportunities, and a wide variety of shops offering goods produced in manufacturing centers across the nation.

Warner Underwood came to Bowling Green from his native Virginia as a teenager, studied law with his older brother Joseph, completed his studies at the University of Virginia, and in 1830 returned to south central Kentucky and opened a law practice. A year later, in the parlor of a small hotel on the town square, Warner married fifteen-year-old Lucy Craig Henry, daughter of an engineer on the Green-Barren River improvement project. Josie was the fourth of their eight children who survived infancy. During the early years of their marriage Warner made several visits to Texas and served as land agent for immigrants bound for the American colony along the Brazos River. He flirted with the idea of moving his family to the Southwest, but unrest, culminating in the Texas Revolution, changed his mind.

Warner and Lucy purchased Mount Air, their home and farm, the year before Josie's birth. Supervised by a white overseer, slaves tilled the land and cared for the stock. The 1860 census taker estimated the family's real property was worth $60,000; personal property, including twenty-eight slaves (ten were children ten years old and under), he valued at about $45,000. The Underwoods were thus among the community's wealthiest residents.

3

Mount Air typified gracious living. Josie's mother furnished the family's two-story brick home in an "elegant" style, and when entertaining guests the family utilized the first-floor parlor and dining room; the wide hallway on the second floor doubled as a ballroom. Extant records do not describe get-togethers with family and friends during the autumn of 1860, but one can assume that the nucleus of any gathering included Josie and her four younger siblings—Warner (fourteen), Henry (twelve), John (six), and Mary (three)—as well as the family of her sister and brother-in-law, Frances (Fanny) and Benjamin Grider and their children, Warner and Judge Loving. Two other sisters and their families, Juliette (Jupe) and William Western and Lucy (Lute) and Ferdinand McCann and their children, Pearl and Underwood, resided out-of-state. In addition, Mrs. Underwood's orphaned niece and nephew, ten-year-old Corrine (Lady) and twelve-year-old Marius, sometimes lived with them. A family friend described the Underwoods as "elegant, liberal and refined" and noted that "if happy they enjoyed it and if in trouble they share it together."[2]

Raised in the midst of her large and loving family, Josie became well schooled in the events and questions of the day, for her father was active in politics and apparently freely shared his ideas and opinions with his family. Warner Underwood served as a Whig representative in the state legislature from 1848 to 1853, and in 1855 and 1857 was elected as a member of the American Party (formerly the "Know Nothing" Party) to the U.S. House of Representatives. The issues that overshadowed all else during his political career were questions concerning slavery and the right of each state to regulate the institution, topics Warner and his family feared would tear the nation asunder. Warner had grown up in a slaveholding family, and slave children had been his playmates and "friends affectionate and true." At an early age he developed a "strange antipathy" to the institution, yet after he inherited several slave families from his grandmother, his attitude changed, perhaps because the revenues from their labors helped finance his law studies. Warner's older brother, Joseph, also inherited slaves. Unlike his sibling, however, Joseph became an active member of the Kentucky Colonization Society during the 1830s and eventually freed most of his chattel on the condition that they go to Liberia. If Warner ever considered emancipation, neither his speeches nor the extant family papers so indicate. In an address before the U.S. Congress, however, he claimed to be a "decided advocate" of colonization, yet viewed "the social comfort and condition" of Liberia "not equal to what I believe it to be here within these . . . slave states." He did not send slaves to Liberia, perhaps assuming that few black Americans really wished to emigrate to the wild and unknown African continent. In their attitude toward slavery, the Underwoods shared a dilemma common to many Kentuckians who owned slaves yet were less than enthusiastic about the institution.[3]

Josie apparently agreed with her father's sentiments relating to slavery, for her diary reveals both patronizing and compassionate views and prejudices. These were typical of many southern women. Although she appeared to be kind and caring, Josie nevertheless took for granted the slaves' role as that of servants created to attend and serve their white masters.

The agitation over the slavery question and the accompanying right of the various states to determine their free-slave status apparently worried Warner and his family more than did the political or moral sentiments concerning the institution. There was nothing "which so much endangers the existence of our institutions as the continued agitation of the slavery question," he told the House of Representatives in 1856. Two years later, in a speech opposing the admission of

Kansas under the Lecompton Constitution, he warned that "to force the LeCompton constitution upon the people of Kansas against their consent . . . will be to sound the tocsin for a wilder, and deeper, and far more pervading commotion than any you have ever known. It will not be confined to Kansas, but, rolling from its level plains, it will sweep through the northwestern prairies and the mountains of New England, until every hamlet and village, and town and county, will be instinct with excitement."[4]

Slavery and the states' rights issues also dominated the 1860 presidential campaign. Abraham Lincoln and the Republican Party believed that slavery should not be allowed to spread into any western territory; some party members indicated they wished to abolish the institution altogether. Illinois's Stephen A. Douglas, nominee of the Northern Democrats, advocated that the slavery question should be settled at the territory level; Southern Democrats and their candidate, John C. Breckinridge of Kentucky, proclaimed that the issue should not be determined until statehood and that a state had the right to secede if federal law threatened its well-being by prohibiting the institution. For those Democrats who could support neither of the sectional candidates, the Constitutional Union Party offered a more moderate platform, with John Bell of Tennessee for president and Edward Everett of Massachusetts for vice president. Bell and Everett ignored the slavery issue and talked of abiding by the Constitution and preserving the Union.

Underwood spent much of the summer and fall of 1860 campaigning for Bell-Everett, and Josie read her father's speeches and perhaps accompanied him on some of his travels. His opinions and words became hers, but the reaction of the electorate to his speeches is unknown. Nevertheless, when they went to the polls on November 6, residents of south central Kentucky supported Bell, as did the majority of the commonwealth's voters, and cast a mere handful of ballots for the Republicans. Lincoln carried none of the slave states, and although he received only 39 percent of the nation's popular vote, he garnered the majority of the electoral votes and became the sixteenth president of the United States. On learning of Lincoln's election, Josie and her family probably agreed with a south central Kentucky physician who predicted that Lincoln's election would "be looked back on as the date of the beginning of the greatest calamities" that ever befell an enlightened people. South Carolina so feared the economic and political ramifications that would result from the Republicans' victory that the state seceded from the Union on December 20. Six other Southern states followed during the early days of 1861—Mississippi (January 9), Florida (January 10), Alabama (January 11), Georgia (January 19), Louisiana (January 26), and Texas (February 1). Delegates from the seven states met in Montgomery in early February, adopted a constitution, and elected Jefferson Davis as provisional president of the Confederate States of America.[5]

Throughout the winter and spring of 1861, talk of secession escalated in the border states and Upper South. Warner toured south central Kentucky during the spring of 1861 and explained why the Bluegrass State must not join the Confederacy. The commonwealth would be more successful, he reasoned, in addressing its grievances as a member of the Union rather than outside it, a sentiment that Josie expressed frequently to her friends. However, not all Kentuckians agreed.

The state's economy and the sentiments of its people placed the Underwood family and thousands of others in an unenviable climate. Family ties linked the commonwealth's residents with those of Indiana, Illinois, and Missouri as well as Virginia, North Carolina, and Tennessee. Kentucky's economic well-being depended on southern and western markets to purchase its agricultural products (horses, mules, hogs, tobacco, hemp, and corn) as well as on northern markets to supply the manufactured items its people needed. Furthermore, Kentucky's slave labor system created a strong tie to the South. In 1860, the state's residents included 225,483 slaves (19.5 percent of the population), worth in excess of $100 million, and 10,684 (less than 1 percent) free blacks. One household in four owned slaves, and the average holding was 5.4 chattels. Thus, with an agricultural economy partially dependent on slave labor, many Kentuckians, even many who owned no slaves, supported the South's insistence that any federal laws limiting or outlawing slavery would violate the Constitution and that each state had the right to regulate its own peculiar institution.

In addition to emotional issues, Kentucky's economic status made the state more important in the nineteenth century than in more recent times. Among the nation's thirty-three states, Kentucky ranked ninth in population, seventh in the value of farms, and fifth in the value of livestock. Moreover, the commonwealth's geographic location placed the state in jeopardy, for leaders of both sides coveted the commonwealth's advantages. Kentucky controlled most of the Midwest's major rivers, which served as highways for antebellum America. The Ohio River flows along the state's entire northern border and then into the Mississippi, which winds along Kentucky's western boundary. The Cumberland and Tennessee Rivers, both navigable for hundreds of miles into the South, pass through Kentucky before emptying into the Ohio. Likewise, the Green-Barren tributary was navigable by small steamboats as far south as Bowling Green. The October 1859 completion of the Louisville and Nashville Railroad through Bowling Green and the March 1861 opening of the line from Bowling Green through Russellville and Guthrie to Memphis linked the Upper South's most important trade and population centers and further amplified the area's significance. Control of Kentucky and of the Bowling Green area guaranteed access to invasion and supply routes into and out of the Confederacy. The Underwoods and their neighbors well understood that both belligerents might invade the area, thus placing their homes and futures in jeopardy. Acknowledging the commonwealth's significance, Lincoln wrote to a friend that "to lose Kentucky is nearly the same as to lose the whole game. With Kentucky gone, we cannot hold Missouri nor, I think, Maryland. These all against us, and the job on our hands is too large for us. We would as well consent to separation at once, including the surrender of the capital." Someone suggested that the president hoped that God was on his side, but that he must have Kentucky.[6]

Josie began her diary during the Christmas holidays of 1860 as she prepared to visit her sister and brother-in-law in Memphis. In the hotbed of Tennessee's secession movement, she attended parties, plays, and parades and received calls from friends and acquaintances. For all, the major topic of conversation concerned secession. As she listened to others proclaim the advantages of separating from the Union, Josie attempted to convince them of the errors in their thinking. One of the discussions among her friends became so volatile it concluded with name calling—and a duel. On another occasion a cousin, a graduate of West Point who had been forced to surrender the U.S. armory at Baton Rouge, talked of his strong feelings of loyalty to the United States and his love for the daughter of a prominent Mississippi secessionist. He painfully warned, "Don't fall in love, Jo, don't fall in love." But she may have—and with a secessionist.

On her return to Bowling Green, Josie discovered that the all-absorbing question in south central Kentucky, as in Memphis, was "the breaking up of the Union and it seems no longer a question but a fact." Schoolboys were ready to fight "at the slightest provocation." One of Josie's younger brothers, for example, became embroiled in a fistfight when his pro-Southern schoolmates called him a "Lincolnite" and an "abolitionist." The lad's father suggested that a gentleman should not engage in "rough and tumble fights with a low fellow"; Mrs. Underwood, however, admonished him to "knock down anyone" who called him such bad names. Even adult friends and acquaintances began to hurl "cutting speech" at each other, and by late spring many families and long-time friendships were breaking up "faster than the Union." Members of Josie's own family suffered from opposing opinions. Her staunch unionist uncle Joseph had an outspoken secessionist son-in-law living in his home; two of her brothers-in-law supported the Union, yet a third was an ardent secessionist. Moreover, Josie's mother disowned a beloved brother and labeled him a traitor because he intended to fight for the South.

War began with the April 12 firing on Fort Sumter. Shortly thereafter Lincoln called for troops from all the states, including four regiments from Kentucky. Four states—Virginia, North Carolina, Tennessee, and Arkansas—left the Union rather than fulfill his request. Kentucky governor Beriah Magoffin replied that the commonwealth would furnish no troops "for the wicked purpose of subduing her sister southern states." On May 16 the Kentucky House of Representatives resolved that the Bluegrass State intended to "occupy a position of strict neutrality" and take no part in the war. The Senate adopted a similar resolution.[7]

Unfortunately, personal neutrality proved impossible. "Every man, woman and child is one or the other," Josie observed. When one of her brothers-in-law announced that he planned to join the Confederate Army, another answered, "all right . . . I'll raise a regiment to fight against you and whip you back into the Union." A third brother-in-law, who supported the Union, moved his family to California and thus avoided taking an active part in the conflict. When Josie tried to learn the sentiments of a family member in nearby Russellville, her uncle astutely advised that "talking too much does a great deal of harm."

Neutrality for the state likewise proved impossible, for control of the commonwealth was vital to both belligerents. During the early summer of 1861, Union and Confederate recruiting stations, located just beyond the commonwealth's borders, enlisted thousands of Kentuckians, and in midsummer the Union began recruiting within the state. On September 4, Confederate forces under General Gideon Pillow moved into the Mississippi River town of Columbus (the terminus of the Mobile and Ohio Railroad), and three days later a Federal army led by General Ulysses S. Grant took nearby Paducah. Kentucky's neutrality had ceased.

On the evening of September 17, General Simon Bolivar Buckner and some thirteen hundred troops boarded railcars at Tennessee's Camp Boone and arrived early the next morning in Bowling Green. On detraining, one of the soldiers climbed to the depot's roof and lowered the American flag. Not satisfied with tearing it down, the lad also trampled on Old Glory. While doing so he fell from the roof and broke both of his legs. The Shaker diary that told of the incident also related that the young fellow "died in a few days and no doubt received the reward of his work."[8]

The anticipated arrival of the Confederates created panic among south central Kentucky Unionists. Many fled or sent their frightened wives and children to areas less likely to attract an army. Believing the military might execute those who opposed them, an elderly, Bible-toting woman surrendered to the first southern officer she saw and announced that she was prepared to die for her country. A block or so away from the depot, a northern man employed at a school for young ladies answered a knock at the door of his schoolroom. After a brief conversation with his visitor, the schoolmaster announced to his class that he needed to "go out for a minute" and that the girls should "sit quietly" until he came back. He apparently left town, and when the dinner bell rang an hour or so later, the young ladies went home and the lunch period lasted for many weeks.[9]

On learning of the arrival of the Confederate troops, Josie lamented, "The Philistines are upon us." Eventually 20,000–25,000 Philistines—members of Albert Sidney Johnston's Army of the West, composed of units from Kentucky, Tennessee, Mississippi, Louisiana, Arkansas, Texas, and Missouri—camped along the waterways of south central Kentucky. Bowling Green served as the army's headquarters, and vacated homes and hotels quickly filled with officers and their families. The soldiers felled trees that obstructed any view of roads, river, and rails leading to the area and built forts on hilltops surrounding the town. Because of its location and fortifications, Bowling Green became known as the Gibraltar of the Confederacy. "They can't whip us here," a young fellow assured his sister. Another cocky fellow boasted, "We are too well fixed for the Yankees to come here," and estimated that it would require two hundred thousand men to take the town. "If they ever come we will give them a genteel whipping," he promised.[10]

Once an attractive community, Bowling Green's "beauteous days" vanished as autumn turned to winter. "Tents in every direction and mud to any extent the most vivid imagination could portray, had rent the town of its loveliness," wrote a Tennessee volunteer. A Texas Ranger nicknamed his station "Camp Mud Puddle" and informed his family that "I know nothing which we could more usefully employ now than a boat in our encampment." A thousand or so of the soldiers erected their tents on the Underwood farm. Josie filled her diary with descriptions of the fright and frustration she and her family experienced as the unwelcome guests trampled their fields, pilfered crops, burned fences, cut down trees, stole food and all else they needed, and violated the family's privacy. One wintry day Josie even discovered a couple of the interlopers warming themselves by the fireplace in her sick mother's bedroom.[11]

As the weather declined, so did the morale of the occupational forces. They had expected a battle at Bowling Green and looked forward to "whipping" the Yankees. Except for a handful of prisoners, however, they had not seen any enemy soldiers. The glamour of soldiering rapidly gave way to the realities of inedible food, abominable living conditions, and poor health. Many of the southern soldiers lacked adequate clothing for a Kentucky winter. Josie pitied the ill-equipped, ill-provisioned, shivering men who bundled up in fancy comforters, "no doubt gifts from their sweethearts and sisters."

Lack of adequate housing during Kentucky's cold and wet fall and winter plagued the army. Consequently, many erected in their tents or hastily constructed huts fireplaces that generated more smoke than heat but on which they cooked their meals and coaxed a little warmth for their living quarters. Furnishings for these drafty abodes generally consisted of whatever could be begged, borrowed, or stolen. A thin pallet of straw covered with a blanket might serve as a bed, but as winter wore on, covering became scarce. Few soldiers had more than one blanket, and straw became so hard to find that there were only "seven straws to nine men and those were pilfered from a half starved horse that stood nearby," a Tennessee volunteer joked.[12]

However, the problems faced by the Confederates stationed in south central Kentucky were no joke. Food, prepared over an open fire by men who lacked culinary skills, usually was over- or undercooked, frequently unpalatable, and sometimes putrid. Because sewage and camp debris often contaminated the water supply, cases of typhoid, dysentery, and other enteric illnesses became commonplace. Epidemic outbreaks of communicable diseases plagued the soldiers, and pneumonia and other respiratory problems became a constant threat. With quarantine impossible, combined maladies almost wiped out the Army of the West. Throughout late November and December one-half of the command at Dripping Springs had measles and scurvy, and three-fourths of the forces at Oakland were felled by measles, dysentery, and pneumonia. In most of the camps only half of the troops were able to stand for roll call. The need for hospitals and professional help overwhelmed.[13]

Military doctors called on their professional brothers in the community for aid and commandeered every available structure for hospitals. Dr. David Yandell, the army's medical director, established a large tent hospital, dubbed Camp Recovery, on the eastern edge of town and pleaded a "pressing need" for more medical officers. In lieu of professional nurses, Lucy Underwood and her friends put aside their political sentiments and provided food, medicines, and care for the ill. When asked why she, a staunch Unionist, aided the sick enemy, Mrs. Underwood explained that as long as any mother's son was ill, she wanted to help; however, she halted her Samaritan activities when a man became able to bear arms against his nation.[14]

Hearing of the soldiers' plight, Ella Newsom, the "Florence Nightingale of the Southern Army," came to Bowling Green in late December and "concentrated her energies" caring for the sick, "often laboring from 4 o'clock in the morning until 12 o'clock at night." But nothing was enough. No records giving an official death count have been found, but a local undertaker who furnished coffins for the army later estimated that about 10 percent of the soldiers died during their five-month stay in south central Kentucky.[15]

Although the death rate among citizens did not escalate, the quality of their daily lives deteriorated. With the area's population greatly expanded, food became scarce and imported manufactured goods were virtually nonexistent. Cut off from all communication avenues to the north, nothing came from Louisville and very little trickled in from Nashville or Memphis. Shelves in local stores stood empty and citizens' root cellars, smokehouses, and pantries were quickly depleted. Living with the enemy in their midst affected every phase of the daily lives of area residents. Rumors circulated, suspicions increased, and tensions mounted. Would Unionists be arrested? Would property be confiscated? Would homes and businesses be destroyed? Attempting to protect his family, Warner Underwood drew up papers that transferred all of his property to his Confederate son-in-law. However, when one of the servants cried out, "Good Lord . . . I never would er [sic] believed Mars Warner you'd sell us," Underwood couldn't—and didn't. General Buckner had earlier assured Warner that he would "suffer no molestation from troops under his command." Nevertheless, in early January the Underwoods received orders that they must evacuate Mount Air; shortly thereafter a friend advised Warner to flee, lest he be arrested for his outspoken support of the Union. Eventually, the occupational forces destroyed Mount Air.[16]

In the early days of 1862, the Confederates suffered reverses in the eastern and western portions of the state. At about the same time, a large Union army moved into central Kentucky. Consequently, the Confederates decided to pull back to Nashville. Dismantling of the camps, storehouses, and fortifications began during the first week of February, the evacuation of hospitals commenced about the 10th, and the last troops headed south on Valentine's Day; many Southern sympathizers accompanied them. "We were told," a local resident later recalled, that the rebels "would burn the town and every home within five miles." Cognizant of that possibility, Confederate general William J. Hardee issued a directive that anyone attempting to fire any building would be shot without a trial. Consequently, although the Confederates destroyed the depot, the railroad bridge, and the wooden footbridge crossing the Barren River, little damage occurred to private property. However, a fire of undetermined origin burned half of the north side of the square, including the small hotel where Josie's parents had married and the building that housed Warner's law office.[17]

The retreating troops destroyed some of their provisions stored in town and abandoned others that could not be taken south. Seeing barrels of flour piled in the square, Episcopal minister Samuel Ringgold claimed them as his "payment from Albert Sidney Johns[t]on for storage." Unfortunately, others also wanted the commodities and began rolling the barrels away. Waving his cane and shouting that the flour was his, the dapper little churchman became a comic sight as he ran from one end of the pile to the other, attempting to protect his cache, to no avail. An Ohio infantryman later exaggerated that the rebels left "enough pork, salt, beef and other necessities to supply our division for a month . . . [but] burned a million dollars worth of stores." Another Union recruit suggested that because of the abandoned and burned stores, which included arms, the injury to the Confederate cause "could scarcely be greater if they had had a thousand men slain in battle."[18]

The evacuation of the hospitals commenced several days before the last Confederates left. Dr. Yandell later reported that 500 ill and 350 convalescents, who were too weak to endure the march, were transferred by rail from Bowling Green to Nashville. Another 1,400 needed hospitalization following the sixty-mile march in the freezing rain and snow. By the time the medical director found enough Nashville accommodations for all the sick, Johnston had decided to move his forces to northern Mississippi.

As the last of the rebel troops left Bowling Green, a large group of Federals arrived on the north side of the river. Lacking a bridge and thus unable to cross, they lobbed shells across the river until they learned that the enemy was gone. Between fleeing secessionists, evacuating troops, exploding shells, and the freezing rain, sleet, and snow, pandemonium reigned in Bowling Green throughout most of February 14. Josie vividly described the chaos and fright experienced by area residents during the Confederates' retreat and Federal bombardment. The following morning, Union troops forded the swollen river upstream and crossed on pontoons and flatboats and entered the town. Local folks who rushed to greet the initial Federal troops were appalled to discover that their rescuers were not Kentuckians, but rather were a group of "hungry coarse *Dutchmen*," German immigrants who assumed that all residents were "dam[ned] Rebels." Josie predicted that "nothing could have been more unfortunate for the Union cause in this town." Another area resident wrote that some of this initial group "rushed into our house . . . opened the safes and carried off everything eatable . . . [and] in every other house . . . went from garret to cellar . . . insulting people in them, particularly those of southern proclivity." Apparently the insulting behavior was widespread, for a farmer living some distance from town also reported being "visited by three ruffins [*sic*] in the dead of night with revolvers cocked and they took just what they wanted . . . and threatened to burn the house and mill if we did not launch out the gold."[19]

Although many of the Federal troops continued southward, several regiments remained to guard the river and rails and to serve the numerous hospitals established in the town. But whether they remained for a few days or many months, they disrupted everyday life. Josie continued to write of humorous, maddening, and heartbreaking events in the occupied town. She laughed about a friend embarrassed by an errant hoop skirt that shockingly revealed her pantaloons. She fussed about animosities that developed between friends and neighbors and fumed over words and deeds of local troublemakers and egotistical, arrogant military know-it-alls. She purchased food for some hungry prisoners of war and she worried because her friends in the Confederate army lacked the heavy overcoats and other equipage enjoyed by their better-provisioned foes. She aided her mother and other women of the town in distributing items sent by the Sanitary Commission, and she grieved over the soldiers' expanding graveyard. As fatalities increased, Josie questioned if "any cause" was worth the lives lost, and on learning of the April 6–7 battle at Shiloh, she pleaded, "God have mercy and stop this cruel war." Unfortunately, the war continued.

Bowling Green remained under military occupation throughout the war. For residents of the area, the same conditions existed under Federal occupation as had delighted or plagued them during the shorter visit of the Confederates. Men in blue held dress parades, parties, and cotillions, but also bivouacked in orchards, drilled in clover fields, cut down trees, burned fences, stole livestock, requisitioned food and forage, destroyed roads and bridges, created frightening sanitation and health problems, violated civil rights, and infringed on the dignity and serenity of civilians. Residents began to agree with the woman who mourned, "I see nothing but abolition soldiers clad in the hateful blue uniforms." Members of the army categorized their hosts as rebels, and many undoubtedly shared the attitude of a soldier from Connecticut who complained that "I cannot get a man here to admit that New England is in any respect superior" to Kentucky. Animosities previously directed at the Confederates soon were aimed at the men in blue. And since their influence lasted longer and touched the sensitive issues of recruiting slaves and using black troops—about two thousand African Americans were inducted at the Bowling Green recruitment station—local feelings for these newcomers from the north declined into hatred.[20]

In the early summer of 1862, Warner Underwood's name was submitted for a consular position, and Josie went with him to Washington to confer with the president. During their visit, Josie delighted in being introduced to many of the nation's political and military leaders. After meeting President Lincoln, she described him as a "common looking man" with a "kindness in his face—that does not fit the tyrant-unfair man I have been thinking of him." Following their official meeting, Lincoln awarded Underwood the position of Consul to Glasgow, a seemingly suitable patronage post for someone without foreign-service experience. The last entry in Josie's diary is dated September 8, 1862, the day before they began their journey to Scotland.

Thus, while their Kentucky friends and neighbors coped with a second army of occupation, the Underwood family adjusted to foreign ways. Little is known of their life in Glasgow. Josie's brother Henry kept a diary of his school activities in the seaport city and fussed when his teacher "criticizes everything that I say and tells me that may be the way they talk in our country but not in thars." His boyish scribbling told of excitement about the marriage of Britain's Prince of Wales, of seeing the blood of David Rizzio at Holyrood Castle, and of playing with his toy boats in the Clyde River. He also related that the family closely watched events taking place on the western side of the Atlantic. "Had the Stars & Stripes up rejoicing over the defeat of Lee [at Gettysburg] & the fall of Vicksburg," the youngster penned on July 20, 1863. Apparently Josie did not keep a diary during her European sojourn—or if she did, it has not surfaced.[21]

Warner Underwood's major consular tasks included reporting on Confederate activities—on ships believed to be carrying rebel goods and on the Clyde River shipyards, which were suspected of building vessels for the Confederate navy—and guarding against any activity that would jeopardize Anglo-American relations. However, he soon grew weary of the skullduggery his duties required and complained to the State Department that his $3,000 salary was not commensurate with his responsibilities as consul and the surveillance of rebel activities; he requested a change in his assignment. When none appeared forthcoming, his homesick family made a brief visit to London, Naples, and Rome, and then left for the United States in the spring of 1864. Warner submitted his resignation shortly thereafter and sailed for home in October.[22]

On their return to the United States, the Underwoods enjoyed an extended visit in San Francisco with their daughter and son-in-law, and in 1866 moved back to Bowling Green. Unfortunately, the family never recouped its prewar status. Their home and most of the furnishings at Mount Air, as well as the outbuildings and fences, had been burned by the Confederates; Union troops had carried off the stock, 450 cords of wood, and 36,000 bricks salvaged from their burned home. Moreover, the Thirteenth Amendment had freed the labor force that once cared for their fields and animals. Despite its war scars, however, Mount Air remained a handsome site for a home, certainly a "handsomer site" than any place they had seen elsewhere. Thus, Warner ran an ad in the paper to sell a portion of his farm. Josie reminded him that he had promised that if she "lived [to be] an old maid," she would "have a home at Mt. Air." She now felt cheated out of both the farm and a husband. Despite her protest, portions were sold and the family made plans to rebuild on the remainder. Underwood reestablished his law practice, and until he could rebuild, he rented a small house in town for his family. Unfortunately, he suffered a stroke in 1868 from which he never fully recovered, and he died in 1872. The widowed Lucy, who had never enjoyed good health, and during her last decade was afflicted with severe palsy, lived with one child and then another until her death in 1893.[23]

In 1870 Josie married New Yorker Charles Nazro in a double ceremony with her cousin "Lady," at Bowling Green's Christ Episcopal Church. Very little is known about Nazro and of the couple's life during their twenty-eight years together. Their four lively children—Lucy (1871), Edith (1873), Underwood (1875), and Frank (1880)—certainly occupied Josie's time and energies. Charles and Josie's brother Henry pooled their resources in the early 1870s to organize Bowling Green's short-lived National Southern Kentucky Bank, for which Charles served as president. Sometime after the bank's demise, the Nazros moved to Ballston Spa, New York, where Charles held an office job and earned about $100 a month. Unfortunately, the transplanted Josie never reconciled herself to a lifestyle of the North or to being strapped for money. Living in a small rented house "that the owner will see fall down before he will make any repairs," the former southern belle complained bitterly about having to do her own housework. "I get so sick and discouraged at spending all my days in such menial degrading work," she wrote. "I was not brought up to such drudgery. . . . My hands . . . are now so rough and swollen and wrinkled . . . that I would be ashamed to shake hands with any of my friends of former days." Sometime after 1889 they moved west, lived in Denver for a few years, and were in San Diego when Charles died in mid-April 1898. His ashes as well as the remains of their daughter Edith, who died that same year, were interred in California.[24]

Josie returned to the town of her birth about 1912. Popular among her peers and considered "one of the brightest women in Bowling Green," she became active in a variety of community groups, including the Daughters of the American Revolution. For a literary club presentation, she prepared a brief history of the town that included some of her memories of the war. The local paper published her article; unfortunately, it contained no discernable quotes from the diary she had kept sixty years earlier.

At her death in November 1923, Josie resided in a small house owned by one of her sons. Her will distributed her most valuable and sentimental possessions among her children and grandchildren—a china tea set, family ambrotypes, her engagement and wedding rings, a sapphire pin from Charles, a few books, and a group of water colors "painted in India by my friend Edwin Baxter." To her eighteen-year-old granddaughter living in Texas, she left her DAR pin and "my journal (2 books) kept during the Civil War. Foolish as are many of its records, it may interest her as a sort of history of her grandmother's young live [sic] and of the exciting time in which much of it was passed."[25]

For students of history, of the Civil War, and even of the problems visited on any civilian group during military activity and occupation, the diary indeed provides an interesting view of exciting times experienced by a family and community when the Philistines were upon them.

❧ CHAPTER ONE ❧

During the hot, dry summer of 1860, politics and the presidential campaign dominated thoughts and discussions, and at the state fair, held in Bowling Green in mid- to late September, they overshadowed all else. Crowds gathered to hear spokesmen for candidates Bell, Breckinridge, and Douglas, and Louisville newspapers carried their speeches. John Bell and one of his supporters, John J. Crittenden, attended the fair, and to appreciative crowds they reiterated the promise they delivered at other gatherings: to preserve the Union and the Constitution. At the fair, and elsewhere throughout the fall, local politicians continued to whip crowds into a frenzy. By the first Tuesday in November, few voters could think or talk about anything except the election and its ramifications. When word of the Republican victory reached South Carolina, the state seceded from the Union. What should and would the rest of the South and the border states do? The question sparked lively discussions across Kentucky and in neighboring Tennessee.

Josie began her diary in early December as she prepared to visit with her sister and brother-in-law in Memphis. The diary chronicled a slave wedding, parties, social calls, and romantic visits that enlivened the holidays, but more serious concerns quickly overshadowed these social festivities. In Memphis, the hotbed of Tennessee's secession movement, she witnessed torchlight parades and became involved in heated political discussions. Despite her attempts to remain a soft-spoken southern belle, the twenty-year-old voiced her parents' opposition to Lincoln and to secession. As one after another of the states of the Lower South seceded, the intensity and anger in these discussions increased.

"Mt. Air" near Bowling Green, December 1860.

Dec. 10th—

Tomorrow morning I leave for Memphis, Tenn. to spend the winter with sister Jupe and Mr. Western. Miss Jane Grider is going with me and we expect a lovely time.[1]

This will be my first visit from home since I finished school last June and became a full fledged "Young lady." Though I felt badly when September came, that I was not to return to the dear old school, I have had a splendid time, especially during the state fair which was held in Bowling Green this year.

Sister Lute and Judge McCann came home from California and invited Messrs. Chamberlain and Massey, two gentlemen whom they met on the steamer, to visit us during the Fair. Cousin Ed Henry from Miss. came *up*—Will and Johnny Bell came *down*, Aunt Hassie, Sister Jupe and Mr. Western, Cousin Jane Todd, Mollie Rogers, and Cousin Mal Gorin were all with us, and last but by no means least, our most honored guest, Gov. John J. Crittenden, who made a beautiful address at the opening of the Fair. He has the biggest mouth I ever saw. Every evening a number of gentlemen came out from town. "Uncle" Lewis [a slave] played the fiddle for us to dance and we had lots of all sorts of fun. I am quite sure there never existed better host and hostess than Pa and Ma, to make everyone have such a good time—with apparently so much enjoyment themselves. Mr. Massey who is originally from Penn. said "Mount Air" was the realization of all he had read and imagined of a hospitable Southern home. I haven't yet gotten quite used to having [Mike] Hall and other old beaus of my sister's treating me with the dignity of a grown up young lady, tho' Hugh Gwyn is making fun of me half the time. I wonder if I'll have as good a time in Memphis. Well, "Nous erons [verrons?]," as my old French teacher is so fond of saying.

CHAPTER ONE

Ma has given me this book to keep a sort of Journal. What I do—who I meet—and my impressions of people and things, so I can read it to her when I return. Dear Ma! as much pleasure as I expect from this visit I feel so selfish and sad to leave her.

DEC. 12TH, 1860, MEMPHIS, TENN.

We reached here safely yesterday. Mr. Western and sister met us at the train, giving us such a hearty and affectionate welcome that we felt at once we were going to have a good time. Their home here on Vance Street is a lovely place. The house sitting far back in a big yard full of Magnolia and other southern trees, beautiful roses and flavoring [flowering] shrubs—many now in bloom— A wide veranda extends entirely across the front of the house, the tall pillars reaching to the roof above the second story. The windows open down to the porch. A wide hall through the center of the house. It is altogether a lovely home and sister and Mr. Western are as happy as can be. Certainly it would be hard to find a more congenial couple.

We had a great time when we left Bowling Green. So many of our friends were at the train to say good-bye. All in fact except Mr. B——, whereupon Hugh Gwyn asked, in the most serious tone, if any one knew the particulars of [Edwin] Baxter's accident. Every body exclaimed, "Why no, we hadn't heard it; what happened to him? Was he hurt," etc. and so on. I was of course as concerned as the others. Then Hugh said, "I am awfully sorry I can't give the particulars, but I know something dreadful must have happened to him, or he would be here. Perhaps Miss Josie can tell particulars as the last seen of him he was slowly & sadly wending his way from 'Mount Air.'" Then we knew it was just another one of his jokes at Mr. B—and my expense. I wish he would stop this everlasting joking which Mr. B, being an Englishman, can't parry and I don't like—yet he is so funny I can't get angry at him. I confess I thought it a little strange Mr. B. wasn't there and was no little amused—not to say pleased—when at the first station 12 miles out Mr. B quietly walked into the car— Much to my annoyance Jane told him all of Hugh Gwyn's nonsensical joke. He came with us as far as Nashville, saw us comfortably on the Memphis train—checked our trunks and, giving me a lovely box of candy, said I should be very glad to hear if you young ladies reach Memphis comfortably—whereupon Miss Jane said, "I'll write as soon as we get there for we are so much obliged to you." His mouth twitched in such a funny little way as he said—"O thanks!" I think she is writing now but she likes to be mysterious about her correspondents.

Dec. 13th—

Mr. Western's partner Mr. T[orian] and wife called this evening. Mr. T. seemed despondent about the country and wanted to talk Politics but Mrs. T. said in a pleasant way, "Please don't you and Will Western spoil our call by political wrangling—you know you never can agree." Mr. Western laughingly replied, "Never fear but he will soon come to my way of thinking." "*Never*! never!" the old man snapped out and his lips almost clicked, he shut them so tightly. Mr. Western thinks the South ought not to submit quietly to Lincoln's inauguration and expresses himself—often in the most ultra fashion—inconsistent, it seems to me, with his usual good sense. Mrs. T's brother [Will Webb] called with them. A young lawyer and pretty bright fellow. He and Mr. Western both got pretty excited over the discussion Mrs. T. had rescued her husband from—

CHAPTER ONE

Dec. 14th—

Several girls called today all enthusiastic over Memphis being the most delightful place in the world as there are 1100 more young men in town than women—a "regular paradise for visiting girls" they said. May we find it so! Mr. Western brought cousin Jack Henry out to take supper with us. He is a son of Uncle Gustavus Henry of Clarksville, Tenn. Tho' born so near us, we've never met before—some sort of estrangement having existed between the families, but I am awfully glad I know Jack now—for he is *lovely*. Like all the Henry men he is fair with light wavy hair, but unlike them, instead of blue eyes, his are the softest dark hazel. His manners are elegant—neither stiff nor familiar. In fact we would not think of *manners* at all in connection with him. His *pleasant ways* are so much a part of himself, such easy grace—withal so modest and unassuming. Not the least bit self asserting, yet even when there are a dozen others in the room, as was the case this evening, even though Jack is not speaking—his presence is persuading. A Mr. Tom Grafton of Miss. and Mr. [James] Witherspoon, both young lawyers here (as is cousin Jack), called after supper—both are bright handsome men and agreeable talkers—though Mr. Grafton gave me the feeling that he was leading me to talk more for his own amusement—than my entertainment, that he was mentally criticizing me though his manner was entirely gentlemanly, almost too deferential. I did not feel at ease talking with him and was glad when the conversation became general. Mr. Witherspoon, on the other hand, impressed me as a frank good natured fellow, with no reserves or hidden motives. They are law partners. Their office [is] in the same building and adjoining Mr. Western. They invited Jane and me to go to the theatre with them tomorrow night. Sister, Mr. Western and Jack are also going. Jane claims to go with Mr.

Witherspoon and I hope it will be arranged that way, for if I were asked which I like best, on such short acquaintance, I think I would say Mr. Witherspoon. Yet, Mr. Grafton interests me most, I don't know just why.

Dec. 16th—

Well, we went to the theatre last night. The play was "The Lady of Lyons" and perfectly beautiful. I had read it and knew all the pretty passages by heart—but Oh! how different to see it played! It was all so real I could hardly believe it was simply acting. We were in a box and I felt like we were part of the play. The only thing that marred my pleasure was Mr. Grafton. He sat there in his immaculate evening clothes, a little bunch of violets on the lapel of his coat. (He had brought me a beautiful big bunch and before we left the house asked for two or three to be pinned on his coat.) Instead of watching the play he was watching me most of the time—infinitely amused at my absolved interest. I have never been to any kind of theatre more than two or three times if so often and it was all new, beautiful and real to me and I could not assume an indifferent air—I wish I could, especially if Mr. Grafton is along. He has lived in New Orleans—travelled a great deal, and of course I am awfully green in his eyes. In spite of him, I never enjoyed anything more.[2]

Dec. 17th—

We dined with the Prestons this evening. Everything was elegant and pleasant till the gentlemen began talking politics—when several of them got so excited it wasn't pleasant at all. If Lincoln's name happens to be mentioned, it's like a match thrown into powder—.

CHAPTER ONE

Dᴇᴄ. 18ᴛʜ—

The weather is mild and beautiful—returned calls and had a lovely drive. After supper, Jack Henry and Mr. Withers[poon] called. Later Mr. Grafton with his Uncle, Mr. Crew—an old bachelor. I like Mr. Crew very much. Sister and Mr. Western make their home so delightful with her singing and his playing so sweetly on the violin to her accompaniments—that never an evening but some young men come out. Often too—the conversation is witty and brilliant—especially if sister and Mr. Crew—take the lead—and can keep away from politics. Tonight we got to talking about the play "Lady of Lyons"—and naturally of love—marriage—love in a hut—or palace—without love and so on. As our discussion waxed spirited, I [was] carried away with my side of the argument—like the simpleton I am—quoted the speech of Ellen Douglas.

> "Rather would Ellen Douglas dwell,
> A prioress in Moravanian's [*sic*] cell,
> Than in realms beyond the sea
> Courting the world's cold charity—
> An outcast pilgrim would she rove
> Than wed the man she can not love."[3]

Then was so mad at myself for doing it—and felt like a fool. When Mr. Grafton said in the cold quiet way he has, "You are sentimental—aren't you Miss Underwood"— Mr. Crew came to my rescue answering—"No, not a bit *sentimental,* but her young heart is full of a true *sentiment* that you *boys* can't appreciate. Come, Miss Underwood, let's you and I join your brother on the veranda—and leave these would be *cynics.*" Offering me his arm with an exaggerated grace we sailed out of the room, Mr. Grafton saying as we left, "A fine trick Uncle—well played."

I spent a pleasant half hour listening to Mr. Crew and Mr. Western talk—Sister Jupe and Miss Jane entertaining the others till time to leave. When they all came out on the veranda Mr. Grafton said—"Well Uncle—have you and Miss Underwood selected what star shall be your home—when love becomes immortal?" "We will forbid him the premises when we do, won't we Miss Underwood?" answered Mr. Crew, and so with pleasant banter the evening ended— But as is always the case when Mr. Grafton calls—leaving me with a feeling of dissatisfaction with myself.

Dec. 20th—

Several gentlemen called. It was dreadful to hear how they talked. Mr. Western and Mr. Grafton did not hesitate to say they would be glad to see the country divided—that there was no similarity of interest in the two sections North and South—no love between them and the sooner separated the better—Worse than useless to be trying to live as one country and forever working against each other. Dear Pa charged me to avoid political discussions but goodness alive! how can I sit quietly and hear such talk as this. Sister, Miss Jane and I are strong union—and Mr. Webb got very much excited as he argued against Mr. Western and Grafton. Though I think all he said was right—he uses such strong terms and gets so excited that he offends and does more harm than good. He and Mr. Grafton had called together—but he made excuse to leave early—evidently as Mr. Grafton as well as the rest of us knew—because he did not want to walk home with Mr. Grafton. I wish I could have heeded Pa's advice tonight—but it is impossible to sit quietly by and hear such talk—if one has any love at all for our country— I was very glad I had read Pa's last speech so carefully—for it seems to me there could be no finer arguments than he made in that for maintaining the Union—and in my excitement tonight they were my best weapons—but Mr. Grafton belittled them and me—by saying, "It is almost pleasant to differ with you—your excitement in defending your cause—brings such a pretty flush to your cheeks."— He makes me so angry by treating me like I was a silly child!

DECEMBER 21ST—

Got good home letters and from John Ward and Hugh Gwyn—John telling me how he missed me—and Hugh telling me other people did—also a paper with a fine article in it, which Pa had written, in maintaining the Union.

DEC. 25TH—CHRISTMAS DAY.—

DEC. 26TH—

I was just dead tired yesterday when all the excitement was over and at last we could go to bed. Such a jolly day as we had, and in all my life I never got so many pretty things. By daylight all the darkies came tipping in, first one then another—poking their black heads in the doors—suddenly calling out "Christmas Giff Mars William—christmas giff Miss Jupe, Miss Jane—Miss Josie, christmas *giff, everybody.*" So we were all "caught," as we knew we would be—and had prepared presents for the occasion. There being no children in the house firecrackers were dispensed with but were popping all around the neighborhood. We had a great time unloading the stockings which we had hung up in sister's room—Mr. Western playing Santa Claus. Breakfast was hardly over before the bell began to ring and we [began] to receive all sorts of pretty gifts, books, flowers, baskets of fruits, cards and calls. After supper ever so many gentlemen called— We had egg nog with the brightest toasts—singing and playing, with a battle of wits between Mr. Crew and Mr. Western which kept us in uproarious laughter. The climax of fun was reached when about 11 o'clock the bell rang and Jack Henry who had left a little while before staggered in with a big gunny sack on his back—marked in white chalk—"For Miss Josie." He put it down in the middle of the parlor—all gathered around whilst I untied the string—When up popped Ed. Norman's [Eckstein Norton] head—like Jack-in-a-box. Out he stepped. Nobody except Jack knew he was in Memphis and they had planned this funny surprise. "What will you do with your present," they all asked, making all sorts of fun at my expense—so I said "I'll get Mr. [Thomas] Carrington (a banker) to lock it up in a safe deposit vault and he answered, "I'll do it with the greatest pleasure." So the day ended—all as merry and happy as Christmas could be—only I wish Ex hadn't come. This evening he called again and asked me to go with him tomorrow to call on some sort of connection of ours 3 miles in the country. Much as I wanted to I could not refuse—but oh! I dread that ride.[4]

DEC. 27TH—

Well, we made our visit and what I dreaded and have been trying to stave off ever since I stopped school has happened—he asked me to marry him. As we started on our return I commenced talking and kept it up in a blue streak—talking about the flowers, the woods, the people we had visited, everything and anything to leave no pause for him to get in a word edgewise. Finally he said, "Miss Josie, I must leave this evening and I must ask you to let me tell you why I came down to Memphis—though I think you already know"— I made some flippant answer, but it was no use. He came to tell his story and I could not prevent him. Good, earnest, persistent soul that he is—I do sincerely and truly *like him* and wish he only cared for me in the same way— I don't love him and can't love him and however "safe" as my dear Aunt Liz says the match would be, I'll never marry a man I do not love with my whole heart and soul. If this be *sentimental* then *I am sentimental.*

DEC., 28TH—

Busy preparing for the Grand Ball at the Gayosa Hotel New Year's eve.

JAN. 1ST—1861—

The Ball last night was the most splendid affair I ever attended. My first big *full grown* Ball. Mr. Witherspoon took Miss Jane, Mr. Grafton was my escort. He sent me an exquisite bunch of lilies of the valley and violets which was all my dress lacked and I had not thought of them. As he put my cloak around me before we started he said, "Always wear white muslin!" The lilies give its chief beauty to-night— I replied, "How did you happen to send flowers so suited to my dress."

He smiled and turning to Mr. Western said, "She wonders how I happen to send *her* lillies and violets." Though they both laughed, I felt approsed [*sic*] and my vanity came to the front for I don't think I ever had quite so pretty a dress. There were two gentlemen to every girl at the Ball and we could not have had a more charming time, though a rather unusual incident for a Ball occurred. The subject of secession like Banquo's ghost *will not [die] down* but will come up—no matter what the place or time—especially if Will Webb and Tom Grafton meet. Last night it was Mr. Webb's bad taste— that started the subject—then we were all off like horses in a race. I as bad as any of them. Mr. Grafton, Dr. [Lunsford]

Yandell, Mr. Carrington and I were talking together during an interlude. When Mr. Webb came up with some would be funny remark about that being a time when he would like to see that trio put their secession doctrines in practice—so the subject started— Mr. W. and I had the worst of it, as the other three are all smart bright men and much better talkers than Mr. Webb. I drew on Pa—Gen. Rousseau and Attorney General Jo[seph] Holt—for all the fine arguments and bright things I could remember from their speeches, getting very enthusiastic not to say excited in defending the Union and very conscious what a poor [?] out of it I was making—when to my great delight, a gentleman about Pa's age—standing so near that he could not fail to hear our talk—came still nearer and bowing in a most courtly way, said—"Permit an old friend of your father's to commend his daughter's loyalty and noble advocacy of his patriotic principles"—and turning to Mr. Grafton said—"Tom Grafton, what do you mean by talking *treason* in this style?" Though he spoke pleasantly and Mr. Grafton smiled, his face flushed and he replied, "You choose strong words Governor,"—then introduced me to *Gov.* [Henry] *Foote* of Mississippi—who told me he served in Congress with Pa and knew him well. We had a very pleasant talk till the dancing began again. As we walked off, Mr. Grafton said—"The Governor and other old foggies like him don't appreciate what the condition of the South will be if Lincoln is allowed to carry out his abolition principles—and I for one am ready to fight to the death to prevent it." But why not fight for Southern rights *in* the Union—why wish to divide this great country that your forefathers and mine sacrificed so much to establish.

"How could Washington dream a Lincoln—a low born clod hopper, would ever be elected president of the United States? And he never was either—only a part of the Country wants him and the sooner we separate forever from that part—the better for the South." I was glad the dancing stopped his talk. It is plain to see that the older—wiser people are for preserving the Union in spite of their antagonism to Lincoln and his party—but it is dreadful to hear how so many of the younger men talk— Mr. Western advocates secession as a fundamental principle for any free country—he and Mr. Grafton are very fond of the expression "A secessionist *per se*." In spite of this episode I never spent a pleasanter evening or attended so brilliant a party.

JAN. 4TH—

Last night the Unionists had a torch-light procession. An immense procession it was too—all the most substantial settled men of the city in it. Women in carriages, too— Sister, Miss Jane and I went— Mr. Western wouldn't go with us, as we wanted to drive in the procession, but we got Mr. Conrad, a great big six foot fellow, who won't say which side he is on— to drive with us, as he *looked* more important than little Mose, the negro driver. We passed Jack and Mr. Grafton and asked them to get in and ride but they, suspecting our intention to drive in the procession, wouldn't do it—saying they "would drive with us a few evenings later—when *"Loyal Southerners* had their show"— I think I will send them a dictionary with the word *Loyal* marked—for they have forgotten its meaning. Will Webb, who is a small man, was conspicuous on the biggest horse he could find, carrying a transparency—"Union Forever" on it—and I could but honor him for his Loyalty tho' his "Zeal is sometimes without knowledge"—and leads him to rash, offensive expressions.

JAN. 6TH—

Yesterday we had a telegram that Cousin John Todd and his mother, Aunt Mal, would be here. They arrived that afternoon— Cousin John was U.S. Major, Commanding the Arsenal at Baton Rouge, Louisiana—which the State troops had taken possession of with all the arms and ammunition—but allowed the garrison to keep their side arms and march out— Dear Aunt Mal—who was there with Cousin John—asked the privilege of having the Old Flag which had floated over the arsenal. It was given her and, folding it around her shoulders beside the Major, she marched out with the troops—as Cousin John said, "The Goddess of Liberty herself—couldn't have done it with a grander dignity." He spent the night with us and left this morning for Washington. Aunt Mal will remain a week before going to Bowling Green and Russellville where her only daughter Cousin Jane Harrison lives. Cousin John is greatly troubled at the condition of things and his own especial situation and we all share his trouble. He is a magnificent man, kindly and affectionate to an unusual degree and loves his people and all his relatives are Southerners—but he is a graduate of West Point—Loyal to his whole country and to his profession and condemns in toto—the action the South is taking—says he does not intend to resign but hopes beyond everything the difficulties will be settled before the army will be called to action against the South. He has a very flattering way, to me, of telling of his love affairs and this evening as he was walking up and down on the veranda after supper, smoking, he called me out to keep him company, saying as I joined him—"Jo" your old cousin is in all sorts of trouble, come and sympathize with me a little bit." "That I surely do," I assured him, then he told me—he was engaged to Miss Lucy Gwin, Senator [William] Gwin's daughter and "By Jove! I love her, "Jo!" was his emphatic expression—her father argues with me—setting forth in his strong way reasons why I should resign. Her mother storms and Lucy pleads—and all say I shan't have her unless I resign and I cannot resign—I would despise myself if I did, even for Lucy's sake." I tried in my poor little way to comfort him by saying—"If Lucy was worth his love she would herself despise him if he gave up a principle, even to win her, and would honor and love him more—if he stood true to what he thought right"— "I am afraid my little Jo don't know the world," and throwing his cigar away he said, "lets go in and see what Will Western has to say—but don't fall in love Jo, don't fall in love."— Nobody else ever calls me "Jo" except Cousin John and I like it from him. We went in and talked until late bed time of the public side of his case— which is that of so many other army men, all of us in deepest sympathy with him, except Mr. Western, who of course with his secession views thinks he ought to resign and side with his section and against the Government that has educated him and which he has sworn to defend. But Mr. Western is too much of a gentleman to have expressed his ideas very forcibly under the circumstances, Cousin John being his guest. I went in Aunt Mal's room with her to see her comfortably in bed—after taking off her dress and upper skirt—she said, "help Aunt get her flame [flannel?] petticoat off and Oh! what a relief it will be, for tho' gold is a great thing to have its a burden to carry"—and in truth the skirt which had a waist, as she always has to her skirts, was heavy enough. There being no safe way to send money from the South now—Aunt Mal had run cases [casings] in the waist of her flannel skirt, which was double and into these cases she had put 20 dollar gold pieces till she had several thousand dollars in gold around her body. When she got to Kentucky she could deposit it in the bank—we decided the best place to put it was—between her mattresses and I would make her bed whilst she was here, or help Emily do it—and the folded skirt would excite nobody's suspicion even if they saw it, so long as they did not lift it—so the dear old Aunt—whom we all love and admire so much—especially for her last heroic act slept as peacefully and *audibly* [sic] as if she were lying on down instead of gold.[5]

JAN. 7TH—

We spent the day listening to Aunt Mal's account of their exit from Baton Rouge Arsenal. We are all anxious and excited—wondering what will come next— I received a beautiful letter from Pa—full of sadness at the condition of affairs—and the unwisdom [*sic*] of the Southern states in leaving the Union—instead of fighting for their rights in Congress and at any hazard *in* the Union, and counseling me not to let my "Noble Loyalty to the Union and my father's principles" waiver, but in all discussion to keep control of myself and not get too excited"—i.e., keep my temper—hard to do.

JAN. 8TH—

The Secessionists had their parade and I was so glad it was such a poor one— Mr. Western, Jack, Mr. Grafton, Mr. Crew and Mr. Carrington—with a few other young men made quite a dashy appearance on the fine "chargers" at the head of the procession—but the most of it, and there was not much—was made up of the "Ragtag and bobtail" of the population. We wouldn't even drive down—but walked and tried to make ourselves as insignificant as possible to diminish even the crowd looking. When Mr. Western came home Jack and Mr. Grafton came with him. We made all sorts of fun of them, which they took good-naturedly saying—"Never mind—it won't be long before the whole town will be on our side—when Lincoln and his abolition gang show their hand." The hardship of the position of the Unionists in Tenn. and Ky., like Pa, Uncle Joe and others is that they are just as much opposed to Lincoln and his policy as the secessionists are and Pa was a Bell and Everett Elector and did all in his power—to prevent Lincoln's election—but he is no less a lover of his country because a party he regards untrue to the constitution were successful. He thinks for that very reason all true patriots should stand true to the old flag and to the whole country and he says—he opposes secession *most*—out of his love for the South, for disunion will be her ruin—for if there is war—it will surely be in the South and the whole land desolated and laid in waste and slavery will certainly go if the Union is dissolved. The only way, he thinks, is for the South to remain in the Union if she would maintain *any* of the "Southern rights" she is clamoring for.

JAN. 9TH—

We lunched with Mrs. Boyd today and dear Aunt Mal was overcome by a mistake she made which amused the rest of us immensely. Mrs. Boyd is a beautiful woman of about 30, married to the most horrid old brute of at least 60—immensely wealthy—and Mrs. Boyd was very poor with an invalid mother—and this old fellow told her how "he wanted to lavish his money on someone who would just let him love them." Ugh! it is disgusting to think of him, and how Mrs. Boyd—who is so pretty, pleasant and bright, could ever have married him passes my comprehension. "The Col." did not get home till we were ready to go into lunch. Before he came Aunt Mal was telling of a couple who came up on the boat from New Orleans—she, such a pretty young woman, and he so old and ugly. None of us could step on her toes or in any way stop what she thought an interesting story—till in the midst of it Col. Boyd came in and Mrs. B. introduced "My husband" to Aunt Mal and could hardly control her mirth as she did it. It was no joke to Aunt Mal, and she couldn't recover from the embarrassment of the situation. Her first words after leaving the house were—"My children, never tell a story till you've seen the entire family." I can't tell you how funny it all was and Mrs. Boyd enjoyed it more than anybody.

JAN. 11TH—

Nothing worth noting yesterday or today. Wrote a number of letters—several of the "don't counts" as Mr. Western calls the gentlemen who come to see us and who make no impression one way or the other—called last night. Dr. Lunsford Yandell with his high silk hat and his light overcoat on his arm—his usual dandified style and Mr. Carrington, stopped by a little while this afternoon to invite Miss Jane and me to go to the theatre with them tomorrow evening. Dr. Yandell is very good looking and very smart but is altogether too well aware of the fact to please me. When he makes a bright remark, as he often does—there is a distinct pause after it—for applause which I take pleasure in not giving. Mean, I know—but I do so dislike conceit—and yet ("Woe unto you hypocrites") I am going with him to the theatre.

JAN. 12TH—

The play was "Ingomar, the Barbarian" and beautiful. The definition of love was especially pretty. "A flame a single look will kindle—yet not an ocean quench," etc. I am really grateful to Dr. Yandell for giving me so much pleasure. He is intelligent and agreeable and didn't appear as conceited tonight. Perhaps I have misjudged him.[6]

JAN. 13TH—

We heard a good sermon today at Episcopal church—but when the Prayer for the President was ended—the silence—the absence of "Amens"—was painfully apparent. I think a good many people said their previous amens—more distinctly just to make their refusing to say Amen after this prayer the more noticeable. We had the usual Sunday afternoon callers and Jack and Mr. Witherspoon took tea with us. Mr. Western and Sister Jupe—could not possibly do more than they do for our pleasure—we are having a delightful time, but I am getting anxious to be at home again— Dear Ma is not very well this winter and there is so much excitement and nobody knows from one day to another—what will happen next—that I think I must bring my visit to an end soon—but Miss Jane says she never had such a good time in her life and wants to stay till spring and as she couldn't well stay if I left, I will have to stay awhile longer, for her sake. She is so suspicious too that she thinks I want to go home solely to spoil her good time—which the next hour she will beg my pardon for saying, as she knows full well—I would make a good many sacrifices for her pleasure.

Jan. 14th—

I finished Phebe's wedding dress today, and the bridal veil and wreath Miss Jane will get tomorrow. Phebe was very indignant when Miss Jane suggested *Pink* roses for her wreath and said she wanted white of the "*Virginest purity*"—so white they will be—she wanted the dress low neck and short sleeves and so I made it. The effect of the black neck rising out of the white muslin is peculiar—she wants white kid gloves also. Mr. Western says he will present these to the "Bride." We are all too anxious to get her settled down to decent behavior— to oppose any little thing like gloves and wreaths.

Jan. 15th—

This morning Mr. Western's cousin Jimmie Lotspitch came. He is going to stay with and read Law with Mr. Western. He has dark hair and eyes, a rosy complexion, is tall and slender with hands and feet disproportionately small—

about 22, a very *pretty* young man without much force, I judge.

Phebe was married tonight and the modest bride-like air she put on was amusing to us who know what a termagant she is—why such a decent negro as Johnson wants to marry her I don't know, for she has made and will make him no end of trouble. Johnson and the negro preacher both looked very nice in swallow-tail coats, & white vests—and Johnson had on white kid gloves also. The preacher read the Episcopal marriage service and didn't substitute the names for the "N and M" in the prayer book, so we are wondering if they are quite married after all. They had a fine supper and a fine time. We went back of the cabins and through the window watched them dancing. It was very funny to see Phebe as she danced, with every now and then a long swoopy glide—as she looked over her shoulder to see her dress and veil trail—but the dance grew "fast and furious" and "Jim Crow" had his day or night till 12 o'clock when Mr. Western had previously told them the frolic must end—and now sister hopes to have peace and quietness in the kitchen for a time.[7]

Jan. 16th—

We were all very much excited today. When Mr. Western came home at noon, he told us the usual crowd were in his office that morning and the inevitable talk on secession came up with more excitement than usual—as a prominent man who had been "Union" had come out for secession. (Mr. Torian is Mr. Western's partner and Will Webb is Mr. T's brother-in-law and though not in the firm has the same office. Jack, Mr. Grafton and Mr. Witherspoon are usually in there a while every day). This morning in the excitement, Mr. Grafton and Mr. Webb got into a personal altercation— Mr. Webb called Mr. Grafton a "*Traitor*" and a "*liar.*" Mr. Grafton jerked up a chair and would have killed Mr. Webb had it come down on his head with the force Grafton's strength was wielding—but Jack sprang forward and caught the chair and the others caught Grafton. Jack, saying as he caught the chair, "No Grafton, we are all *your* friends, Webb is alone—you can't strike him." Grafton furious, marched out glaring at Webb, as he left saying—"This is not the end, sir."—"insignificant as you are, pistols make us equal"—and now we are all scared to death for fear they will fight a duel—but Mr. Western thinks not and charged us not to mention the matter if we see either of them, as they hope to settle it without notoriety.

JAN. 18TH—

I couldn't write last night. Too much happened and I was too excited. When Mr. Western came home, we of course hoped to hear more of the trouble between Mr. Webb and Grafton. We all like Mr. Grafton best but sister Jupe, Jane and I being Union, are more in sympathy with Webb's principles—though he is so excitable and uses such irritating expressions. He never will call secessionists anything but "Traitors." Mr. Western said nothing more had happened *worth speaking* of. We know now what the worth speaking of meant. After supper, sister Jupe and Miss Jane went down to the Gayosa Hotel to spend the evening with a Mrs. Dockery, a bride and a cousin of Miss Jane's from North Carolina. I did not care to go as I wanted to write some letters. Mr. Western said he had some business down town so he would drive them down and bring them home. So I was left alone. I had just sat down to write when the bell rang and Ed. [a servant] came and told me Mr. Grafton was in the parlor. I got in such a tremor of nervousness, I could hardly quiet myself. What would he say? What would I say if he mentioned the trouble? When I went in he was standing before the fire—with a little picture of my mother (which in a little frame stood on the mantle) in his hand. After the usual greeting, I said, "I am sorry sister and Miss Jane are not here, they went to call at the Hotel." "Yes," he replied, "I saw them"—looking up with a smile he so often makes express almost more than words— still standing looking at the picture he asked, "Is this your mother?" "Yes," I replied, "and the dearest, best mother that ever lived"—and Oh! how glad I was we had struck such a safe subject. "How happy you must be," he went on—with father, mother, sisters and brothers—so many to love you—"I have *no* one," and putting the picture back he sat down—an expression of great sadness on his face. "Then is your mother dead," I asked. "Yes—she died when I was too young to remember her and my father shortly after—I never had a sister or brother." "You are indeed alone," I said, "but you have so many good friends—and your Uncle—Mr. Crew"— "he is my mother's brother and the only relative I have in the world— but—if I should die tonight—or tomorrow (after a pause he added) what difference would it make to my friends and tho' Uncle might grieve a little he would really be benefitted." (Mr. Grafton is wealthy.) "No, Miss Underwood, my death would make no difference to any one." "You are unjust and unkind to your friends," I replied—"I am sure we would all be very truly grieved if any misfortune came to you and it *would make a* difference to all your friends to miss you from their lives." "Oh! if you would only change the pronouns in that sentence and instead of *we* and *their*—say *I and My.*" "That is easily done," I said. "*I* would be very sorry if any misfortune came to you (or any of my friends) and it would make a difference to *me* to miss *you* (or any of my friends) out of my life—but why are you so sad and serious tonight?" Then I was awfully sorry I asked that but I was nervous and was trying to make talk—for I saw he was sad and feared if he told me of the trouble, not being in sympathy with his secession ideas and being in sympathy with Mr. Webb's unionism, whilst liking Mr. Grafton so much better, I might yet say something to hurt him so I wanted to avoid the subject—especially as Mr. Western had charged us not to seem to know anything about it. To my last speech he answered, "You've spoilt it all by that "any of my friends," then went on—"Miss Underwood, I generally take life as it comes to me and waste no time in self pity but tonight I felt so unutterably lonely—I felt a great longing for my mother (whom I never knew), for a sister, for someone who loved me—to whom I could unburden my heart— knowing right or wrong I would find sympathy. Then in my loneliness my heart turned to you— I did not mean to say all this or tell you of my sadness, in fact I meant *not* to do it. You have given me a proper reprimand— I am only one of your *many* friends—nothing more to anyone in all the world." Then indeed the flood gates of my sympathy were opened and I told him—how it grieved *me* to hear *him* talk that way— how we all liked him better than anyone who came to the house—that he was the most agreeable young man we knew—we all thought that and I said every nice and kind thing I could to comfort him and all I said was true, too. Then he replied whilst he knew all I said was the effort of my tender heart to drive away his sadness—it awakened a hope of joy he could not suppress and told me he had intended simply to say good-bye as he expected to leave town the next day—but—then he told me in words—I can't write—that he loved me—that it was wrong for him to tell me—as he had already offered himself to his state as a soldier when the inevitable fight came and he could not ask any bright young life [be] tied to his but he found he could not leave me for that or *any other absence* without trying for the happiness of winning a little word of love from me. I don't know just what I said—I don't know just what to think of myself—whether I am capable of loving or not—for whilst I admire him so greatly, I don't feel as he feels toward me. I wish I did—for he seems to me everything a girl might love except, alas! his desire to break up our country, which is a broad gulf in our sympathies. I tried to explain to him that I liked him better than any man I knew—but did not love him as I wanted to feel toward the man I gave my heart to. He said "if he lived he hoped to win that—that hope gave him a desire to live that he had not when he came" and taking my hand—he kissed it and said good-bye—asking me in a solemn sort of way to "Pray for me tonight—I have no mother to do it";—and certainly I did with the best of my poor faith. He is a man whose appearance pleases me extremely. He is about 5 ft. 11 inches, splendidly proportioned—large but not at all fat—has a very easy walk and carriage. No appearance of trying to stand straight and yet is straight, his head the least little bit inclined forward. His hair is about the color of a chestnut hull, evidently well kept but never very smooth—his head is rather large—his brow broad—neither high or low—his eye brows more straight than arched and his eyes the clearest blue grey with dark and long lashes—his nose straight and not too large—his mouth good shape, rather large with regular white teeth and a firm chin—his face clean shaven, neither mustache or beard. The expression of his face is in repose, serious almost sad, but he has the brightest, most expressive smile I nearly ever saw. His dress is always perfectly plain—but one cannot fail to notice the immaculate neatness of his linen. His manner when I first met him though perfectly gentlemanly irritated me—with me it was like a big New Foundland dog playing with a kitten and seemed to say "don't be afraid, I won't hurt you, I just want to amuse myself a while." And I really think that was the way he felt. When he left last night I was all excited and didn't want to talk about him or his visit to Miss Jane or sister Jupe—so I practiced a little deception by jumping in bed (I had undressed in preparation for this) when I heard the carriage drive in the gate and when they came in the room pretending I was fast asleep. Sister Jupe thinking I was asleep said, "I won't wake her, so goodnight," and went to her room and Miss Jane kindly following her example came quietly to bed for which I was duly thankful—though it was long in the night before I slept. This morning with questions I started her talking about her cousin, the bride and was amused when she said, "Aha! you missed something by not going with us—we had a nice little talk with Mr. Grafton"— "If that is so I'll go next time," I said, and felt hypocritical and safe. When we went into breakfast this morning Emily said Mr. Western had his breakfast early and had gone and told her to let sister Jupe and us sleep as we were tired. I couldn't help feeling uneasy, just why I couldn't say— when he came at noon—he told us—Mr. Grafton challenged Mr. Webb the morning after the fight, yesterday and all day the seconds, Mr. Roland and Jack were arranging matters and they were to go across the river at sun up this morning and at a selected place fight a duel! Then it all came over me what Mr. Grafton meant by "if I should die tonight—or to-morrow and any other absence" "I expect to leave town to-morrow." I was thankful when Miss Jane asked "Are they dead?" Mr. Western answered "No, neither." My heart gave a great throb of joy. He continued, "They went across the river with seconds—Drs. and two or three friends on either side for they are both very popular"—and with so many interested it somehow ("Thank the good Lord") leaked out and the officers got wind of it and got across the river just in time to stop the awful murder and suicide, for that is just what a duel is— Mr. Webb apologized to Mr. Grafton and so "honor is satisfied." How absurd dueling is! Mr. Webb left on the noon train for Hopkinsville, Ky. and we are all awfully thankful it ended as it did. After telling us all this Mr. Western looked at me and laughingly said, "Now, I wonder if anybody can tell where Grafton was last night when things were arranged he disappeared and none of us could find him." Miss Jane said, "Why we met him in the hotel," and alas! for my tricks at secrecy—Ed—(waiting on the table) said, "Mr. Grafton was out here Mars. William. I let him in myself." Then I *was* unmercilessly [*sic*] teased in spite of Mr. Western's kindly efforts to come to my rescue and I realized how worse than useless any efforts I can ever make at deception are—for anything I try to keep—like murder—will out.

I have forgotten to say Aunt Mal left day before yesterday.

Jan. 20th—

The usual day. Sister Jupe, Miss Jane and I enjoy each other's company and never lack for pleasant subjects of conversation as we sit together sewing and it is funny how if any one of us is reading or writing the three sided talk goes on just the same. This evening several gentlemen called; the secession feeling is increasing and it is impossible to keep it out of social talk and our discussions get more and more excited often approaching a disagreeable point. Mr. Western is always so considerate for the feelings of others that he is never disagreeable though he is the most radical secessionist I know. In every letter Pa charges me not to get excited in arguments but I can't help it— I read all his speeches that he is making all over the district—every opportunity that offers and get my best arguments from them—for his desire to keep the South in the Union and his best arguments to that end—are prompted by his love for the South. He knows she can but suffer most in any effort to break up the Union. He opposes Lincoln's policy as much as anyone. Gen. Lowell Rousseau's speeches are fine, too and he and Pa both being Southern men with all their interests in and with the South nobody can attribute any other motive than love for the south and her best interests to them.

Jan. 22nd, 1861.—

Last night Mr. Grafton called and shortly after three other gentlemen and I was thankful, that the conversation was necessarily general.

Jan. 23rd—

Rainy day which gave me a good chance to write home letters.

Jan. 25th—

Last night had the usual calls and exciting discussions. I am getting very anxious to go home. Ma isn't very well and Pa is evidently greatly troubled about the condition of the country and I want to be with them—so we have decided to leave here next week. I received a letter today from John Ward—which I wish he hadn't written—it troubles me no little— John is one of the best fellows in the world and I like him so much, ever since he came to Bowling Green years ago and went into Pa's office to study law—we have had such good times together—without any sentimentality or thought of love making—I called him my "brother friend." Now he has spoilt all that—he always has an idea he must define his position and he has done it this time much to my discomfort. I hardly know how to answer his letter without grieving him and goodness knows—I don't want to hurt his feelings. He is a noble true patriot and after writing about the condition of the country and his determination to "stand by the Union and give his life for it if necessary" and of a fine speech Pa

made at Brown's Lock[8]—he says he was out at Mount Air—he
and Hugh Gwyn, and learned from Ma that I would soon be
home and "after giving the matter deep thought"—he felt
he could not with honesty go on as he had been doing and
felt it best to "define his position" before I returned—so that
when we met—he would no longer keep up a pretense of being simply my "brother friend" as my absence had revealed to
him what he had long suspected, that his feelings were very
different from that of a friend or brother and he wanted me
to know when I met him again—I would meet "a man who
loved me with the most intense and pure devotion a man
could give a woman"—but if I could not return this feeling
and still regarded him simply as a friend—he would strive to
maintain that status with all the fidelity of our past friendship
and endeavor not to grieve me by intruding his love—which
would only hallow our friendship, etc. *Now isn't that a pity!*
He has always been my confident, in a way— I have told him
more freely than anyone else (except of course Ma) of all
of my beaus and what I thought of them and how I liked
them all so much but didn't love any of them—and now I do
wonder if ever I said anything that made him think I might
love him. Surely I never did anything so foreign to my feelings—he is neither vain or conceited—in fact I believe he
knows as well as I do that *I do not love him* and has written this
letter, because he has that fine—if Quixotic idea that he must
never seem what he is not—so as soon as he suspects himself
of any other feeling than unallayed friendship he would feel
himself a hypocrite if he didn't tell me at once for his own
comfort and honor—but I wish he hadn't—for now our intercourse can never be without an undercurrent of reserve—for
I, at least, must hereafter be guarding my words—lest when
I would be kind, I be cruel instead. I thought he loved Jen-
nie Stubbins and hope yet he will find, what seems so plain
to me—that her nature is gentler and far more lovable than

mine and she and John seem to me just suited to each other. Our home is so lovely and Pa and Ma so delightful and make it so pleasant for everyone who comes to "Mount Air" that knowing my own deficiencies so well—I can't help thinking sometimes—young men imagine they are in love with me—when it is my environment that captivates them—and wondering if they would think they loved *me* if I were old Caplingers' daughter.

Jan. 27th—

The young men here have organized a Company called the "Shelby Grays"—and all our secession friends have joined it. Mr. Witherspoon told us—when they voted for Captain—each man wrote his vote on a slip of paper which was dropped in Dr. Yandell's high silk hat—and then counted—and when the count was made every single man had one vote, except Jack Henry—who had none—so knowing every man except Jack had voted for himself they made Jack Captain. They are organized as state guard but do not hesitate to say—they will fight against the Union— I asked under what flag and Mr. Grafton said "A Banner with the Virginia motto "Sic Semper Tiranus," on it and *your* friend Lincoln for the prostrate figure would please us best"— He knows I dislike Lincoln as much as he does and speaks of him as "your friend Lincoln" just to provoke me and then laughs when I get excited— This is one of the hard things for the Unionists to contend with—so many of them don't approve Lincoln's course and have to fight his extreme views as well as the secessionists.[9]

Jan. 29th—

I went down town yesterday to do a little shopping—sister Jupe and Miss Jane did not go and the day was so beautiful and mild I walked— when I was starting home Mr. Grafton joined me and asked to carry my little packages and walk home with me— I could not say him nay— when we got out on Vance Street where we met almost no people—he told me again how much he cared for me and when I tried to tell him that I did not love him—he would not let me go on—but asked me if I loved anyone else— I told him no— I liked a great many but felt no love, such as *I* believed in & *he* had laughed at "for anyone"— "I no longer laugh—you are avenged," he said—but listen to me and don't answer me now—I cannot take no for an answer—so I listened and he talked so beautifully—telling me of his lonely childhood, of his life as a man—he is now 28—of his longing for love and home—asking me to let him write to me and by and by come up to see me at my home and meet my father and mother and to withhold my answer till then—when I would know him better—then I reminded him that my father was a strong Union Man and had no sympathy with his secession ideas— "Don't let's talk of differences now," he said, and so we did not and I consented to write to him—to all he asked about not answering him yet—for truly I don't know whether I love him or not— I know I don't feel as I want to feel towards the man I would marry but maybe there is no such exalted love as I imagine; yet I would not be satisfied with less—and his secessionism is a great barrier between us. He is not my hero with his disunion ideas. Well—I will wait—Oh! I wish he was a Patriot like John Ward— Miss Jane and sister Jupe too—were very curious to know what we were talking about walking all that way home and I remembered Talerand's [*sic*] speech that "Words were used to conceal thoughts" and talked so much about my shopping, the beauty of the day—the walk and Mr. Grafton too—that they forgot they had asked what he was talking about.—[10]

CHAPTER ONE

J<small>AN</small>. 31<small>ST</small>—

Last night, sister Jupe invited the girls and gentlemen we have known best—about 30—to spend the evening and we had a most delightful time— Mr. Western and sister are perfect hosts—and the house was lovely—with the windows open and the sweet odors of flowers floating in—everybody expressed regret that we were so soon going away—and mingled with my pleasure at getting back home. There are many regrets that I may never see again so many of the pleasant people I've met here.

Mr. Grafton leaves tomorrow for his plantation in Miss. and we go next day. I am quite sure he has made a confidant of Jack—for last night Jack managed in such a funny way to get us away from the crowd a little while— It was near the close of the evening. Mr. Crew and I were standing near one of the low French windows, Jack from the outside of the window pulled my sash—saying, "I wish you could help me a little—have you a pin"— Mr. Crew and I both supposing he had met with some accident, that a pin could remedy—I quietly stepped out through the window—having taken a pin from my belt—as I did so, "What can I do?" I asked. "Give it to Grafton," Jack said smiling and quickly stepped through the window into the Parlor—leaving me alone with Mr. Grafton—who had a few moments before bid good-bye to sister and Miss Jane—in the other parlor and made me wonder, as I saw him going out the door with his hat—why he had not bid me good-bye too. "I thought you had gone," said I. "I could not say good-bye to you, in there," he replied, and then in broken sentences with feeling repeated what he had before told me and taking my hand—lifted it quickly to his lips and was gone. As I lingered a few moments on the piazza—hoping the cool night air might banish the flush I felt burning in my cheeks— Jack came out and after walking up and down a little while we went in. The only reference Jack made to Mr. Grafton was to say, "That's a fine fellow, cousin, don't be too hard on him." Then changed the subject to the scene about us. I was glad when everybody went home—for it was hard to talk and be pleasant to people when my mind wasn't on what I was saying and I am afraid the last hour I was far more excited than brilliant.

FEB. 1ST—

Busy packing with a number of interruptions from friends calling to say good-bye. Jack and Mr. Witherspoon took tea with us.

✎ CHAPTER TWO ✎

On returning to Bowling Green, Josie discovered that the major topic of conversation in her hometown, as in Memphis, concerned the pros and cons of secession. To her friends she repeated the fears and opinions expressed by her parents and praised the attempts of rational residents to curb the growing hostility. She also lamented the refusal of others to measure words in light of their explosive potential.

The April 12 firing on Charleston's Fort Sumter marked the beginning of war, and throughout the summer Kentucky's opposition to secession increased, as did the fear of invasion. Appreciating the volatile sentiments of its residents as well as the state's precarious geographic position, Kentucky's governor and the legislature proclaimed that the Bluegrass State would never send troops to fight against her southern sisters; the commonwealth would remain neutral.

"MOUNT AIR," FEB. 3RD—

Home again with the best father and mother that ever lived and the dearest old home in the world. It is worth going away to make everybody so glad to see me back again. We had a grand time when we left Memphis. Mr. Western and sister Jupe went to the train with us and there we found Jack—Mr. Witherspoon, Mr. Crew, Mr. Coward, Mr. Roland and Mr. Carrington waiting to see us off—some with flowers and Mr. Crew with a big box of candy for us. They made a big to-do about our having no escort—said "it would never do to let young ladies leave Memphis without a gentleman to look after their comfort—such a reflection on the gallantry of the City would never do." Mr. Witherspoon and several others offered to go— Then Mr. Crew said the jealousy of those left behind would be too greatly excited if any but a relative went as escort—so Jack must go—which he expressed himself glad to do—only he hadn't his overcoat. Off went Mr. Witherspoon's overcoat—which Jack put on, feeling in the inside pocket with such a suggestive air—that Mr. Crew immediately handed him his purse—as did several others. He took the bills from Mr. Crews—handing him back the empty purse, and so after much pleasantry we left with Jack as escort—which contributed no little to the pleasure of the journey and I was particularly glad—as I wanted Pa and Ma to know him and thus further heal the breach that had existed between our two families. When we reached Bowling Green—the evening had grown chilly and dear Ma was there in the carriage to meet us and Cliff Rhodes for Miss Jane. Ma had had a chill that very morning, and did not look at all well and my heart smote me with remorse—that I had staid away so long. Hugh Gwyn and John Ward were also there to welcome us home and Mr. Baxter had gotten on the train at the [Memphis] Junction, 5 miles out—so we had a jolly home coming, in spite of some awkwardness on my part in greeting John Ward. Sister Fanny—Mr. Grider came out to take supper and spend the evening and Jack staid all night leaving this morning for his home in Clarksville. I was so proud of him and so proud of my own dear father and mother too— for though Jack's father, Uncle Gus Henry, is one of the most elegant and accomplished men of the day—he is not one wit ahead of dear Pa—in all that makes up a courtly christian gentleman. When Jack asked Ma and Pa if I might visit them at their home in Clarksville during the Fair this summer—he did it in such a way as to say plainly, "This means that we want to forget the old trouble and be friends," and Ma's gracious consent to my going was an acceptance of his friendliness. There was of necessity some talk of the condition of the country—as Pa wanted to get from Jack the sentiments of the Tennessee people but both appreciated the situation as guest and host and there was no objectionable excitement. I have kept this Journal that I might recall things to tell Ma of my visit and it seems a very egotistical affair—only of I, I, I—but if I had written of Miss Jane's doings as well as my own, it would have taken more time than I had to spare so I have left her to tell her own story which may be far more interesting than mine.

Feb. 5th—1861

It is so good to be at home. Sunday we all went to church and heard quite a good sermon from Mr. [R. K.] Smoot, the Presbyterian minister. Sister Fanny, Mr. Grider and their boys Warner and "Judge" came home with us and spent the day. Uncle Henry Underwood is here—Pa's dear old bachelor brother whom from my earliest childhood I have longed to see. He came whilst I was in Memphis—bringing a young Mr. [Tom] Rutherford with him. Mr. R. is about 22, well educated and poor—he is staying at "Mount Air" reading law with Pa. He seems a quiet gentlemanly fellow. Uncle Henry is about 70 with gray hair and mustache—a large man with the kindest face—and blue eyes—which like Pa's easily overflow with tears. He talks very little and that little in short sentences—but never seems morose—his quietness is more that of gentleness—perhaps sadness or lack of self appreciation. My heart already goes out to the dear old man and I hope I can bring a little happiness into his lonely life—coming as he does—in his old age—penniless and as he feels, a failure to live with his more successful brothers. But if he were a prince he could not find kinder welcome to hearts and home than he finds here—in fact—his poverty and lack of success make a warmer place for him in the tender hearts of dear Pa and Ma whose doors have ever been open to the unfortunate.

The all absorbing question here, as in Memphis—is the breaking up of the Union and it seems no longer a question but a fact—though Pa seems to think if the border states stand firm it may yet be saved. In the hope of saving Kentucky and preventing her passing an ordinance of Secession, Uncle Joseph Underwood and a number of other prominent old men of the state who had retired from politics have again entered and been elected to the Legislature of the state (after having been U.S. Senators and Supreme Court [Kentucky Court of Appeals] Judges) so that they can save her from the hot-headed action of secessionists—who don't realize—that in event of war, Kentucky would be rebaptized—"The Dark and bloody ground."[1] They are trying to keep Kentucky *neutral*—but this is pretty hard in these exciting times when every man, woman and child is wrought up to the highest pitch of excitement. Mr. Grider thinks it impossible and he and dear Ma, who is the most intense patriot I ever knew—think it a shame for any state to stand neutral when the destruction of the Union is at stake—Pa, Uncle Joe, Col. Henry Grider, Judge Loving—here and the older and conservative men of the state think it the only way to keep Kentucky in the Union—as the Gov., Beriah Magoffin, is known to be in sympathy with the secessionists and his influence and that of the hot-headed young men in the Legislature—would probably get an ordinance of secession passed—if any other policy were adopted now. The policy of the *state* is neutral but the people are not—goodness knows. Every man woman and child is either "Rebel or Union." All the older and thinking men—who have most at stake and love their country best and as Pa says—know disunion means ruin to the South and her "peculiar institutions" and a terrible war—want to preserve the Union. The unthinking hot-heads and blatherskites are in for secession. They want change and excitement and "War" (Warh) as that simpleton Bob Cox says. He never did a day's honest work in his life—owns nothing and lives on Uncle Joe—(his brother-in-law). Uncle Joe rises early and sits up late trying to preserve Kentucky to the Union and save the country from war. Bob Cox rides into town about 10 o'clock, on one of Uncle Joe's best horses, puts it up at the Livery stable, at Uncle Joe's expense, and stands around the streets (in clothes Uncle Joe has paid for) all day—talking secession and abusing Union men. I don't see how Uncle can be so tolerant— If I were he—Mr. Robert Cox would have to secede from my home—pretty quick or keep his mouth shut—whatever he chose to think— Ma has always been the most intense Southerner I ever knew and hated Abolitionists as envious meddlers and had little use for anything above "Mason and Dixies Line" and she says now to think that the South will be so foolish as to break up the country for which their fathers fought, bled and died and give up the old flag, to the Yankees—instead of staying in the Union and fighting for their rights under the Constitution of our fathers—is more than she can bear. Her grandfather Gen. William Henry was in Washington's army and he and his six sons—her father, Mathew [*sic*] Winston Henry (one of them) fought through the war of 1812 and she has inherited the combined patriotism of the family. It nearly kills her that Uncle Gus Henry of Tennessee (Jack's father) and Uncle Pat of Memphis should favor secession and she glories in the fact that "Uncle Wint," her youngest brother, is at West Point and in case of War will be ready to do honorable service under the old flag and yet it is so hard to think the South so wrong. Today she said, "O, if it had been—Massachusetts and Connecticut that seceded how happy I would have been." Pa's love for the South is just as great and he has not a relative or personal interest above the Mason and Dixon's line, but his patriotism transcends section and personal interest and he cannot bear the thought of seeing this great country with its glorious future among the nations and influence in the world if she holds together—broken up into insignificant provinces—for he says "the doctrine of secession once admitted and established means continuous deteriorations and he can see only evil to the whole country and absolute ruin to the South—in a division of the country—on the basis of any state seceding whenever they have a real or supposed grievance." He gets letters continually from his friends throughout the South—men with whom he served in Congress—Senator [William] Gwin of California—[James Murray] Mason and [Robert Mercer] Hunter of Va.—[Felix] Zollicoffer—whom Pa loves, as David did Jonathan—all setting forth their views of the situation and trying to bring Pa to their way of thinking—but dear Pa—cannot agree with them. He cannot on any grounds think it right or best for the country or any part of it to break up the Union and hard as it is for him to be separated in thought and action from so many he loves—he must stand firm to the principles he thinks right and many sad hours it brings him. Emerson Etheridge of Tenn. agrees with Pa—and I am always glad when a letter comes from him for though I do believe Pa would stand firm and true to his own conviction of right if all the world were against him. It is hard for one who loves his friends and section as Pa does to go against them. I am glad he has the comfort of most of the prominent men in Kentucky being Unionists. Men like Gov. (now Senator) John J. Crittenden—Joe Holt, (Attorney General), [Robert] Mallory—most of the Congressmen from this state—George D. Prentice, editor of the *Louisville Journal*, most of the prominent lawyers in the state and *all* of them in Bowling Green are strong Union men. In fact all the men in Bowling Green of any position or prominence whatever are Union men—and yet many of these men have—wild reckless unthinking inexperienced sons—who make so much noise [about] secession as to almost drown their fathers' wiser council. Marius Henry said a very good thing yesterday— He is staying at "Mount Air" now and Warner, Henry or Marius ride into town for the mail, as soon as they can get their breakfast. Yesterday Marius went—nobody starts at anything till the mail comes and somebody sends the news out, from the *Louisville Journal*—for the situation in South Carolina is of all absorbing interest. When Marius came in as he threw the little bag of mail on the table before Pa he said, with great excitement, "Uncle Warner, the Union people got to have more 'Rowdies,' they can't succeed 'thout more rowdies—I went up to the Depot when the train came in and all the "riff raff" in town was up there and when the train came in and when it started off they all yelled, "hurrah for Jeff Davis," and yelled and yelled—till the train was gone and every man on that train will think Bowling Green is *Rebel*—when she's *Union*—can't we get a pack of rowdies somehow—Uncle Warner, to yell Union at the trains." Everybody agreed that was not a bad statement of the situation, for though the Union sentiment is much the greatest in Kentucky, the Rebels have so many rowdies they make the most noise. Then they have the advantage of having admiration and enthusiasm for the man Jeff Davis—at the head of their cause—whilst the Kentucky Unionists despise Lincoln and fear his policy and it is doubly hard to stand firm for a principle and true to the Union under these circumstances and requires a high order of patriotism to be a Kentucky Union man.

Feb. 10th—

We are all as absorbed in the general and public interests that little personal matters are of no consequence—though our pleasant home life goes on as usual. Mr. Rutherford teaches the boys and we have at last persuaded little Mary to go over to the School room (in the overseer's house) for a little while each day. She didn't want to go to school with "the boys." Mr. Rutherford is evidently beginning to sympathize with secession though he don't say much about it—but talks about going back to Virginia this spring. I asked dear old Uncle Henry what he thought about Virginia leaving the Union and he said—"I don't know daughter, I don't know—I don't want to think about it at all." There begins to be unpleasant feelings between old friends who take different sides. When Lizzie Wright and I met today we both got too excited—just what we said I won't try to recall—but when we parted I had a hot feeling through me and Lizzie's face was flushed and though we were both polite—we did not kiss each other as usual on parting. We have never had a disagreeable word pass between us in all our lives before. I'll be careful not to let it happen again.

John Ward and Hugh Gwyn come out as often as usual—but not always together as formerly. John is strong Union and Hugh is a Rebel and when I go in town they are often in different groups of young men, which never used to be the case— Hugh is so opposed to anything disagreeable—that however he differed with an old friend he would try to be pleasant—and when he is out here—and the subject of secession comes up—if the discussion begins to be warm—he manages to change it with some joke—I got a beautiful letter from Mr. Grafton today—but he takes such a queer view of things—he does not want me to answer him yet—wants me to wait till he comes up next summer—says he does not think I yet begin to comprehend what my love for him would mean or to understand his for me—. He makes it hard for me to answer his letters and is making me treat him unfairly—for so much as I admire him—I am quite sure I do not love him—for if I did I would feel worse at being separated from him and this I want to tell him, for I should despise myself if I trifled with a true affection or flirted with a pretended love.

Feb. 14th—

Sister Fanny with her dear little boys came out to spend a few days—whilst Mr. Grider is away— Mr. Grider is away for a few days at a time quite often now and Ben Bristow is at his home quite often and there is something mysterious in their confabs and goings and comings. They are both opposed to neutrality though they have to submit to it—openly—but I believe some way they are organizing Union men. The young men—secessionists—all over the state are flocking to join Buckner's "State Guard," which everybody knows is a subterfuge for organizing the secessionists and getting them armed by the State. Pa is making speeches on every possible occasion and continually writing letters for various newspapers throughout the state to break Union sentiment and hold Kentucky in the Union. Spring is coming fast and when one looks over this beautiful country, it is hard to realize the dissensions and bitterness animating the people.[2]

Feb. 18th—

We had an exciting and disagreeable talk this evening over an editorial in the town paper of which Henry Skiles is editor. There is never any doubt about what Ben Grider thinks on any subject and if there are two sides to any question—he is decidedly on one side or the other and lets everybody know where he stands and he never can see why everybody else can't be as positive as he— Henry Skiles, on the contrary, always sees a little good in everybody's opinion and is not overly positive in his own, so he is naturally sorely perplexed at this time how to write his editorials so as not to offend anybody and he accepts Kentucky's neutrality with thankfulness—so today Ma and Mr. Grider were very severe on Henry. Mr. Grider said "he was a man without prejudice or principle and a coward"— I like Henry very much and tried to defend him and Pa tried to moderate the severity of Mr. Grider's denunciations—which were brought to a sudden and amusing halt—by the entrance of Belle Skiles (Henry's sister) who had come to spend a week with us.

FEB. 20TH—

Old Aunt Phillis, the oldest of all the negroes, died yesterday and was buried today. She has been too old to work ever since I can remember and her sight was almost entirely gone. Her chief occupation was telling tales to the children, who—both white and black—loved to gather in her cabin and listen to stories of Old Virginia about when "your Pa was little and I '*nussed* him,' or the fox hunts and company keeping at the 'great house' in Virginia when Miss Betsy was Mistis and things *wus* fine in them days." She was too old and feeble to go to church and it was one of my daily duties—which I shall miss now, to read a little in the Bible to her every afternoon and I will never forget how the dull old black face would light up—with religious ecstasy, almost beautifying it—as I read to her the Psalms of praise and the glorious promises. She had a pet Frog—that would hop into her cabin and sit on the hearth close beside her—now and then turning its head to look up at her—a strange sympathy and I sometimes fancied even a resemblance between them—not long ago the poor old woman ever thinking of the past—said, if she could just see "little Jimmie Alsop—who must be *'bout* a man now—she wouldn't ask nuthin' more." Jimmie Alsop was a cousin of Pa's—whom Aunt Phillis nursed when he was a baby at least

50 years ago. So sister Jupe dressed up in cousin Bob West's clothes—shortly afterwards and rushed into Aunt Phillis' cabin, saying, "how'dy Aunt Phillis don't you remember Jimmie Alsop"? She certainly remembered Jimmie and shook his (sister Jupe's) hand, and patted his back and felt how tall he was—asked all sorts of questions about *Old Virginny* and *was happy.* Sister gave her a present and regretting she couldn't stay longer—went and changed her clothes, making everybody promise they would never let Aunt Phillis know she had not really seen Jimmie. When Pa heard of it, he was very indignant and tried to scold sister Jupe for "deceiving a poor old blind negro"—but sister being always equal to any occasion answered, "Now, father—how strange it is that you would want that poor old blind negro to go all her life longing to see Jimmie Alsop and be so cruel as not to gratify her—*now,* she thinks she has had a visit from him and is happy. If you want to take her pleasure all away—you can tell her it wasn't Jimmie at all, but I don't see how anybody could be so mean as that." Nobody was and Aunt Phillis talked of Jimmie's visit to the day of her death. A few years ago she and old "Uncle" Nat Payne—who was as old and almost as decrepid [*sic*] as Aunt Phillis—got married, much to the amusement of the other darkies—and Uncle Nat, after that, took up his abode at Mount Air with Aunt Phillis. Pa and Mr. Payne had some pleasantry about Mr. Payne making the match as the best way to get Uncle Nat taken care of, but no doubt the two poor old souls were a sort of comfort to each other and I trust they are both happy in Heaven now. The funeral sermon was a good deal better than many white men could preach.[3]

FEB. 25TH—1861

Pa had a letter from Wint [Winston Henry]— He says the Kentucky Cadets at West Point are awfully anxious to know what Kentucky is going to do and he wanted to know what Pa would do or advise him to do in case she seceded. Pa wrote him, he should stand by the Union and the Old Flag and hoped Wint would do the same and never help destroy a government his father and grandfather had fought so bravely to establish and from which he was receiving an education and a profession. Things are getting worse and worse; everybody fears war and the country is holding its breath as it were—so intense is the interest in the situation at Charleston. More and more of the young men of the State are joining Buckner's "State Guard" and Gen. Rousseau has established a camp across the river from Louisville where Union men can join his "Legion"—and neutrality seems harder and harder to maintain and dear Pa is more and more troubled and less hopeful that war can be averted.

E. Norton stopped over a day on his way to Russellville and took supper with us. He, too has gone over to the secessionists and I was indignant at the way he talked last night, knowing Pa is a Union man and being at his table. It was unlike E., who had heretofore been so mild— If he had had any sense he would have seen what a fool he was making of himself from the dignified way Pa declined discussing the question with him. But dear Ma couldn't help hitting back—for Pa's sake—and when we rose from the supper table she said, "Mr. Norton (she had always called him E. before), you will excuse me from going in the Parlor with you—and of course you would not wish to be asked ever again to become a guest in the home of Unionists after the sentiments you have expressed." Poor E. almost lost his breath and stumbled over—"I did not mean to offend," and I got us into the parlor as best I could, where the hour we spent wasn't very pleasant though I couldn't help feeling sorry for his awkward position—for I knew he hadn't considered the significance of his words— but Ma has taught him a lesson he isn't likely soon to forget.

The feeling is growing more and more bitter between Union people and secessionists, try as we will to maintain the same outward show of friendship—there is a lack of sympathy in hopes and fears that is felt when not expressed.

FEB. 28TH—

Hugh Gwyn came out this afternoon and the day was so pleasant we took a horseback ride and he stayed to tea. When we were alone together I said something about secession and he instead of continuing the subject, said, "Now look here—that is just one subject I won't talk with you about—for I am determined not to lose my old friends and if I can help it nothing disagreeable shall ever interfere with the pleasure it gives me to visit Mount Air—or with my friendship with you," which was very wise I could but grant—and we spent a very delightful evening. He read out to me "Maud Muller" and he read it beautifully. We also looked over "Richelieu," the play we are going to read at our next Club meeting. I am to read the part of "Julie" and Hugh says Mr. Baxter is to have the part of De Maupont [de Mauprat]. I hope not and believe Hugh himself has it. Mr. Baxter has a long ways more literary ability and sense than any other man in the Club but he reads with a slow English draw—that is not agreeable to listen to.[4]

MARCH [?], 1861—

We are expecting sister Lute and Mr. McCann with their two children, Pearl and Underwood. They are coming home from Kansas where they have been for the past year—hoping to be satisfied to make a home there but neither of them like it and after making us a visit they will go again to live in far off California, which has been Mr. McCann's home ever since he went out there in 1848 and he can't be satisfied anywhere else.

MARCH 6TH—

Lute and Mr. McCann arrived well and making us all happy to see them and their dear little children, the brightest little things I nearly ever saw. Sister Jupe and Mr. Western are coming up tomorrow from Memphis, so as to have a family reunion—before sister Lute goes so far away and Mr. Western wants to talk with Pa, and very sad it is going to make Pa to hear him talk as he does about the advantage of disunion. But whilst Mr. Western is very decided in his own ideas, he is so tolerant of the opinions of others and so amiable and perfectly lovely in disposition, that I am sure he and Pa can discuss matters without any ill feeling and surely when he hears Pa's arguments he must see how dreadful it is to try to break up the country, as he advocates.

MARCH 10TH—

Warner had a fight yesterday with one of the school boys who called him "A Yankee and Abolitionist." Warner knocked him down—and says he told him "he would teach a low down cur who didn't know which side of the line he was born on and never owned a mule, much less a negro, how to call him a "Yankee and Abolitionist, because he was Union." The Union boys were very proud of Warner and though Pa talked to Warner about a boy of 14 who counted himself a gentleman having a rough and tumble fight with a low fellow—Ma's admonition to "knock anybody down who called him such names" carried more conviction I am afraid.

March 12th—

Mr. Western and Sister Jupe got home today, bringing with them "Lady" [Corrine] Henry, whom they had with them in Memphis, thinking perhaps they might adopt her as they have no children—but Lady is a headstrong, quick-tempered little body and sister Jupe does not feel equal to the undertaking, so she will continue to live with sister Fanny and Mr. Grider, Mr. Grider being her and Marius' guardian.

March 20th—

The letters I receive, those I write, the visits I receive, and make and all my personal doings are of no importance even to myself or worth recording—in the midst of the universal anxiety over the condition of the country. We have every phase of sentiment represented in our own home, though all are southern born. Pa being a Virginian, Ma a Kentuckian, Mr. McCann a native of Baltimore and Mr. Grider, born here in Bowling Green and Mr. Western in Hopkinsville, Kentucky. Dear Pa believes in maintaining the Union—for the good of the *whole country* and thinks any division of the country will hurt the South far more than it will the North—in fact will *ruin* the South and he still hopes if Kentucky does not secede she may some way avert a war and bring about reconciliation between the sections. Mr. Grider and Mr. Western from different standpoints, hoot at the idea of any patched up peace— Mr. G. says, "*Whip* the South back and give her her rights and kill off the fire eaters north and south and maintain the constitution as it is and uphold the old flag against traitors north and south" and dear Ma agrees with him—both opposed to any neutrality. Mr. McCann does not believe in slavery—though he thinks the Government had no right to meddle with it in the States where it already exists—

but thinks the South should not be allowed to seceded—for admitting that doctrine is ruin— Mr. Western believes slavery an essential condition of the inferior races—ordained by God, and he also believes in States Rights and secession—so the arguments rage in one way or the other all the time—but thank the good Lord no personal animosity yet enters into them, and no own brothers could love each other better than Mr. McCann and Mr. Grider and Mr. Western do and no father be fonder of his own sons than Pa is of them all. Dear Warner, who is as noble a boy as ever lived, too young to join in the argument, has his opinions just as decided and expressed them with force today when he said, "I don't care what anybody says, if a war comes I'm going to fight for the Union," and so saying marched off with his fishing poles to the river. God defend us from ever having that dear boy a mark for bullets.

MARCH 25TH—

The situation in Charleston harbor is getting more and more intense—all the family gathers on the front porch after breakfast and eagerly wait the coming of the mail—no matter what letters we get, nothing is read till the news from Fort Sumter is heard. Mr. McCann, who is the best reader takes the *Louisville Journal,* and reads it out. Then all the other news and the editorials by Geo. D. Prentice—and we all hope as long as no gun is fired there are yet hopes that war may be averted.[5]

MARCH 30TH—

I've been out to Aunt Lucy Ann Skiles' for the past week. Belle and I had lots of fun. She is the most sentimental, impractical mortal I ever knew except in the evening when she is driving up the geese—then when the old gander stretches out his long neck, hisses and runs at her, she runs faster than I do to get out of his way. Aunt Lucy told her if she would take care of the geese, she might have all the money she could make out of them and she is making a desperate effort to have the crop of feathers as large as possible. I never can solve the mystery of how a gentle little Christian woman like Aunt Lucy ever married such a profane old blunderbuss as Uncle "Ham." He promised me he wouldn't swear whilst I was out there and when I told him good-bye said "I am awfully glad you are going for I be —D—if I wouldn't have *busted* if you stayed a day longer." When I go out there and see and hear him storming around, albeit he does it in good nature—I feel very sorry for Belle and am more than ever thankful for my beautiful loving home and for my father and mother, of whom I am always so proud.

March 28th—

We were all invited over to Uncle Joe's yesterday to have a sort of family party—but Uncle Joe was in Frankfort in the Legislature; after having been a colleague of Henry Clay in the U.S. Senate or Supreme Court [Kentucky Court of Appeals] Judge—he takes this minor position that he may serve his state and country. Pa had gone up to Scottsville where he makes a speech and Mr. Grider was too busy—so Ma, sisters Fanny, Jupe, Lute and I with Mr. McCann and Mr. Western went and had a pleasant day with every good thing imaginable to eat—and delightful music. Robert Underwood and Mr. Western playing beautifully on the violin, Aunt Liz Underwood accompanying them on the piano and sister Jupe and Lute playing and singing— Aunt Liz does not know a note and yet by ear, she plays exquisitely and as Mr. Western plays the same way on the violin, I thought their music had more melody in it and was sweeter than all the rest. I was glad

Bob Cox wasn't there. He is always polite enough but he is my ideal of pretentious unworthiness and I don't like him. John Underwood is at the [Rensselaer] Polytechnic Institute in Troy, N.Y. Dear Uncle Henry was with us and had brought his carpet bag, having decided by much persuasion that he ought to stay a while with "brother Joseph and sister Elizabeth," but when we came out to get in the carriage, there was Uncle Henry sitting beside "Uncle" Lewis the driver, his carpet bag pushed far under the seat and when Aunt Liz in her fussy sort of way said, "Why, brother Henry we expected you to stay," he said, "I'll come again, bye and bye." When we drove off he said to Ma—"I'm going to *stay* with you sister Lucy, sister Elizabeth *bothers me*. Dear old man! Ma understands him as she does everybody and she makes him perfectly at home as a member of the family and he knows she likes him— Aunt Liz makes company of him all the time—. Ma answered, "That's right, brother Henry, Mount Air is your home and there is no use your going for long visits anywhere, you can go over to see your brother Joe and sister Liz for a day or so when you want to—that's enough." "*Yes, 'tis*," he said and was comforted and Ma in her own easy way had settled for him a question that was giving him much perplexity, when he came out from Virginia. (The dear old man has no means whatever.) It was rather understood that he was to live half his time with Uncle Joe and half with P [Pa] and he has had the feeling that he must live up to this idea—but he feels lonely and poor over there—here we all make much of him and he is and feels at home and loved;—and Pa and Ma, too, are glad to have him here instead of alone, old and poor in Virginia.

MARCH 31ST—

Another month gone! More and more states are seceding. Sumter has not been fired on yet and we pray it may not be—though a good many people are just as anxious that it should be and "The Ball opened" as they say—not realizing what a dance of death—war between the North and South would mean. Major [Robert] Anderson who is in command of Fort Sumter is a friend and distant cousin of Pa's and that fact gives us all a personal as well as national interest in the situation. Pa thinks him a very brave man and Patriot.

APRIL 2ND—

Last night Annie Hawkins spent with me; after supper Hugh Gwyn and John Ward came out and we spent a very pleasant evening. This afternoon Annie's uncle Mike Hall drove out for Annie, Mr. Baxter coming with him and staying to tea, after Annie and Mike left. Annie is such a bright natural girl and we are all so fond of her. All the family like Mr. Baxter very much too—he is such a well informed man and such a refined gentleman—but however much we like him—nobody can help being amused at his awkward English ways and he embarrasses me by his straight forward attentions—no matter how many others may be present. Then I get teased about it afterwards.

APRIL 5TH—

Our Shakesperean Club met at sister Fanny's and we had a delightful time mainly because our President, Professor Le Compte, announced in his funny French way "now the reading is over we will haf [*sic*] a little social time, but the *politic is Taboo.*" The most pleasant evenings we have are always when we meet at sister Fannie's. She is such an affable and elegant hostess and in spite of the rule to the contrary, manages to have some delightful refreshment—an offense easily excused.

April 6th—

Pa had a letter from Cousin John Todd—he is greatly troubled about the prospect of war—but determined not to resign from the U.S. Army. In our family everybody from Pa down to the youngest child expresses their opinion on every subject that comes up—so Cousin John's resolution comes in for full share of comment—Pa and Ma—the boys and I—Sister Fanny, Mr. Grider—sister Lute and Mr. McCann approve his course—Mr. Western thinks it disloyal to his section, and sister Jupe, as she says is pretty strong on both sides. Pa gave us an eloquent statement of how much greater was loyalty to the whole country and government—than to any sectional feeling—dear Pa! to a man who loves his section as he does—it is very hard to have his convictions of right make it impossible for him to side with what he calls her "Suicidal actions."

April 8th—

The excitement and intense anxiety about Ft. Sumter grows greater every day— Mr. McCann and sister Lute will stay with us till this crisis is over— God only knows how it will end.

Received a long beautiful letter from Mr. Grafton. He has withdrawn from "The Shelby Grays" and joined a Mississippi Regiment and has been made Major of the Regiment—as he says—"hoping the North will recognize the right of the South to withdraw from a hated Union—without bloodshed—but ready to give his life for the principle of States rights in case she does not." God help the country nobody knows what's going to happen and everybody is upset and excited—fearful—except such people as Robert Cox—who as he says—"have nothing to loose and all to gain and long for any change that will make chances."

CHAPTER TWO

April 13th—

It has happened! For Sumter was fired on yesterday!—when Major Anderson refused to surrender. What an exciting time we had; when the news came we were all waiting on the front porch as usual—when Marius who had gone for the mail came galloping furiously up the road—waving the paper and hollering out the news long before we could distinguish a word he said. As he came nearer we heard—"Fort Sumter fired on! One *woman* got hurt. Harriette Lane shot in the Stern! What was a woman doing there anyway!" Harriett Lane was the name of a vessel—but Marius' funny mistake made us all laugh and relieved the dreaded news of its first horror. Mr. McCann read every detail as we all listened with intense interest—as he finished he said, "Well, we must leave for California as soon as Lute can get ready— I want to be with my state in this"— Mr. Western was as quick to say and "I'll go to Memphis and arrange to fight with the South—for that's what she will do now"— Mr. Grider (who is devoted to Mr. Western and Mr. Western to him) said "All right Bill—I don't reckon Kentucky can stay neutral now—and I'll raise a regiment to fight against you and whip you back into the Union"—and so in spite of the warmest affection between all—the talk got excited almost to anger—till dear Pa said—"Boys! boys! it grieves me beyond measure to hear you talk so. Let us consider these questions seriously," and so they did, for long after the boys had gone to school and Ma, sister Fanny, sister Jupe, Lute and I had gone about our feminine duties—there they sat all the morning discussing the situation with painful earnestness—but nobody's opinion of what they intended doing was changed for Mr. McCann and sister Lute have determined to leave next week for California, sister Jupe and Mr. Western go a few days after to Memphis and dear Pa and Mr. Grider remain to meet conditions as best they can. Sister Fanny and Mr. Grider went in town to their home after dinner and when Pa came from town he was grieved greatly to find the firing on Sumter had turned a number of waivering people to secessionists, for they argue now there is no chance of saving the Union and right or wrong they want to go with the South. But the staunchest and most prominent men in the town—are all determined still to stand by the Union, and save the country from being broken up like South America—as is inevitable if the right of secession prevails—but oh! how they wish they had a less Ultra partisan than Lincoln, at the head of the Government. Pa knows Lincoln well and whilst he does not agree at all with his ideas—and as a Bell and Everett elector did all in his power to defeat him for President—he thinks him honest in his convictions and his desire to do what is right—however his ideas differ with the great Union party of Kentucky and other conservative states— He knows Jeff Davis very well too—served on the same Committees with him for several terms in Congress. He says Mr. Davis is a man of great general information and as far as education goes, much Lincoln's superior— but he knows now from recalling many conversations with Mr. Davis—that he has long been anxious to see the Union dissolved.

April 15th—

For two days Major Anderson and his brave garrison resisted the firing—then, alas, had to surrender and yesterday (Sunday) fired a salute to the Flag with his last powder—gave up the Fort to Beauregard— Oh! I wish I could see Major Anderson—the brave man to hold out so nobly for duty and country!

CHAPTER TWO

APRIL 16TH—

I took a horse-back ride with Mr. Baxter this afternoon. The air was so balmy and sweet. The country so lovely with the Red bud and Dogwood in blossom among the fresh budding green leaves of other trees and "Mount Air" as we came home just as the sun was setting, the most beautiful place in the whole country round. The peach trees all in blossom made it look like a huge bouquet of pinks and the perfume of the early honeysuckle was wafted to us on the gentle breeze just as we rode up the Hill from the front gate—never was there a more peaceful happy home and never I believe a happier girl than I. It is too horrible to think of war devastating this beautiful land and that is what dear Pa dreads for he says if there is war—the border states will have to bear the brunt of it.

APRIL 17TH—

Lincoln has issued a call for 75,000 troops! This means war surely— Warner wants to volunteer! Think of it, a boy only 14; of course Pa won't hear to such a thing—even if Kentucky were not still trying to remain neutral. But that position can't be held much longer and is really only in name—for every man, woman and child is on one side or the other. Every day we hear of some one we know going to join the Rebels in Tennessee or the Union Regiment camped across the Ohio at Louisville. Mr. Grider and Ben Bristow have more mysterious meetings. I am quite sure they are quietly enlisting men— John Ward was out today to say goodbye—he is going to his home in Greensburg—to see his father and he told me he would join the first legally organized troops Kentucky furnished to fight for the Union. Mr. Rutherford is going back to Virginia next week. He says, though he is opposed to

77

secession as a principle he wants to go with his state. Dear old Uncle Henry says very little but when Mr. Rutherford said that—his blue eyes filled with tears and saying, "I wish I was young enough to go with you, Tom"—he left the room and later I saw the old man going slowly towards the river without his fishpole, which showed he was much troubled in mind.

Dear Pa's position is so hard and yet he does not swerve from his duty in being true to the preservation of the Union—and yet his love for the South is just as great. In fact *because* he so loves the South, he does not want her ruined by disunion and giving up the old flag and government. Ma puts the situation very strongly when she says—"she never will as long as she lives consent to be driven out of the Union and give up the Flag and all it stands for, for which her father and forefathers fought, to a lot of meddling Yankees and she never will forgive the hot-headed fire eaters of the South for going out of the Union and giving the Northern fanatics such advantage.

April 18th—

Uncle Wint writes from West Point that his class which would graduate in June is to be graduated ahead of time, to help organize troops. It is the greatest comfort to Ma—that Uncle Wint stands true to the Union. The little Zouave Company here of which Will Hobson is Captain and brother Warner, 1st Lieutenant, has had a good many new members lately—but not as many as if the boys knew "which way the cat will jump," for though Will and Warner are strong Union boys some of the others are as strong "secesh." They gave an exhibition drill today and I was so proud of Warner, I thought he did better than any boy in the company and he has such a beautiful, earnest face. Henry would like to join the company but he is still a little under the age admitted. The Captain, the oldest member being only 18.[6]

April 20th—

We are all busy sewing, helping sister Lute get herself and her dear little children ready for their long trip to California. They go to New York and from there by steamer—a three nearly four weeks sea voyage and it takes a good many clothes to keep children clean on such a trip. The feeling between Union people and secessionists grows more and more strained and friendships are breaking faster than the Union. I get too excited whenever the subject comes up—in spite of all my resolutions not to, but when they slur at southern men "who side with the North against the South" I can't take it quietly—the secessionists intentionally put it all the time that it is just *North* against the *South,* when that isn't it at all—but it is the South against the established government based upon the Constitution—which they and the fanatics at the North are trying to overthrow to the destruction of the whole country and which sound-thinking men throughout the South deplore *most* because it will ruin the South, far more than it can hurt the North—no country can amount to anything if any part of it is allowed to secede whenever things are not going all their way. What government institutions, forts or buildings could be put in states if at any time they could secede and claim all government property as exclusively their own. These are Pa's arguments of course and I am sure they are good ones.

April 23rd—

Hugh Gwyn was out today and just as pleasant as ever. He says most of his friends are Union people and he does not question their right to think as they please since he claims that privilege for himself—but he will not uselessly discuss questions upon which he and his friends disagree, and as long as he can find pleasanter things to talk about he is not going to row his little conversational boat on shoals that will wreck friendships. He is a great admirer of sister Lute's and is coming out tomorrow with several other friends of hers to spend a last evening—before she leaves.

April 26th—

Will Rochester and wife, Agatha Strange, Fanny Porter, Cousin Jane and George Rogers and Julia Cox, Mike Hall, Cooper Wright, Hugh Gwyn and Mr. Baxter spent the evening with us before sister Lute left. Everybody tried to forget all disagreements and the sadness of sister Lute's going so far—when everything is so uncertain and we may never all meet again. Sister Jupe and Mr. Western played—Lute and Fannie Porter sang and we all had a happy evening. This morning, sister Lute and Mr. McCann and little ones left and it was a sad time for us all. Too sad to write about— God grant we may all be spared to meet again in more peaceful times!

May 2nd—

Sister Jupe and Mr. Western left today for their home in Memphis. I believe Pa was almost more troubled in seeing him go than he was to say goodbye to Mr. McCann. He knows Mr. Western is going into secession heart and soul and it seems such a wrong and disastrous attitude for him to take. Mr. Western said when they were parting, "No matter how we all differ or what comes—nothing can ever happen to lessen my love for you all and dear old 'Mount Air' and not one of us but felt the same way towards him.

CHAPTER TWO

MAY 5TH—

Pa has gone up to Louisville and Frankfort to be gone a week. The Union men are making every possible effort to keep Kentucky in the Union and it is to that end this trip is made. Dear Ma is not very well this spring. She has headache much oftener than formerly, being frequently confined to her bed several days with it. The excitement grows greater and every day seems bringing war nearer and friends farther and farther apart.

MAY 8TH—

The days are beautiful and "Mount Air" never seemed so lovely to me. Everybody is busy gardening and all day I spent with Ma trimming and tying up the vines and rose bushes. In all the fields plowmen may be seen turning up the rich brown earth. The boys and Uncle Henry go fishing almost every day—after they make a pretense of having a few lessons which Uncle Henry hears, for since Mr. Rutherford left, they will not start to the school in town till next session. But the days occupations are never begun till the mail is brought and the *Louisville Journal* read and the news it brings goes with us all the day no matter what else we are doing. Even the negroes are getting restless—anxious to know the news from Washington and "if any more states done seceded." In town there are always people in groups, earnestly talking, and it is easy enough to tell the Union and secession groups. Certain women, too—Mrs. [Larkin] Baker—"Miss" Polly Grider (nobody every thinks of her as Mrs. Tobe [Tobias] Grider), cousin Jane Rogers and a few others—may usually be seen in their *Rockaways*—neither vehicle, horse or little negro driver showing much care—driving restlessly around stopping here and there, more to gather up sensations than news and the first two flinging in some sharp cutting speech with their greetings. Mrs. Baker is "Union" and "Miss Polly" secesh and the bitterness of this difference is added to their former dislike of each other. But I am not the one to comment on the short comings or sharp speeches of others—for I was anything but mild when talking with Web Wright today, about a speech Will Dulaney had made—in which he spoke of Pa's "Unionism" as the result of association with [Owen] Lovejoy and other Abolitionists in Congress. Contemptible young ignoramus! He has no better sense than to think the way to advance his own cause is personal abuse of the most prominent men opposing secession. Lovejoy was in Congress when Pa was and they are merely acquaintances, but Will Dulaney said he met a man, from Indiana, who said he heard Lovejoy say Mr. Underwood of Kentucky was one of the brightest men in the House and he argued, "*Lovejoy* wouldn't have spoken that way of a consistent Southerner." Fine logic he is starting out with! Somebody told me of his speech and when Web Wright asked me if I knew Lovejoy—I knew why he asked it and I let my temper and my tongue loose at the same time—and when I met Will Dulaney shortly afterward and he spoke—*I didn't see him at all,* and sailed on "like the Queen of the West unheeding" till I met Mike Hall a few steps further on and stopped to shake hands and have quite a little talk with him so that Will Dulaney could see plainly it wasn't *hurry* that made me pass him.[7]

MAY 15TH—

This afternoon Mr. Baxter came out and as we sat in the summer house where the violets and lilies of the valley were all in bloom about our feet and the sweet honeysuckle blooming above us—the combination of fragrance was something delicious and the sun setting in glorious beauty made the whole scene lovely beyond description. Nobody could help feeling sentimental at such a time and place. Mr. Baxter did not try to but told me he loved me and in words of too much earnestness and feeling, for me to write, asked me to marry him and go to England with him away from all the discord brewing here. I felt so sorry for him, for I can't help believing him sincere and I do truly wish I loved him—for I do not believe anyone will ever be as devoted to me as he is—and why I do not I can't tell—for he is such a perfectly honorable, true gentleman—but I do not—though I like him so very much—and I could only tell him frankly how I feel— I wonder if I am hard-hearted? *No*, I am sure I am not, but I have my ideal of what love should be and of what I want to feel for the man I would marry and whilst I do sincerely like so many, no man I have ever met has aroused this feeling in me. Mr. Grafton comes nearer to it than anyone else—but he too fails to unloose the fountain of the deep love I know myself capable of feeling. No, I will wait till I find my own true Prince—or till he finds me and wait forever—unless he comes.

I am going to Russellville, to stay a few weeks. It will be a little easier for Mr. Baxter if I am out of town for awhile; though he says this shall make no difference in our friendship.

JUNE 13TH—

I returned yesterday from Russellville having had a very pleasant visit. Aunt Martha and Uncle George Norton treat me always as though I were their own daughter come home again and I am very fond of the dear children—especially Juliette and Minnie, who are growing to be such interesting girls. Minnie is beautiful and Juliette's ugliness has an individuality that makes it attractive. It isn't at all commonplace, ugliness—but character ugly—big mouth, high forehead—

intense eyes and an amusement and excitement about everything that is funny and interesting. Ernest is very handsome,
too handsome to have a strong face as my dear brother Warner has— Uncle George won't talk politics at all and holds
Ernest's tongue in as with bit and bridle. He reads all the
exciting news in silence.,—When I was bursting to hear it
and have him express himself, and Aunt Martha is just as
circumspect. Once I said, "Uncle George, which side are you
on—you surely don't believe in secession do you?" His answer
was, "I deplore the condition of affairs and hope I may never
do anything to add to the trouble, but talking too much does
a great deal of harm, Josie—a great deal of harm," and so
I got my answer and my reproof at the same time. All my
old schoolmates flocked to see me and I found it best for all
parties to take Uncle George's hint—for many of them are
as strong secessionists as I am Union and discussions would
only have made disagreeable times. But Mollie Williams,
daughter of "Gen. Sierra Gorda [Cerro Gordo] Williams,"
Lucy Bell and I *had* to let ourselves out once or twice—for
we couldn't stand not knowing how each of us stood. All the
young men in Russellville with one or two exceptions are in
sympathy with the Rebels—and most of the boys from the
South who attended Bethel College when I was at school
in Russellville—have already joined some company to fight
against the Government and every day more and more Kentucky boys are flocking to Camp Boone—just over the line
in Tennessee. They are watching eagerly for some violation
of Kentucky's neutrality so they can rush into the state and
more and more it is becoming plain that neutrality can't be
maintained—much longer—for while the older conservative
men think it the best means of preventing the Legislature
passing an ordinance of secession, all the young men in the
state are eager to be decidedly "in the fight" on one side or
the other. Mr. Grider is away a great deal of the time and

now I know he is organizing men to spring forth, as Roderick Dhu's men, the moment they can legally do so. John Ward is doing the same thing up about Greensburg. Dear Pa is getting more hopeless of avoiding a horrible war and distressed at the destruction he believes it will bring upon the South but does not waiver in his allegiance to the old Constitution and his determination that he will do all he can to preserve the Union and bring the seceded states back.[8]

JUNE 20TH—

The times are so exciting I can't half describe anything—all thought of ordinary things is upset—and we are living in a state of nervous tension that makes everybody excited and restless. The streets are crowded with farmers and country people, who ought to be plowing their fields and working their gardens—but how can they go quietly about such occupations till they have come to town to get "the news" and getting it the discussions and excitement keep them there all day and fights are constantly occurring. The school boys all "carry chips on their shoulders"—ready to fight at the slightest provocation. Henry was awfully excited when he came from the Post office this morning; some "secesh" boys had shouted at him, "Ab—Ab"—meaning Abolitionist and that is what no southern boy will stand being called—so Henry pitched into the crowd—several other Union boys joined in and the fight was "fast and furious." The Union boys—whipped, so Henry says and was very angry that somebody stopped the fight—before—they could "wipe that secesh crowd out." We were all excited about it— Pa charged the boys—"not to demean themselves by getting in street fights" and Ma told them at the same time, "knock down any boy that called them 'Abolitionist,' and so it goes. The Southern Union men having all sorts of unjust charges hurled at them.

JUNE 28TH—

Mr. Grider was away and I spent the past week with sister Fanny—the dearest, best sister in the world. I helped her make a lot of waists and pants for little Warner and Judge and we got all their summer clothes finished. I had several delightful horseback rides with Hugh Gwyn—who has a beautiful dapple gray horse and is one of the handsomest men I ever saw on horseback, for he rides beautifully. Mr. Baxter and Mike Hall took tea with us one evening. Sister Fanny thought a special invitation to Mr. Baxter would make it easier for him to have things appear as formerly so no one would make remarks uncomfortable for him. She likes Mr. Baxter very much and he returns her admiration with interest. Annie Hawkins was also there—we wanted to ask Lizzie Wright and Cooper—but Mr. Grider and their father had such a hot discussion last week, we thought best not to— I am very fond of Lizzie—and like her brothers Cooper and Webb well enough—in fact I liked them very much till lately—they talk so outrageously and foolishly too— Web said "*he* would be the Robespierre of this Revolution." I never saw Mr. Baxter so amused for whilst the Wrights are clever enough people—everybody knows "Wright" is just another name for coward. When Webb said that Mr. Lacy, who is a funny fellow from New York, offered to bet half his salary—if war comes to the worst, Web would never fight. Hugh Gwyn with his usual tact changed the subject to one less combustible.[9]

JUNE 30TH—

Ma had a letter from Uncle Wint. When his class was graduated three months ahead of time, he was sent to Missouri to "fight mit segal" [Franz Sigel] and has had a stirring, active time and "seen more service" already than many an older Army officer and strange as it is, he seems to think it a great thing to have been in fights—shooting at other men! I don't see how he could do it, such a tender-hearted fellow as he always was. I know I get awfully excited and talk like a simpleton not to say a fool—about what ought to be done with people trying to break up this Government—but when it comes to actually shooting anybody—that's too horrible! Imagine myself shooting at Will Western, Jack Henry or Tom Grafton or letting anybody else do it if I could prevent it—not for my life! Wint is an officer so didn't have to do any shooting himself, which isn't quite as hard—though it amounts to the same thing—if he commands it done. The weather has been so horrible and he so exposed to it that he has had several attacks of rheumatism. He writes if it gets much worse—he won't be able to attend to his duties. Dear Ma is so proud of his serving his country—for it nearly breaks her heart that Uncle Gus and Uncle Pat Henry and so many of her relatives have gone against the Government.[10]

JULY 2ND—

We had letters from sister Lute and Mr. McCann and from Sister Jupe—California,—Mr. McCann says is strongly Union and Lute grieves that she must be so far from us all in these trying times and can only sniff the battle afar off—for California is too far away to have any personal fear or part in the troubles, though of course her allegiance to the Union is worth a great deal morally. Sister Jupe writes a funny letter and says as Mr. Western and everybody around her are secessionists and abusing the Union—she is bound to take up for the "Absent party" and so long as Pa is of that party she is Union heart and soul—especially as she is with Mr. Western—but if she, was away from him and among the Union people—she would have to defend his side and be strong for secession, "so she stands on the line—one foot on either side"—a position more natural than graceful for my dear sister. She writes that a great many of the young men I knew who were strong Unionists—have gone over to secession and even Will Weber—has returned from Kentucky and joined the "Shelby Grays"— I wonder if they gave him Mr. Grafton's place. Something Lincoln did turned him. It takes more sense than he has—to be true to the country and government as my dear father is and opposing Lincoln at the same time and that makes it so hard for the truest Patriots.

August 1st—

July is ended and the most horrible month ever, I suppose, known in this country. War in all its horror! Brother against brother, friend against friend, the children of this great country fighting to destroy it—the fighting in Virginia is something terrible. The places in old Virginia, familiar and hallowed to Pa and Uncle Henry by all the memories of their boyhood, now the scenes of bloody battles. Poor old Uncle Henry says but little, but as the news is read the tears roll fast down the furrows of his cheeks. Today Pa said "it is hard brother that we are not younger men." Uncle Henry said, "Maybe it is best for us that we are not, Warner." I am quite sure the dear old man was thinking he would be in the Rebel army and he knew Pa's loyalty to the Union could not be shaken. Oh! it is a hard question and hardest of all for the man who loves the South as Pa does and yet cannot accept secession—as his love for the whole country is greater than for any section and he knows secession means continued degeneration. More and more Kentuckians are going to the Rebel camps in Tennessee and more and more Union men flocking to Rousseau across the river from Louisville. Kentucky cannot maintain her neutrality much longer. The Union men feel that, but are thankful through that policy that they have been able to prevent an ordinance of secession. It is distressing how friendships are being broken up—nothing is talked of but War! war! and it is impossible (for me anyway) not to get too excited and say things that offend and hurt. The lines between secessionists and Union people are more and more marked and the Union or Rebel feeling is drawing people together who never before had any association. None of my friends have fallen away as yet—except Lizzie Wright does not come out as often as formerly—neither do Web and Cooper. Hugh Gwyn comes as usual and is always pleasant—but I *feel* a difference. We are always trying to avoid the subjects we are each most interested in—which spoils a friendship— hitherto so full of frank confidence—. On the 4th of July there was a flag raising over the round house at the Depot. Pa made a *grand* speech and the enthusiasm of the Union people was tremendous, though the crowd was not as large as we hoped it would be—the secessionists most of them staying away. Annie Hawkins and I drove up there in a buggy with Mike Hall. After getting the buggy in a good place for us to hear, he left us and Mr. Baxter came and sat on the side of the buggy with us. Cooper Wright, Will Dulaney, Hugh Gwyn and several others stood off on the outskirts of the crowd and only Hugh came to speak to us and he only stayed a few minutes and I knew they were just there to criticize and condemn and I couldn't bear for dear Pa's grand patriotic speech to be listened to by such unappreciative opposing men.

August 10th—

Mr. Western has joined the Rebel Army—*Forrests'* command! When we were in Memphis, Forrest had a "Negro Yard" where negroes were sold and no decent people had anything to do with him—now—he is a *Gen.* and Mr. Western is in his Brigade but nothing Mr. Western can ever do will alter my love for him—for he was always like a good brother to me and is altogether the most lovable disposition I ever knew a man to have. Ma is terribly distressed about his *fighting* against the Union, as we all are.

August 13th—

Uncle Wint arrived today on his way to the Hot Springs of Arkansas—he is all crippled up with rheumatism and is on a leave to go to the Springs and get cured. He gave us a very interesting account of the war in Missouri.

August 15th—

Uncle Wint left today. Pa had a long earnest talk with him—fearing when he got among his secession relatives he would be persuaded to resign from the U. S. A.—but he declares he never will and said never could he be brought to advocate the cause of secession. Pa fears however the influence will be too strong for him.

August 16th—

Sister Jupe writes she has been having a terrible time in her heroic efforts to befriend a Union man and wife;—a Presbyterian minister by the name of Bateman—he had charge of a church in Mississippi—but was a New England man from Mass., I believe. The excitement became so great against him because he was a Union man that he with his delicate [pregnant] wife were compelled to leave, without preparation and little money. They got as far as Memphis and had not enough money to go further and no one would take them in to board, fearing the consequences of befriending a

Union man driven from a southern place. Sister Jupe heard of it, got in her carriage—went down town, found them, and brought them to her home where she did everything to make them comfortable as though they had been her own brother and sister, for as she wrote she thought all the time "suppose my own father should be treated so because he is Union." She told them they must stay with her till they were entirely rested and she would let them have the money to get to their own home. They had no time to write to their friends for money before being driven out. They staid a week with sister before they could get on. In the meantime, delegations of secessionists waited on sister to protest against her—the wife of a secession officer sheltering Union refugees—she declared her father was a Union man and any Union man in the position of Mr. Bateman could find shelter in her house. Then they tried to scare her, saying excited people might burn her house down. She said, "Let them burn ahead"—she wouldn't turn a man and especially a woman in Mrs. Bateman's condition, out of her house—and so no threats or persuasions could induce her to do so till she could see them started safely on their journey North. She says their gratitude nearly overcame her—she has since heard of their safe arrival in Boston and the birth of their first baby a few days after their arrival, a little girl, whom they have named Juliette Western Bateman, as a constant recognition of her heroic kindness to them—not many women would have had such courage—or such sympathy for those persecuted and distressed, and there is no doubt Mr. Western will commend her for her action, for his heart is as generous and true as hers.

AUGUST 25TH—

We are all distressed and dear Ma is heartbroken. Uncle Wint has resigned! He wrote "he had not before understood the true conditions of the conflict and as much as it grieved him to withdraw from the service of the government that had educated him and the profession he loved—and above all to go against the opinion and advice of brother Warner (Pa) whom he honored and loved above any other living man—he could not conscientiously fight any longer against the South—so had sent in his resignation." Pa said, "just what I feared," and tried as best he could to comfort Ma—who wept in terrible distress just as though Wint were dead—and indeed said over and over again, "Oh! if he had only died or been killed defending the flag and the country for which his fathers fought—before he turned traitor"—"to think of my father's son fighting against this country" and so she grieved in a heartrending way—for all her patriotic family pride had been centered in Wint and his resignation nearly kills her. She begged us all never to mention his name to her again—to let him be as one dead. Too bad! too sad! How can we do that, for he has always been like our brother. How bitter, how hard everything is getting—and yet—how beautiful the world is—as I look out from my window—the glorious sunset—illuminating this dear old home with a splendor indescribable, and as far as my eye can reach—only peaceful beauty to be seen—the flowers bloom—the grain ripens, the trees "bring forth fruit each after his own kind"—and man only seems not to fulfill the will of God. His evil passions alone spoil the happiness of this beautiful world— I can't understand why God permits it so to be for the Angel song of "Peace on Earth, good will to man" seems forever hushed.

August 26th—

Got another beautiful letter from Mr. Grafton. Ma thinks I ought not to write to a man fighting against the Union and I suppose I ought not to, but he is so alone, as he says "no

woman in all the world except his old black 'mammy' to shed
a tear for him and never a letter in a woman's handwriting except mine." It seems cruel not to write to him—even if I—

August 29th—

Belle Skiles has been spending a week with me. She is the
most impractical mortal I ever saw and does so many silly,
imprudent things, that mortify her brother Henry so he can't
bear to have her come to town—but I told him today—that
he ought to blame himself more than Belle—for staying out
in the country so much where she never saw anybody or has
any pleasure—if he would take more trouble to get something into her life—she wouldn't act imprudently in her efforts to have a little pleasure when she is thrown with people.
She is just as bright and pleasant and pretty as she can be and
I don't believe ever had an evil thought in her life—no matter what silly thing she does. Her heart is just full of poetry
and sentiment and not having found the right object to lavish it upon—every man she meets she imagines her hero— I
made her promise this time she wouldn't grow sentimental
and poetical with any of the clerks when we went into the
stores or waste her sweet smiles on any man she hadn't been
introduced to—so Henry hasn't scolded her as much as usual and we have had a real good time, together. All the family
are down on Henry because he does not come out stronger,
in his paper for the Union— His editorials are pretty luke-
warm but he is in a trying position for a man who has many
good qualities but isn't suited for conflict or being a Standard bearer. Ben Grider, talking against neutrality, said, "It
is very well suited to Henry Skiles—but [t]he rest of us can't
stand it much longer." It makes him so mad that Henry don't
use his paper to better purpose for the Union, so long as he
says he is a Union man. Everybody is afraid Kentucky can't

pursue her neutrality much longer and the feeling is growing that it isn't desirable—though we are all afraid of the consequences—when the Rebels at Camp Boone in Tennessee and the Union troops across the river from Louisville shall rush across the lines to meet in Kentucky. Everybody seems to think when they do, Bowling Green will be the meeting point and a battle will be fought. How horrible to think of it. God forbid it! but we are all getting used as I never thought we could, to thoughts and realities of war. Conditions are more and more horrible in Virginia—feeling grows more and more bitter between Union and "secesh" here and dear Pa is graver and sadder. Ma does not cease to grieve over Uncle Wint's resignation—though she hasn't mentioned his name since and when we heard he had joined the Confederate army, she cried again like her heart would break—saying over and over "O that I should live to see the day that my father's son would fight against this country!"

August 31st—

It has been a hot—hard day. The secessionists are exultant—the Union people depressed—everybody is excited—nobody can confine their attention to any ordinary things. Even the negroes—naturally too—can't half do their work. They, poor souls, have more reason perhaps than anybody to be anxious and eager for news. Everything anybody says or does—is construed to mean more than the act or words signify ordinarily. If we see a group of secessionists laughing we are sure they have some news good for their side and they are as evidently suspicious about us. Today I happened to go to the post-office. The office was crowded and when Mr. Donaldson handed me the mail, a large long envelope—addressed to Pa—containing some Law paper—looked official and I could see plainly that it had excited the curiosity, if not suspicion of all who happened to see it and most did see it and not a few tried, very adroitly as they thought to see what it was and I amused myself by holding it and trying myself to look as though it was important and indeed I did not know until I got home but what it was, for dear Pa is continually receiving letters from John J. Crittenden, Attorney General Joe Holt, our congressman and others as to the best policy to keep Kentucky in the Union. Mr. Grider and Mr. Bristow have more frequent confabs than ever and Mr. Grider is now away from home and sister Fanny and the children are staying with us this week. This is the anniversary of Pa's and Ma's marriage and I don't believe any two people could be more perfectly mated. Their dispositions are different and the difference makes them more suited to each other. If I ever found anyone who was as devoted to me as Pa to Ma, whom I loved and trusted as Ma does Pa—I would not hesitate about entering into "that most solemn State."

September 12th—

I have had a pleasant visit in Russellville. Pleasant because Aunt Martha, Cousin Jane Harrison and families and all the friends of my school-days seem so glad to have me with them and treat me so nicely in every way. Ex. Norton came for a few days whilst I was there— I have a suspicion that Uncle George Norton wrote him to come. He has his heart set on making a match between us and does all he can to throw us together—believing with Byron (it seems) "That accident—blind contact and the strong necessity of loving will remove antipathies, etc. etc."—but his efforts are all useless. I like Ex. very much—he is kind and amiable as can be—but he is just the kind of man I could not possibly love. He never has told Uncle George of his proposal and my rejecting him—neither have I mentioned it and in our efforts to appear the same as before, we got on very well. Most of the young men I knew—are with Gen. Buckner at Camp Boone—just across the line in Tennessee—and most of my old schoolmates are secessionists and that marred our intercourse no little. I am not going down there any more—till these troubles are over. I don't care how much they oppose my Unionism but when they say mean things against Kentuckians who go against the South and mean to hit Pa, I can't and won't take it quietly. It is so easy to go with the people and section one loves and so hard to be true and loyal to principles and whole country against all personal interests and this my noble father is—and he knows, he sees the end from the beginning, that secession will be ruin to the South. George Todd is living in Arkansas and has joined a Rebel regiment. He wrote his sister that he supposed of course Cousin John Todd—would resign from the U. S. Army, if he hadn't already done so. Cousin John hasn't resigned and don't [*sic*] intend to—so there is the horror of the war—brother against brother.[11]

September 15th—

Our Literary Club decided last night to meet no more for the present. Professor Le Compte the president—is going away—so many of the members have already gone and those remaining are getting more and more strained in intercourse. We can't talk of indifferent things when the war is the all-absorbing subject of our thoughts and we can't talk without getting excited on that subject.—and Kentucky can't preserve her neutrality much longer. She must take sides as a state. Hugh Gwyn and Mike Hall took tea with us tonight and afterwards Mr. Baxter came out. Mike is a strong Union man, Hugh a secessionist and Mr. Baxter an Englishman. I was foolish enough to say "we have all phases of opinion represented here tonight." Mike replied, "No, there is no northern fanatic, who I think is just as disloyal as a rebel; secessionist and abolitionist are both equally opposing the constitution and Laws"—whereupon Hugh's face flushed and for the first time he got excited and he and I cut each other in a way we were both sorry for and even Mr. Baxter's and Mike's kindly efforts to change the subject did not quite clear the atmosphere. When they left however, Hugh laughing, held out his hand saying, "Shake hands and I won't do so any more." But the fact remains that all sympathy and accord of feeling between us *is gone* and it is hard to have in its place merely a thin crust of amiability and regard for the opinions each of the other.

The hilltop fort on the north side of the river, built behind the home of Larkin and Polly Baker, overlooked the railroad, river, and road coming toward Bowling Green. Apparently drawn from a description rather than from a photograph, the engraving omitted the hill and its Fort Lytle on the southern edge of town (now part of the Western Kentucky University campus). *Frank Leslie's Illustrated Newspaper,* March 15, 1862.

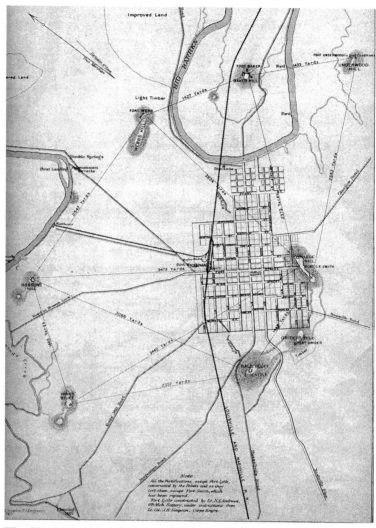

The Union Army's 1863 map documented the fortified hilltops, including the fort built behind the Underwood home. Partial remains of Forts Webb and Lytle still stand. *Atlas to Accompany the Official Records of the Union and Confederate Armies, 1861–1865* (New York: Julius Bien, n.d.), Plate CI.

The night before the Confederates left Bowling Green, a fire destroyed a portion of the north side of the town square. The courthouse (built about 1812) and small log jail were torn down a few years after the war's end. Today the area is a small park. *Frank Leslie's Illustrated Newspaper*, March 15, 1862.

MARTIAL LAW PROCLAIMED!

This town is declared under Martial Law. All citizens and soldiers except the guard, will retire to their quarters at 8 o'clock, P. M. A strong force will be stationed in the town. All persons found in the streets will be arrested.— Any one attempting to fire any building will be shot without trial.   W. J. HARDEE,

Bowling-Green, Feb. 13th, 1862.   Maj. Gen.

"Martial Law . . ." broadside. Courtesy of the Kentucky Library and Museum, Western Kentucky University.

BOWLING-GREEN, KY.

Before they evacuated the town, the Confederates destroyed
the wooden footbridge across the Barren River; the Union army
replaced it with a pontoon bridge. *Harpers Illustrated Weekly*, March
15, 1862.

Because the bridges had been destroyed, Union troops forded the river and crossed on long rafts and flatboats. In the background stand the supports for the footbridge and the railroad bridge destroyed by the retreating Confederates. *Frank Leslie's Illustrated Newspaper,* December 6, 1862.

Lucy Henry
Underwood (1815–
1893). Courtesy
of the Kentucky
Library and Museum,
Western Kentucky
University.

Warner Lewis
Underwood
(1808–1872).
Courtesy of the
Kentucky Library
and Museum,
Western Kentucky
University.

In 1860, Kentucky controlled the major waterways west of the Appalachian Mountains. The newly constructed L&N Railroad, completed through Bowling Green shortly before the war began, connected the Upper South's three major cities (Louisville, Nashville, Memphis) and could provide a "shortcut" from the Ohio to the Mississippi River. Daniel Boorstin and Brooks M. Kelley, *A History of the United States* (Lexington, Mass.: Ginn and Company, 1983), 283.

⇜ CHAPTER THREE ⇝

War and occupation by a large military group changed life for all residents of south central Kentucky. For many, the pleasures of life ceased. Josie wrote that daily existence went from "bad to worse," as "more soldiers are continually coming into town." The Philistines "invaded" the Underwoods' farm and home and restricted those activities she and her family normally enjoyed. For some, however, the army offered welcomed amenities. Soldiers held drills, sham battles, and colorful dress parades to which flocked denizens of all ages. Officers sponsored cotillions and socials, where they and young lasses enjoyed each others' attentions. One of Josie's contemporaries proclaimed that these were "days of happiness . . . the happiest of my life, for the intellectual & beauty of the South clustered here."[1]

SEPTEMBER 20TH—

It has come! "The Philistines are upon us!" Kentucky's neutrality is over! On the morning of the 17th, [Simon Bolivar] Buckner with his hosts of disloyal Kentuckians and other Rebel troops—rushed up by rail from Camp Boone and took possession of the town. Henry had gone to the post-office and we were all out on the front porch, waiting his return when we heard, shout after shout and continuous shouting rise from the town. Getting the old "Spy Glass"—Pa looked to see if he could distinguish a cause for the shouting. Quickly his eyes and ours without glasses were caught by the Flag over the Depot, which alas! and a shame! was coming down and a new and strange one run up the pole—when again shout after shout rent the air. Too well we knew what it meant. The Rebels had taken possession of the town. Heavens! how I felt. I never before realized that The Flag meant anything special to me—*that I loved it*. It was simply a pretty Banner pleasing to see waving in the breeze. But to day—when I saw that Flag with drooping folds coming slowly down and that other run up quickly to flaunt gaily in its place—I verily believe, girl as I am had I been in that crowd I could have *shot* the man who pulled that Old Flag down, and all day long & now—late at night my heart feels like it was held in a strong terrible grip, that will prevent its ever beating free again.[2] Dear Ma sank into a chair, white as though she would faint. I rushed for water for her. Pa quickly put his arm around her and whilst the tears rolled down his own face, said, "bear up, my wife" (as he always calls Ma) we need all our courage now. Warner said, "*Now,* father you'll surely let me join the Army *now*"—I remembered afterward that Uncle Henry said, "Too bad *we* couldn't keep the old Flag," and the *we* told where his sympathies are—though the dear old man said so little. The negroes hearing the shouting rushed from their various places and work to the front of the house and there long we stood looking wondering what next and waiting for Henry, who soon came galloping up the hill at a break-neck speed—yelling the news as far as we could see him and long before we could hear what he said—though we knew without hearing. Then Pa ordered his horse and he and Warner went to town—Henry, Marius and Uncle Henry soon following and I longing to go with them—but we did not know what soldiers would do and it was best for Ma and me to stay at home as women must—*wait*. It wasn't many hours till we saw 3 or 4 soldiers in gray coming up the yard—we were all on the lookout, for we could do nothing but watch that day. When they reached the porch dear Ma's voice trembled as she asked what they wanted—for we hadn't the slightest idea and all was dread—and we were relieved when they said—something to eat, if she would give it to them. She had Jake bring them cold ham and biscuit and milk and gave them fruit and then her loyalty and courage coming back in full force, she said: "I will never refuse a hungry man food—but you must excuse me from asking into my house, men who have helped pull down our country's flag," and with that she walked into the house. The men, common soldiers they were—still they ought to have appreciated such a sentiment—laughed as they turned away and I heard them say "Yanks" as they strolled on down through the orchard. I felt like shooting them! Pa came from town at dusk—depressed and heart sore. He learned that the intention of the Rebels was to rush on to Louisville—but Union troops were as quick and a little quicker than they, and knew the minute they entered Kentucky and then rushed in and reached "Muldros Hill" first—had a fight, killed the rebel Gen. [Benjamin Franklin] Terry and held the position, the rebels falling back to Bowling Green—which Mr. Web Wright exultantly informed me this morning would be "The Gibraltar of the Confederacy." I replied I suppose you will at once offer your services—as a soldier to defend this Gibraltar! He is the biggest coward in the universe! It seems to me I met every secessionist I know this morning and they all bowed with a smile and an expression as if to say: ah! ah!—what have you got to say now, and the gray uniforms were everywhere. There was no train from Louisville and no *Journal*. We are cut off from out side and "*know nothing*." Pa does not know what he can do—but one thing he knows, he will never accept secession and no force can make him disloyal to his country.[3]

September 21st—

I started into town this afternoon on my beautiful horse, "Walker," Warner riding with me—on black Bess. Near Bob Strange's we had to stand aside and wait till thousands of men in solid phalanx marched by, where they were going, we did not know, but supposed they were just drilling on the road. Till my heart gave a great frightened bound as I saw our big gate opened and the whole army march into our front field of 100 acres, in beautiful red clover, I couldn't go on to town, fearing they might go into the yard and house, too, so turned back, having to pass quite near some of the troops, who were standing, whilst others marched farther into the field. One Captain took off his hat and bowed to the ground almost again and again. Then, several others in the line, lifted theirs and waved them around once or twice. They were too far for me to recognize and I merely bowed with what dignity I could and rode on home at a pretty fast gallop.

September 23rd—

Yesterday I drove in town and whilst sitting in the carriage a man in Captain's uniform, came up to speak to me and I recognized Terah Freeman, whom I had not seen since I was at school in Russellville and he at college there. The soldier's dress, a moustache and two years had changed him quite a little. It was he who had bowed so low the day before, and two other Tennessee boys I had known in Russellville. He asked me if he could call. I told him "Not in that uniform," which surprised him no little, and he said, "He supposed of course I was a Rebel," and I answered, "Why should you have supposed that? Did you ever in the old school days hear me express great admiration for Benedict Arnold?" and then I told Uncle Lewis to drive on; feeling everything is going wrong I

looked out the back window and there Terah stood where I
left him staring at the carriage, and I wished I hadn't said it.

SEPTEMBER 25TH—

Yesterday I got a note from "*Major*" Carrington, saying he
and "Capt." Williams (both I knew in Memphis) as plain Mis-
ters, were in Bowling Green with their Regiment, the 23rd
Tenn. and asking if they might call. Ma decided they should
not, so we kept the messenger waiting a long time whilst I
wrote note after note, tearing up one and writing another,
trying to write a refusal, without offense, finally settling upon
and sending one saying: "Respect for my father's Union principles, in which I intensely share, makes me feel it best to
decline visits from Rebel officers. Sincerely regretting these
sad conditions, I remain, your friend

Josie L. Underwood."

This afternoon, the thousands and thousands of troops
came out again to drill and it seems our front field is to be
the established drill ground. The beautiful clover is already
trodden down and ruined. We sit on our porch watching
them and it is indeed a grand sight if we could forget what
it all means. General Buckner, on a beautiful white horse,
looks particularly fine, as he is a handsome man and rides
superbly, but I can't forget how he has betrayed Kentucky's
trust, turning all the State Guard under him over to the
Confederacy. It is a grand sight to see but so sad for dear
Pa to sit here helpless seeing his farm and crops ruined. He
goes into his office every day and by his firm courage and
unswerving Unionism in the midst of this Rebel army, gives
courage to weaker men who otherwise would fall away from
the faith.[4]

September 27th—

I was taking a horseback ride yesterday with Hugh Gwyn, when out on the Nashville Pike, "Major Carrington" joined us. He had met Hugh and I could but have a suspicion, that his overtaking us had been prearranged, when this suspicion in my mind, I looked at Hugh, I was amused at his quickness in reading my thought, for he said at once, "You are mistaken, it just happened, don't be cruel," I had no desire to be so and to own the truth was glad it had "happened." Major C., after saying he hoped we would permit him to ride a little way with us, as his regiment was in camp, out that way, said "You don't mean to tell me, Miss Underwood, that you are going to cut all your old friends, because they are Rebels? You are riding with Gwyn who is as big a Rebel as I, and yet you declined seeing me at your home." Yes, I said, "and I feel a traitor to my father's principles to be riding with you now. Mr. Gwyn perhaps cannot control his feelings but he is not in arms, fighting against our country and flag as you are." Hugh spoke up quickly saying, "Let me defend my position, Major. I must, at the risk of losing privileges I so greatly prize. I have not joined the army, because as yet my services are not needed, and I would not burden the cause with even a small useless expense, but I stand pledged a soldier of the confederacy, as soon as I am needed." "May that never be," I said, for surely the South will see her madness soon and come back into the Union." "Never!" both men said. Then Hugh said, "but we are two to one and that isn't a fair fight" and lightly turned the conversation, and I was glad to ask Major Carrington about my Memphis friends and was thankful to hear that Jack and Tom Grafton were ordered elsewhere, for I don't see how I could refuse to see them; and that I will not receive visits from Rebel officers, I am decided—and Ma is still more so, and it would not be proper respect to Pa, who God knows has already enough to bear.

SEPTEMBER 29TH—

Indignant! distressed! helpless! that's what we are and the words very faintly express my state of mind. This afternoon, the whole brigade of infantry marched straight through our yard to pitch their tents in our barn lot—and the Pond Orchard—and there they are camped for God only knows how long and already the new chestnut rail fence, around the orchard, is fast vanishing and being burnt in their camp fires. The soldiers are everywhere, even in the kitchen and the best stables in the barn they have appropriated for the horses of the officers. These are Missouri troops and I am glad I don't know any of them.

SEPTEMBER 30TH—

This morning Aunt Liz could get no milk from the cows, and when she was milking, soldiers gathered around, making what they thought, witty remarks on her efforts. She found the poor cows had no more milk to give as they had already been drained dry by soldiers. This happened just before breakfast and Aunt Liz had hardly gotten through telling us, when Aunt "Dams" came rushing in the dining room, calling "Mars Warner—Mars Warner—make somebody kitch that solger—he's got the breakfast!" Then she told how he came into the kitchen, talked pleasant-like and asked if he might sit a little while by the stove—"just to smell the odor of homemade coffee and good ham"—and then when she went in the pantry to get some eggs, he emptied the pan of biscuits into the skillet of ham and took the whole thing and "put out with it as hard as he could tear." What can we do! Pa went to

see the Col. about it. Col. Rich is his name and a contemptible puppy he is, too. He told Pa "he would see what he could
do, but southern Union men needn't expect much respect
shown them or their property." Pa replied, "he had hoped
southern men might retain their honesty even though they
had lost their loyalty and was grieved to find himself mistak-
en. But what was the use. We are humiliatingly helpless—
when Pa told us of his interview, Ma said, "I bet anything that
Colonel's mother was a Yankee!" And this afternoon it was
funny, I went out in the garden with little Mary, when he and
another officer came out from the summer house, where I
had not seen them. The other officer very politely asked me
for some flowers. I handed him the rose-scissors, telling him
to help himself—he smiled saying he hadn't much practice
flower cutting—so I cut a pretty bouquet for him whilst he
talked in a pleasant gentlemanly way. I managed to ask Col.
Rich where his troops were from and then if he were a Mis-
sourian also. He said his father was but he had the misfortune to have been born at his mother's home in Ohio, but
he had always lived in Missouri, and was doing all he could to
wipe out that misfortune. I could not help saying—"I don't
believe you can do it, for I heard a bet that your mother was a
Yankee. *We southerners,* you know—notice characteristics that
would be imperceptible to you—'Yankees.'" Oh! but he was
mad! and the other officer laughed—and now I am scared
for he is no *way* a gentleman and I am afraid he will take
some mean revenge for my foolish speech. Oh! me! me! I
wish I did not get so angry. I am trying all the time to "hit
back" for the indignities my dear father has to bear and I
just make matters worse. Ma's health is very poor and all this
excitement is dreadful for her. To see our dear old home being completely over-run by soldiers and none of our rights
regarded, almost kills her. We have no privacy in the house
or out. Soldiers as often march right through the hall if the

doors are open—as going round the house. Our cows are milked—our hen-house robbed—the eggs laid in the barn are of course taken. Aunt Damsel has to watch and hide what she cooks and we find no appeal to the officers helps. We have tried, Ma and I, speaking to the soldiers themselves and this does do a little good. The young officers are always coming to the door asking for water or some foolish thing, evidently trying to get acquainted, and sometimes in spite of the line of conduct I have set for myself—baring social intercourse with them, we have rather pleasant little talks, and dear Ma as indignant as she is, at the way they are treating our home and as much as she feels that loyalty to her patriotic ancestry and to the Union and Pa's position against secession and rebellion requires condemnation of all *rebel soldiers,* her tender heart goes out to every pale sick looking fellow she sees and she is constantly making broth, soups and hoarhound [*sic*] syrup for the sick men at the hospital on the road to town and rarely goes by without taking something nourishing to leave there for them. The other day as we stopped there to leave some hoarhound syrup for some poor fellows who were getting over measles and had dreadful coughs, a very nice looking young officer, a surgeon, I think, took it and said, "I have often thought, Mrs. Underwood to call up at 'Mount Air,' to thank you for your kindness." Ma smiled very sweetly as she replied, "That would be unnecessary trouble, sir. I am very glad to do anything I can for *sick* men, no matter who or what they are; but when they are well enough to fight against their country, I want nothing more to do with them." My dear mother is the tenderest-hearted woman to all suffering humanity and the most loyal to what she regards right, I have ever known. She could be burned at the stake without flinching for a principle—and would sacrifice all her own comfort to spare anyone else suffering. It is good for a child to admire as well as love father and mother as I do mine.[5]

OCTOBER 1ST—"MOUNT AIR," NEAR BOWLING GREEN, KENTUCKY.

"Gorgeous are thy woods October,
Clad in glowing mantles sear
Brightest tints of beauty blending
Like the West when day's descending
Thou' art [*sic*] the sunset of the year.

Fading flowers are thine, October
Droopeth sad the sweet "blue bells,"
Gone the blossom April cherished
Violet, lily, rose all perished
Fragrance fled from field and dell.

Saddest sounds are thine, October
Music of the falling leaf
O'er the pensive spirit stealing
To its inmost depths revealing,
Thus all gladness sinks in grief.

I do love thee, drear October
More than budding, blooming Spring;
Hers is hopes [*sic*] delusive smiling,
Trusting hearts to grief beguiling
Memory loves thy dusky ring."[6]

Another beautiful letter from Mr. Grafton today. I can't keep up this correspondence longer. It isn't fair to him, for now I know I do not and never can love him, with the love—his feeling for me, desires. If he were not fighting against our country this might be possible but that will come between us and any thought of him as "my heart's hero." He persistently ignores this but I cannot. My answer to this let-

ter must be my last to him and how I am to write it is hard
to think.

OCTOBER 3RD—

Everything goes from bad to worse—more soldiers are
continually coming into the town. I must give up my horseback rides, unless with an escort, and I do so love to get on
my horse and ride out the country roads—towards the creek
and Ewings Ferry, with only my own thoughts for company.
Pa thinks this no longer safe. Mr. Baxter kindly (?) offers his
services whenever I want to ride and Warner or Henry can
go with me—all very well—but I resent the thought of danger—where all has been so safe for me heretofore. Mr. Baxter comes out oftener than ever now—in that way showing
his sympathy for all we are enduring—of petty annoyances
and dear Pa's larger trials. Mr. Grider is at Columbia mus-
tering in the men he has been all this time quietly raising.
He had 1500 enrolled. Has formed a regiment and handed
the surplus over to Ben. Bristow who hadn't quite a full regiment. Mr. Grider's is the 9th Kentucky, John Ward's is the
27th Kentucky. Brother Warner is nearly crazy to get through
the Rebel lines and join Mr. Grider's regiment. He isn't 15 till
Dec. and Pa thinks him too young and don't want him to try
getting though the Lines without a pass. Henry says if "Warner goes he is going too for he can shoot as well as Warner, if
he *didn't belong to the Zouaves*"—he is only 13—dear boys—we
are uneasy about them all the time as it is, for with soldiers
all about us and every word anybody says being exaggerated
and misconstrued, it is hard to make them prudent in talking. Henry specially takes delight in proclaiming his Unionism and "sassing the secesh" and saying "Pa says this and Pa
says that." Sister Fanny with her two little boys and Marius
and Lady Henry are staying with us. She is very anxious to

get through the Lines to join Mr. Grider. It is doubtful if she can get a pass.[7]

OCTOBER 5TH—

Yesterday, another brigade marched up the hill and camped in the fruit orchard and the few apples left on the trees are fast disappearing. These troops are from Mississippi—are better looking than the Missouri troops and better mannered—but [have] not much more regard for fences and have been sauntering about the yard and garden and several came to the door to ask for milk—but did not push into the house as the others do and doff their hats as far as they see Ma or me—maybe when they find out where the cows stay, they won't anymore *ask* for milk.

SUNDAY—

A quiet beautiful day—but Pa could no longer take all the children black and white, and saunter along the river bank and through the woods and fields. We are too hemmed in by troops and he would be suspected of "taking observations" to report—as he was the other day when he, with the rest of us were sitting on the front porch watching the drilling. They were having a sham battle and we were wondering how many men there were—when Pa made a sort of estimate and said he judged there must be about 30,000.[8] We were standing down by the gate at the time, where we had gone to get a better view, and a good many other people from town were there in carriages, on horseback and foot, watching the drilling. The next day, a rebel who is indebted to Pa for many kindnesses told him—it was reported at headquarters that he was estimating the troops and was acting for and communicating with the Union forces and was being watched, so he had better be careful or he would be arrested and sent South. I wish to the good Lord *we were* in communication with the Union troops and the outside world. We hear nothing except what the confederates want us to hear and I don't believe the accounts published in the papers we see are true. Rarely, we get a *Louisville Journal* which somehow has been smuggled in and is passed around clandestinely among the Union people—till it is worn out, and no letters except in the same way. Pa is continually getting letters from his old friends in the South. Many of them just as much opposed to the doctrine of secession as he is—but have yielded to the pressure of circumstances and gone over to the rebels and they advise and plead with Pa to do the same thing as the "best policy"— I cannot conceive of my father giving up a principle for "Policy's sake"—and he thinks the course the South is pursuing the *worst policy* on earth for the *South* and will bring ruin and desolation upon the South in the end if she succeeds in directing [dividing] this Union—which may God forbid! When we went to church this morning and passed by the orchard and the camps of this Mississippi brigade, it was funny to see some of the soldiers or maybe they were officers, tipping about in the mud (for it rained yesterday) in velvet smoking jackets and embroidered slippers—whilst their negro valets—were blacking their boots before or behind the various tents. They looked more like they were out on a pleasure camping than preparing to meet bullets and death. How horrible it all is! How too, too horrible! and they are gentlemen, too! This evening one of the darkies came up to the house with a big sack of the nicest pippin apples, saying, "Col. Love had had them gathered for Mrs. Underwood and sent them with his compliments and regrets that his regiment must intrude upon private premises." Dear Ma sent her thanks to Col. Love and a jar of peach preserves for his supper—for the courtesy and the *regrets* won her tolerance as no assurance of possession and power could have done.

OCTOBER 9TH—

I started to make some calls today but didn't get very far in the list. There is no use trying to keep up visiting with the "secesh" girls—and we are too intensely interested, too wrought up too suspicious, too distrustful of each other to make any intercourse pleasant. We are not in sympathy—on any subject— I don't care so much for any of them except Lizzie Wright—but it hurts me to be out of accord with her. We have been such good friends all our lives till now, and I am sure she still loves me, as I do her—but there is restraint in our intercourse now—for in the present state of affairs— what makes her glad, distresses me and so visiting together isn't so pleasant. Mollie Hobson and her family are all Union and her brother Will is in the Union Army but Mattie Cook, her cousin, who lives with them is a rabid secessionist—very pretty and has a great many rebel officers visiting her—in spite of her Uncle's opposition. Hugh Gwyn has always been very fond of her and I have sometimes thought they were engaged—though it looks now as if she were more pleased with the gentlemen in gray uniforms. When I called this afternoon, I met a Captain White, of Buckner's staff, who politely helped me in the carriage and asked might he call— I told him I was a Union girl and did not receive visits from Rebel officers. The rebel officers are far more pleasant and tolerant than the rebel citizens—who are very disagreeable to the Union people—more in their manner of triumph than in anything they actually say. I love to go up to dear old Mrs. Hall's—for all the family feel just as we do—southern people loving the south—yet opposing the breaking up of the Union—with friends and kinsfolks on both sides— An-

nie Hawkins, the grand-daughter, whose father is Col. of the
11th Kentucky and her sweetheart Major Mottley of the same
regiment is so bright and delightfully original and Mike Hall
as good as gold, a strong Union man, longing to offer his
services to his country but compelled to stay at home to take
care of his old and invalid mother and widowed sister and her
two little boys and Mrs. Hawkins and her two daughters—besides an orphan niece—Nannie Smith. He has the care and
the self repression whilst others far less loyal and brave go
"where glory awaits them" and alas! it may be death and a
soldier's grave. But his is as noble a sacrifice and a harder
and rarer one.

OCTOBER 12TH—

Nothing new has happened today. The same trying in-
trusions and annoyances as from the soldiers about us and
the continued sorrow at seeing our dear old home being
so destroyed. The fields all trodden down and fences being
burned. But tonight as I looked out from my window at the
tents shining white in the moonlight, with here and there a
camp fire, and hear the various bugle calls from far off and
near—there is something thrilling and beautiful in it all, in
spite of the underlying and ever abiding sadness.

OCTOBER 14TH—

Today we had a trial almost too great for dear Ma to endure. Shortly after breakfast a hundred men with gleaming
axes marched up the front walk and instead of going around
the house, marched straight through the hall and out the
back door in to the barn lot where they commenced cutting
down the grove of walnut and oak trees—which all now lie
low on the ground. Pa had gone to his office in town and

could not have stopped it anyway. Dear ma and I went out and asked why they were doing it and begged they would desist—but they had to obey orders and so the cutting down the trees went on all day. Ma went to her room and locked her door, she could not shut out the sound of the blows, and the falling of the big trees as they crashed down to the ground was as though her heart were crushed. We learned they are going to build a Fort back of the barn and these trees would obstruct the range—the site commanding the Railroad and the Louisville Pike, and also the Scottsville road. Warner went to town to tell Pa. He came home but what could he do? Nothing! only bear with his best strength his helplessness and comfort Ma, as best he could for she loves this old home and especially it's beautiful trees with a passionate devotion. He had hardly gotten in the house—when old Uncle Todd—weighing nearly 300 pounds—poor fat old negro—came toddling and I may say *roaring*—towards the house—saying, "Whars Mars Warner? whar is he? The sojers gwine ter tar my cabin down. Come, stop 'em Mars Warner," he appealed—as Pa went out to see what the trouble was. The darkies can't yet understand that it is possible for their "Marster" to be so "run over" and it was a very sad sight to see and hear the old darkie and dear Pa's explanation to him of how powerless he was to prevent the destruction of his cabin. He said the soldiers said they were going to make a Fort where his cabin stood (on the highest point) and he asked them "just to make it a little furder down the hill and leave his cabin"—but they laughed and told him to "git out." Pa went to see and found it as Uncle Todd had said and the cabin already being torn down so all he could do was to send men, the boys and all the little negroes helping to bring Uncle Todd's belongings to a cabin in the yard. The poor, old fat negro sitting on a fallen tree near by—cursing—fussing and almost crying all the while only exciting the amusement of the soldiers. What will come next I wonder and *dread*. Ma's health is in such a precarious condition, we fear she can't bear up against so many trials and all the nervous strain it costs. The children, white and black, are on the lookout all the time and constitute themselves a gang of excited reporters—all day rushing in with one tale or another—"The *soljers* are digging taters at the bottom of the garden." "Theys got one of we'all's pigs—cause I heard it squeal," and then the boys—go after them and can do nothing if they find it all true and we have told them we can't help it all but we can't stop the excitement that pervades everybody on the place.[9]

October 16th—

Pa got a kind good letter from Mr. Western, deploring the troops camping at "Mount Air" and just as affectionate as any son could write. He asked how Pa would like to sell Mount Air to him and Mr. Soryann [Torian]—his partner. They would take it just as it stands, all the negroes too, so they would not feel any change and things go on with them the same as ever and they could raise mules and corn to supply their big cotton plantation in Louisiana and it would be, if he owned it, the same hospitable home for the family whenever they cared to come to it. He said he realized what it would mean to Pa and Ma to sell Mt. Air and only made the proposition in hopes of relieving Pa and the family of the unpleasant conditions—as he felt to get away from them was almost essential to Ma's health and many kind things he said. Pa, Ma, Sister Fanny and I have talked long and anxiously about it. It is a new thought—selling Mount Air! that never entered anybody's head before and a very hard one to consider—for dear Pa and Ma and for us all—but it was at last decided worth considering. Mr. Western said if Pa should consider the proposition they were prepared, to pay him $50,000 in gold, *cash*, for the place, negroes—stock. Pa said he would not consider it a moment if it were to sell to anyone, not a member of the family. Then as he looked so tenderly and anxiously at Ma, I could see why he continued, but it would be a great thing if we could get away somehow—and charging us not to mention the subject to children or negroes or anyone, we parted for the night—but not much sleep for any of us with so grave a question to consider. O! if the Union army would only come and drive these rebels from our home and give us peace again! I never dreamed it possible we could have war in this country, brother against brother, friend against friend, as now. We drive in town almost every day for the anxiety to see and hear what's going on, so as if possible to gain some knowledge of how long this is going to last or if there is any indication of vacating the town. If there is, it is not apparent, and all the hills around the town are being more or less strongly fortified. People seem to think there is danger of a big battle here—as it is likely the Union army will try to advance on this line—but all is speculation. We know nothing.

OCTOBER 20TH—

Dear sister Fanny at last succeeded in getting a pass for herself and children. (Mrs. B. C. Grider, children, negro driver, and carriage) I believe it read, so yesterday after an early breakfast she started. Warner wanted to go with her and it was best he should for though he is but a boy, so he can go on the pass for "children—he is very brave—manly and sensible and if anything happened on the way, he would be of great help and he can return with the carriage and Uncle Lewis; that is, if he means to return—which I don't believe the dear boy has any idea of doing for young as he is, not quite 15, he has an intense desire to "join the army and fight for his country" and the way the rebels are ruining our dear home makes him more than ever anxious. I asked him if he was going to come back with Uncle Lewis and he said, "now sister *please* don't put that notion into anybody's head. I can't tell and I don't want Pa and Ma to put any *embargoes* on me"; and their anxiety about sister Fanny and her little ones made them very glad that Warner could go with her. "Lady and Marius Henry will stay with us. We will be very anxious till Uncle Lewis gets back for there is no way of hearing a word from sister Fanny—till then.

OCTOBER 22ND—

This morning Henry and I drove to town with Pa to bring back the buggy and "see what we could see," which is the same thing—soldiers everywhere—cavalrymen dashing about—officers riding round, whether to show themselves or on duties I don't know—and the secession people—getting more and more arrogant in their manner toward Union people. Whilst sitting in the buggy—at the post-office, waiting for the mail—which, Pa had gone in to get—Col. Carrington, Lieut. Williams and Capt. White all came up and were talking to me—when Mat Jackson and Belle Smith, passed by, with little rebel flags stuck in their hats. I spoke to them as a matter of course. They returned my "good morning" with quite a toss of their heads and as they passed said loud enough for all to hear, "Josie Underwood won't receive rebel officers at her home—but I take notice she always has them hanging round when she comes to town." Capt. White said quickly, looking at them, "Small favors thankfully received," and I said, "gentlemen, hadn't you better leave me and join those ladies who are evidently so in sympathy with you." (They had stopped in the Post-office door) and if they heard his "God forbid," could not have been much flattered. Some of the

"secesh" girls—Lizzie Wright, Mattie Cook and some others are naturally having a good time but they act like ladies
whilst another crowd of loud talking, common girls flaunt
around making themselves conspicuous and ridiculous and
whilst they certainly attract attention, fail of the admiration
they might otherwise win. I think it best that I should not
receive visits from the rebel officers and I don't' want to—for
we know Pa is being spied upon all the time and we are all so
opposed to secession and the breaking up of the Union that
we don't want to treat the rebels as though we approved or
countenanced them in any way, and yet, I confess, I do enjoy
the chance talks with them even though we give and take
pretty sharp thrusts in defending our different principles.

November 1st—

Since I last made my records here, so much has happened I hardly know how to write. I am so wrought up and
in such an unnatural state of excitement all the time, as is
everybody else, that I make no effort to describe my own feelings—but just record happenings and things that will help
me to remember—what I do not want to forget. A few days
after sister Fanny left, Pa wrote to Uncle George Norton—
telling him the condition of affairs here and how we were
surrounded and overrun by soldiers and asked him to take
"Lady" and Marius to stay with them—as their schools in Russellville are not broken up as they are here and their home
is as peaceful and undisturbed as before the war and Aunt
Martha is younger and well—whilst Ma's health is very poor
and she is compelled to be in bed a great deal of the time
in very critical condition—and Pa thought as the children
were the same kin to Aunt Martha as to Ma and they were
in so much better fix every way—it would be best for Marius
and Lady to be with them. But Uncle George answered it

was against his ideas of what was best for his own children to have other children brought up in the home with them and as sorry as he was for the condition of affairs at "Mount Air," he must decline—taking "Lady" and Marius— I wonder what would have become of all the orphan children in the family if my dear generous wholesome father and mother had acted on the same principle—never do I remember the time that some one outside of our family was not living with us—with every home privilege that any of us had with a place in our hearts as well as in our home. So the children remain with us. The most important thing is what dear Warner, brave, patriotic boy that he is—did not return with Uncle Lewis. When he got up to Columbia, Mr. Grider put him to drilling men in the manual of arms—as Warner is well drilled from his experience in the Zouave Company and when Warner declared his intention of joining the army and sister Fanny and Mr. Grider could not dissuade him—Mr. Grider took him in his regiment—instead of letting him join some other, as he was determined to enlist— I felt he would not come back— when he told me good-bye—he said, "You had better kiss me twice, sister and looked so serious though he laughed. I did not tell Ma my fears, fearing it would only add to her anxieties and I so wish I were a man that I might do something for my country that I could not blame Warner. Now it is done—whilst Ma is anxious she is so proud of Warner, she is greatly comforted and Pa would be too, except he knows Warner is too young to endure the hardships of camp life, and yet I see that he too feels Warner has done only what his *age* prevents his doing—and more than his age, the many entirely dependent on him and the fact that he can help the Union better in other fields—since he has no military knowledge. All about Warner and a good many other things we learned through a letter Uncle Lewis brought and several [news]papers—which he had concealed in the slide of the carriage where the window lets down and he could not get them for us till late the night of his return—when no soldiers were around the carriage house and he sneaked them out and into the house to us. The papers have been circulated around clandestinely among the Union people till they are worn out and we all feel helped up—by the hope that it may not be so very long before we are "delivered from the hands of our enemies."

NOVEMBER 5TH—

My birthday. I am 21 today. Pa gave me $20; Ma gave me a very pretty set of white furs and Henry, dear boy, gave me two beautiful wings of a "Yellow Hammer" he had killed and saved the wings for me. Mr. Baxter sent me a lovely engraving of the "Choirester Boys"; "Aunt Sis" gave me 21 spanks—"my last whoopin"—and I have everything individually to make me as happy a girl as ever lived to be 21—the best father and mother on earth—loving brothers and sisters—hosts of friends and my beautiful home, in spite of the vandalism of the rebels, for though the fences are burned, the fields trodden down and worst of all, the trees back of the house cut down, those about the house and yard still standing and there is no place so "beautiful for situation" as dear old "Mount Air"—my birthplace and life-long home. I cannot bear the thought of the place being sold—even to Mr. Western and yet—I know it would be best, if Pa could get out of the confederate lines and Ma away from all the excitement and constant and trying annoyances and indignities we are subjected to. Pa can't get his consent yet to give up the dear old home but the question is being seriously considered.[10]

Every day we hear of some Union people who have weakened in their loyalty and gone over to the rebels—but all the best men in the town still remain true. Pa, Uncle Joe, the Griders—Judge Loving—the Rodes—the Halls and Hawkins—the Hobsons—the Baker family and the Claypoles and Hiram and Mrs. Smith—Mr. Smoot, the Presbyterian minister, pretends to be a great Union man, but I can't help doubting his sincerity. He is a queer man—smart—but there is something in his face, I don't like and a sort of lisp in his pronunciation that maybe he can't help—but is bad in a woman and much worse in a man. Uncle Joe is in the Legislature, after having been U. S. Senator and Judge of the Supreme Court [Kentucky Court of Appeals]—but for such wise statesmen and patriots going to the Legislature, Magoffin and his gang would have carried Kentucky out of the Union long ago.

NOVEMBER 8TH—

A brigade of more soldiers have camped around our house and over towards Jim Ewings—taken possession of the old Simmons house and are fast pulling all the planks off the barn and even the house for camp fires. It is a good frame house of 7 rooms—but that too is likely to be destroyed. No protest on Pa's part avails. Instead, the knowledge that the property belongs to Pa, the man who has opposed secession so strongly, makes them more anxious to destroy anything they can belonging to him. They forget that he did all he could to prevent Lincoln's election and opposes fanatics North as well as South.

NOVEMBER 9TH—

I had such an absurd letter from Capt. White today, commencing, "My dear Miss Underwood:— A concatenation of infelicitous circumstances prevents a personal declaration of the feelings this letter must feebly declare," and so on—in such grandeloquent style that I had to get a dictionary to read it and was surprised that a man so pleasant as Capt. White had appeared the few times I have met him, should have written such a letter— I can't think he feels any such "intense devotion" as he declares—but fancy he wants to amuse himself with a flirtation with the enemy—a sort of sham Romeo and Juliette affair—to vary the ennui of camp life. I don't care to *play* the game. Then, there's Tom Grafton—if I did—as much as I would like to see him and Jack Henry, I hope their regiments will not come to Bowling Green for I don't see how I could refuse to see them. It is funny the excuses the young officers make to get into the house—those who are really gentlemen and will not intrude as many do without excuse.

NOVEMBER 20TH—

Dear Pa's position is getting harder and harder—powerless to prevent the steady devastation of our beautiful home and unable to take us away from the many hard things we daily endure, which are all so bad for Ma in her present health. Nearly all the fences are gone—burnt, by the soldiers in their camp fires—we have to keep our milk cows in the garden and the railing from around that and the yard are being pulled off. These soldiers respect nothing they want to use. This afternoon Mr. Baxter came out. I was more than usually indignant and excited over some new depredation and could not help expressing what I felt. The dear true-hearted fellow that he is said, "O! if I could only persuade you to leave all this and go to England with me!" I said, "And thereby win your everlasting contempt, for you could feel nothing else for me if I were willing to leave my dear mother and father or my country at such a time as this." This he said he knew I would not do. Then I tried to tell him as gently as I could that whilst I honored and liked him so very much, he must give up any hope of my ever having a tenderer feeling for him. Then he told me he was going to Louisville and thence to Columbia and would offer his services to Mr. Grider (Now Col. of the 9th Kentucky Infantry) in any capacity he might want him; being an Englishman, he can easily get a pass through the lines. He said he would gladly take letters for us and most delicately expressed the fact that they must contain no information regarding the confederate forces, since getting through on a pass, it would not be honorable for him to carry such information. I am quite sure he would not hesitate to give up his life rather than do a dishonorable thing—but no information we could give would be of any benefit, for all we know is that the rebels are here and seem preparing to stay. Citizens know really very little of their intentions—especially Union people.

NOVEMBER 22ND—

A letter from sister Jupe says she, Mr. Western, and Mr. Toryan [Torian] will be here Saturday. Then the matter of selling this dear old home will have to be settled. Another *beautiful* letter from Mr. Grafton. Mr. Baxter came out to say good-bye. Alas! alas! how our friends are one by one leaving us. Hugh Gwyn still comes out and is always pleasant, though it is harder and harder to steer clear of our differences and we could not, but for his genius in turning serious things into jokes.

NOVEMBER 23RD—

We had great excitement today which came near resulting in old "Uncle" Todd's death— He hasn't been well since the soldiers tore down his cabin to build the Fort where it stood. This morning Ma gave him some medicine to take and some liniment to rub on his rheumatic legs—the poor old fellow rubbed the medicine on his legs and took the liniment which had some whiskey in it so he took a double dose, which would have been the death of him if it hadn't happened that Dr. [Lemuel] Porter was out here to see Ma, so got to him in time. We were all mighty amused when as soon as he could talk, he said, "What in the name of Gawd anyone go waste whiskey in liniment fur—*dat* whut get me in de trouble."

NOVEMBER 24TH—

One day telleth another and all are sad for us—though full of excitement. Pa had a letter from [Felix] Zollicoffer today. They were in Congress together on the same committee and are devoted to each other. The letter was loving and kind as a brother could write, grieving that Pa, all of whose interests are in the south, could not go with her now— Hard as it is for Pa to go against his friends—his section and his personal preferences—How can he assent to what he thinks wrong—unconstitutional and ruinous to the South? He cannot do it, and at whatever loss must stand true and loyal to the Union.

NOVEMBER 26TH—

Our friend Mr. Emmerson Etheridge of Tennessee has been arrested for a Union speech and put in prison in Paducah—Ky. There is another southern man brave and true enough to his country to stand firm against those of his own people and section who are trying to destroy it— God help these brave few—and give victory to the right! but alas for southern Unionists, so many we love are with the rebels. That we look with equal interest and sorrow at the lists of wounded and killed on both sides. No victory without its sorrow for us.

CHAPTER THREE

NOVEMBER 30TH, 1861—

Well, Mr. Western and Mr. Torian have come and gone—
sister Jupe will stay longer with us—and what a trying time
we've had! They brought with them a common old carpet
satchel, with $50,000 in gold in it to pay for *Mount Air!* All
the gold in the Universe could not buy—the dear associations—joys and sweet memories of the old home. Long and
earnestly did we talk—sister Jupe, Ma & I—joining in the
consultations of Pros and Cons. with Pa, Mr. Western and Mr.
Torian. It was growing dark when at last Pa and Ma decided
it would be wisest to accept the offer and the deed was drawn
up but not signed—Pa asking till the next morning to make
the final decision— That night after supper, Mr. Western and
Mr. Torian having gone to town, Pa sent for Uncle Lewis,
Uncle William, Aunt "Sis," & Aunt "Dams" to come into the
Library; with serious faces they came, knowing there must
be something unusual and important to demand their presence. Never will I forget that scene—as those faithful servants
and friends sat there listening whilst dear Pa staited [*sic*] as
best he could the situation, in all its bearings upon us, them,
and our home. All of which they knew in a way—but when he
began to tell them how Mr. Western being in accord with the
powers there, could prevent many annoyances that he could
not and gradually made it known to them that they would
remain on the old place just the same and Mr. Western and
Miss Jupe wouldn't be like strange masters and explained the
proposition and that he had decided best to accept it but
wanted to consult them first and explain it all to them. They
took in the central idea at one grasp and all else was as nothing to them and from one and another came exclamations.
"Sell us Mars Warner!" "Good Lord"—"I never would er believed Mars Warner you'd sell us!" Dear Pa could not stand
it—The trial was more than he could bear—bursting into

generous tears—"And I never will," he said and snatching the deed from the table he threw it into the bright blazing fire. "We will do the best we can together—come what may, I give you my promise."—"Bless the Lord! Mars Warner, we believes you," they said and we all cried together— When the negroes went out—Pa said, "Western and Torian will think me a fool no doubt, but I can't help it," and I am sure we all felt relieved— I can't imagine ourselves without Mount Air," and the good faithful darkies around us. The plan was for us—to get through the lines to Louisville where we would be free from all danger and trouble and Pa might be of some service in the Union cause. Mr. Western and Mr. T. think the success of the confederacy assured and that Ky. will go with the south at last, for the Ohio would be the natural dividing line. and Pa's career would be ended, he having been a Union man, and so it would be best for him to sell out whilst he can— All very fine from their standpoint, but we don't grant their premises at all— The south will ruin herself and is ruining us but I don't believe and I won't believe that this great country is going to be broken up and what's more to the point, Pa don't believe it either. He says the south will only succeed in ruining herself, but the government must and will be victorious and she will have to come back into the Union after all the sorrow and death and destruction. O, what a pity South Carolina and Massachusetts couldn't—like David and Goliath—step out between the contending forces and fought it out by themselves whilst the other states looked on in peace. On what would have been much better for the country. Like Milkenny [Kilkenny] cats—till there was nothing left of either of them.

December 1st—

Brother Warner's birthday— He is 15 today. The dear brave boy with a man's courage and patriotism— He has been mustered in as lst Lieut. in the 9th Ky. Infantry and there will be no man in the regiment who will do his duty as soldier better than this blessed brother. May God spare his life and health. How I wish I could see him in his uniform. We haven't heard a word from him or sister Fanny since the letter Uncle Lewis brought back with him.

December 3rd—

It is cold and sleety and a sad sight we saw as we came from town this evening. Bob Strange's Cooper shop has been taken for a hospital and as we passed there we had to wait to let soldiers bring out to a wagon, the body of a poor fellow who had just died, with measles which ran into pneumonia a soldier told us, and whilst we waited it was pitiful to hear the poor fellows in the hospital coughing and to see the pale forlorn looking men who were regarded able to be up and think of how little of needed care they could have in such conditions. Dear Ma—whose heart is always touched by suffering, waited to ask if she might send them some soup and hoar hound syrup. A permission readily granted.

December 4th—

Ma had at least 5 gallons of nice chicken soup and almost as much hoar hound syrup made today and Uncle Lewis took it down to the hospital and brought back a most grateful and gentlemanly note of thanks from the Surgeon and Dr. in charge. I am trying to teach the children a little every day—but it is impossible to do it with any regularity and an almost useless undertaking— Neither they or I can confine ourselves to lessons when we hear the bands playing and see the soldiers marching drilling and having sham battles in our front field and all around the place—before I can stop them the boys are off to see and hear and "Lady" and I are at the windows to do the same. Dear little Mary is the only one who gives any attention to her lessons—being too little to know that these other things are unusual.

DECEMBER 8TH—

It has been snowing and raining a cold sleety rain, first one, then the other for the past week, till the roads are all half frozen slush—the streets are horrible—our yard is so tramped over that it is scarcely any better. The poor Miss. soldiers in the front orchard look too forlorn, bundled up to their ears with all sorts of fancy comforters—no doubt gifts of sweethearts and sisters and most of them have dreadful colds. Their coughing appeals to Ma and when she sees a poor pale fellows coughing she is sure to say come up to the house and let me give you some soup and something for your cold—till I think they have "caught on" as the boys say, and when they see her get up a hard spell just for her benefit or their own, more properly speaking. These Miss. soldiers don't intrude on us as the Missouri troops camped back of the house do. They are gentlemen one can easily see—the others, from their Col. (Rich) down are anything else and take pains to do everything possible to annoy us and destroy the place; they have burned all the rail fences—on that part of the farm—cut down most of the apple trees and are now burning the railings round the garden—though Pa told them they could cut wood in the "woods pasture" the other side the pond, which would make better fires—they burn the fences instead.

DECEMBER 10TH—

I am so indignant and heart sick tonight and so helpless. Dear Ma was so ill today and she had to keep [to] her bed and especially needed quiet and privacy—she was sleeping and I had gone up stairs a little while, leaving little Mary quietly playing with her dolls in Ma's room—when she ran to the foot of the stairs calling, "Sis Josie, the soldiers in Ma's room."— I went quickly down and there, making themselves at home in the two big rocking chairs—sat a Capt and Lieut.— One of them rose (The Lieut) as I entered. The Capt. rocked himself in a satisfied way—and said, "We were taking a short cut through the Hall and this fire looked so tempting we just came in to enjoy it awhile"— I said, "This is my mother's room and she is ill, in bed." I said it with all the dignity and sternness I could, thinking of course they would go, and the Lieut. seemed about to do so—but the Capt. said, "yes, I see—but we won't disturb her," and rocked on and the Lieut. took his seat— Then my anger got the better of me and I said, "Since you are not gentlemen enough to understand my meaning, and leave my sick mother's bed room—perhaps regard for your own comfort will induce you to go into the next room (the dining room) where there is a better fire" and I opened the dining room door. The Lieut. rose—but the Capt. impertinently rocked on—and with a smirk said— "A better fire perhaps but not such good company." What could I do! Ma had wakened and rousing up said as I went over to her, "What is it? Has the Dr. come?" Then the Lieut. said, "Come Capt. lets get out," and they went—the capt. saying as he went, "We will call again soon"— God forbid! I was only thankful Pa had gone to Scottsville on business, for if he had been at home, he could not possibly have refrained from kicking them out and then that would have been an excuse to have arrested him and sent him to some southern prison, as they are so anxious to do—for they say his still maintaining his Union principles in the midst of the Southern Army encourages and keeps up the Union sentiment of others. How long, O Lord how long!

DECEMBER 15TH—

Henry and Marius came from town today very much excited. They saw a squad of soldiers carrying about 20 men to jail and following along learned that they had been captured up in Hart County where they had a recruiting camp for Union men. They had not yet been organized or uniformed and the boys said most of them were in their shirt sleeves and brown Jeans trousers and altogether forlorn looking—and cold—several had no hats on—

DECEMBER 17TH—

Ma drove to town today and she and Mrs. Hodge went to headquarters and got permission to send those Union men captured, the other day, some comfortable clothing as they had nothing but what they had on when captured, and that isn't enough to keep them from freezing [in] this cold weather in that old jail. Getting the permission, Nannie Smith and I took the carriage whilst Ma staid and rested at Mrs. Halls, and went round to the Union ladies and got good warm underclothing—a coat a piece—(there are 19 men) and more pants and other things for their comfort—one lady gave us a lot of night shirts! poor fellows. They have no beds, and are just huddled in one room to sleep on the floor as best they can— This we saw when we took the clothing to them—after we had sorted them out at Mrs. Halls, Ma and Mrs. Hodge, Nannie and I being allowed to take them in the jail to give them to the men, a guard escorting us, and Uncle Lewis, Nannie and I carrying the clothes, the guard looking over each piece before giving it to the men, fearing something to help them escape might be concealed— As Ma and Mrs. Hodge had given their word before they could get permission to take the clothing, that they would give neither information or

anything other than wearing apparel, they were disposed to
be indignant when the guard commenced looking over the
things—but recognized "the military necessity" of such pre-
cautions and were only thankful that they had been granted
permission to make the poor fellows comfortable. I believe
some of them appreciated the combs and brushes we took
them more than they did the coats, for they had none and
their heads were just tangled mats—uncombed and uncut.
Little "information" could we have given them, for we have
had no Union news not even a smuggled *Louisville Journal* for
a month.

December 19th—

I was so happy to get a long letter from Mr. Baxter. How
it got through I don't know—for it was a drop letter, with no
other Post Mark than Bowling Green and how wonderfully
smart it was worded nobody would have told whether it was
written from a Union or rebel camp and yet how clear it all
was— Dear kind good Mr. Baxter, I wish, indeed I truly wish, I
loved him—and I do in a very sincere way—but not that other way that comes at no man's bidding—or woman's either.
He wrote that my brother W. (dear Warner) had been ill with
Typhoid fever in a mild form—but was then up and out of
all danger and enclosed a note from sister Fanny saying how
devoted Mr. Baxter was in his nursing Warner constantly or
sending (to Louisville) or L. as they put it for all sorts of nice
things for him. They both said they could not say when they
would see us, that all our friends were well and did not think
it would be very long before we would see them—and O how
much of hope that gives us—that the Union troops will soon
advance and take Bowling Green—but that will mean a battle
and that means death to some, it may be many we love—
There is only sorrow and horror in it all. The Queen has

issued a proclamation that all her subjects must remain neutral—so Mr. Baxter who is still an English subject and never wants to be anything else—could not carry out his intentions of "fighting for the cause we all love" but may still do what he can to make it easier for those who are not so restricted. We are all so relieved to get these letters, but we can't help feeling that dear Warner just a boy, only 15, a few weeks ago, is too young to endure the hardships of camp life.— O may God defend him from the horrors—of War.

DECEMBER 29TH [20TH]—

Ex. Norton passed thru B. Green today—he called but Ma forbid me asking him to stay to tea— I was glad when he told me he had only an hour—to stay, as he had to go on the next train, so he could not have staid—for I wouldn't like to hurt his feelings for he is a kind good fellow and can't help preferring to buy cotton rather than enlisting. Since if he did, it would be on the rebel side—I hope he will continue buying cotton— I was very indignant the way he talked the last time he was here but he was very sorry for it, and I am sure didn't mean half he said—like me, he can't fight and has to express himself some way— I think of Ex. differently from what I think of other men— I do not believe he is a coward— I think he is morally brave—but constitutionally so tender-hearted that it would be impossible for him to hurt anybody, no matter what the principle involved—and yet—"The bravest are the tenderest. The truest are the daring."

DECEMBER 22ND—

"The days are cold and dark and dreary— It rains and the winds are never weary— the vine still clings to the mouldering [*sic*] pall— While thick in the blast the dead leaves fall— and the days are dark and dreary."[11]

DECEMBER 23RD—

Gen. Hardee is a gentleman. Today I went with Ma and Mrs. Hodge to headquarters to ask permission to take the union prisoners something nice for Christmas— He said it was impossible, to let us do this Christmas—why he did not say—but that we might on New Year's day—if we would call then for permits— Ma and Mrs. Hodge think he is just putting us off and won't give the permits then. But I don't think so— He was so polite and courteous and escorted us himself to the carriage, helped us in and said he wished the rebel ladies were half as anxious to do something for the sick soldiers and rebels in the guard house. The Union prisoners are all in one room of the jail and the rest is used as a guard house for rebel soldiers guilty of all sorts of misdemeanors. Well, we will see if he was fooling us with nice speeches.

DECEMBER 25TH—1861.

[Christmas] Night! What a sad contrast to all former Christmas' days at Mount Air— No family gathering—only dear Pa, Ma and Me to make a strain of merriment—to make the children and negroes happy— Uncle Henry is with us— but the dear old man is much troubled for Virginia though he says so little— Last night the children hung up our stockings as usual in Pa's and Ma's room and all the little darkies hung theirs around the fire place in the dining room—and found them full bulging with candy and some simple gifts, an orange at the top. "Lady" and Mary were delighted with the dolls I had dressed for them and the boys and I had no cause to complain of our gifts— I had made Ma a soft Gray flannel wrapper and knit Pa a pair of riding gloves—and as one little darkie said—Old Santy Claus got through with his pack [in] spite [of the] secesh"— The older darkies came tipping in early, grinning and happy to catch Mars Warner and Miss Lucy—"Christmas gift"—"Chrismas gift Mars. Warner"— "Chris'mas gif Miss Lucy"— Then tipping up stairs popping their heads into my door with "Chris'mas gif Miss Josie"—we had our egg nog which nobody can make so good as Ma— and the boys have had a good time popping fire crackers, with the soldiers helping them—so the day passed—till the children and Uncle Henry went to bed—and Pa, Ma, and I sat long into the night talking of those wont to gather with us on this day and of the sad condition of our country and our own home—and then we three knelt together—Whilst Pa prayed earnestly for Peace, God's guidance for us all and I kissed them, and left them and my heart almost breaking for their troubles. "Peace on Earth, Good will to men!" Alas! how the song of the Angels is mocked by the present condition of the country.

DECEMBER 26TH—

I have been looking over old dresses today and ripping them up to make over, as all sorts of goods are very high and scarce and we will have to make what we have last as long as possible— Our coffee is nearly gone too—when the rebels came into the town we had nearly a full sack which Ma has divided from time to time with others—many people have used parched beans and mixed other things with the coffee to make it last longer. This Ma has not done, saying she would have the pure coffee as long as it lasted without spoiling it and when it was gone then get the best substitute she could— In writing of Christmas day I forgot to say—we had kept one lone turkey gobler [sic] to have for our Christmas dinner—keeping him in as secret confinement was compatible with turkey health— Last night when no soldiers were prowling about—"seeking what they might devour"—Uncle Lewis went to get the gobler—when lo he was gone and no doubt some Army men had our Christmas dinner—.

December 28th—

This morning Pa got a note brought out by a soldier asking him to come to headquarters at 1 o'clock. no explanation of what for was given and we were dreadfully anxious till he came home at 4 and told us— Gen. Albert Sidney Johnston whom Pa knew well and liked was there and they had been in earnest consultation all that time—Johnston trying to bring Pa to see the advisability and advantage of his (Pa's) giving up his unionism and going over to the secessionists—or with his section as the Gen. put it— If Pa could do this how greatly in every way it would be to his personal advantage— This my dear brave true father knows well enough and bravely told Gen. Johnston he should forever scorn himself if for the sake of personal advantage he were induced to advocate secession, which he thought a wrong and destructive principle or to uphold and side with those trying to break up the Union—which the south could not do and her course was only bringing ruin upon herself— Gen. Johnston said he feared Pa could not much longer be permitted to maintain his present attitude in the face of the southern army and so a very great dread of what that means and what will happen next possesses us.

December 28th [29th]—

Col. Love came up to the house this morning to offer Ma the negro boy he had brought from Miss. with him as body servant. It was funny to hear him tell how he and his regiment started off from home—many of the privates with their attendant negro boys—and now they didn't know what on earth to do with them. He said his boy "Wilse" was a fine fellow and a splendid butler and was at Ma's service—whilst the regiment remained, but little use have we now for a butler other than Jake—for it is hard enough to know what to do with our own negroes—with the whole place so overun with soldiers—so Ma declined his offer—much to the Col's regret and Wilse's satisfaction—for he grinned from ear to ear—as the Col. said, "come on Wilse, I can't get rid of you."

December 30th—

Whilst I was waiting in the buggy at Pa's office for him, Col. Carrington and Capt. Williamson came up— they asked if I wouldn't let them call at Mt. Air, New Year's Day—just for the sake of last New Year in Memphis when we had such a happy time at Sister Jupes in Memphis— They said I might put my flag over the door and they would march under it without a word and sing the star spangled banner—with me or anything else—I might decide if I would only let them come— We had a good many pleasant times on the subject before I told them—Ma and some other Union ladies had gotten permission to take some "refreshments" to the Union prisoners in the jail—and I must decline seeing them for the greater pleasure of going with these ladies— Then Pa came, and they were so deferential to him and such gentlemen in every way—that I felt very much like making exceptions to my rule.

December 31st—

We have worked all day preparing good things to take to the prisoners tomorrow and have arranged to take it in as much "style" as possible so that they and more especially the Rebels will see this small evidence that the Union people are the nicest people in town. We have made nice cakes—boiled a ham—made into beautiful thin sandwiches with salt-rising bread—Mrs. Hodge secured a turkey—we have the stock all ready for elegant gumbo soup—as nobody can make equal to Aunt Dam's and tomorrow morning are to make a quantity of Beat biscuit and real coffee— Mrs. Hodge is to bring pickles and jellies— we have the dishes all packed in the clothes basket—and napkins too— Uncle Lewis and Jake are to carry the things in the jail and Nannie Smith, Annie Hawkins and I with Ma and Mrs. Hodge are going in the Jail with Capt. White and a guard to serve them— I invited Col. Carrington and Major W. to dine with "these Union gentlemen"—but they couldn't come—so now I must go to bed and rest for tomorrow— The last night of this sad trying most eventful year of my life—and our country's life. God grant us Peace before another shall end!

1862—

JANUARY 2ND—

My heart is too full of sorrow—to write—but I must record what has happened to us, as best I can— Yesterday New Year's Day as arranged we drove in town with all our good things for the Union prisoners—got Mrs. Hodge and the girls and went to the jail where Capt. White and two soldiers were awaiting us—the prisoners had a feast such as they never had before and were so gratified that several of them were almost too overcome to thank us. The Rebel soldiers (in for misdemeanors of various kinds) crowded to the doors of their rooms holding out tin cups and dirty hands—"We are union prisoners too," give us some soup"—which we gladly did—

for we had enough for all and left a good many good things besides for the Union men and nice clean napkins for them to tie it up in— We were all so happy with the day and Ma and I stayed with Mrs. Hall and Mrs. Hodge talking over all the incidents till it was nearly dusk—Going home then, eager to tell Pa of the day's doings— As we approached the house our hearts sunk within us for at the front door—near the porch—a soldier stood holding horses and dear Henry who was on the lookout for us, said "get out quick"—there are soldiers in the library with Pa." We did indeed get out quick and going into the library—never shall I forget that scene. Three soldiers standing in the glare of a bright fire—my dear father seated on the opposite side of the hearth with a paper in his hand, evidently a military paper, leaning toward the fire so that the light of the blazing logs would fall on the paper that he might read it. Little Johnny by his side with his hand on Pa's chair and in the background, Jake with some plates and a tea [cup] in his hand—for he was setting the table and had come in the library naturally curious. Just as we entered, my dear father looked up from the paper, to the soldiers, saying, "Immediately is a quick word, gentlemen, to a man who has lived at a place 40 years." "What is it," we asked—going to Pa's side, taking Ma's hand in a strong loving and supporting clasp, he quietly held the paper so we could see it and this is what we read:—"Warner L. Underwood and all persons occupying the buildings on Underwood's hill, commonly known as "Mount Air," are required to vacate the premises *immediately* by order of the General commanding, etc. etc. It was like a blow that stunned us. Ma sank in a chair, white and speechless. The orderly I think he was, said, "I am sorry sir to deliver such an order—but had no choice." Pa ordered his horse—saying, "I will ride with you to headquarters—we cannot leave tonight." The soldiers went out and waited around the porch till Pa's horse came. Pa comforted Ma as best he could and we waited anxiously for his return. When he came we knew before he spoke that the order remained, only the time was extended to the 3rd, tomorrow, when we must go, God knows where or for how long—perhaps forever. This morning a drizzling rain was falling and still comes down steadily cold and sleety. Dear Pa got up before day and he went up into Allen County to find a place to take us to and secured an old cabin, 15 miles from here, belonging to "Si." [Josiah] Osburne. Several of our friends hearing of the order asked us to come to their houses—but that isn't best for them or us. All day we have been trying to pack our things—dismantling the dear old home—not knowing where we are going, how long will we stay—or to what we are leaving Mount Air. It is hard, hard work, and these vile Missouri soldiers and even their officers—are just taking possession of the house—tramping all over it—handling things and twice today I took things out of the hands of men who were evidently going to pocket them. A Captain came up the steps to my room, when I was trying to pack things, marched in without knocking and when I arose indignantly and said, "Well, sir," he stood looking around and said, "Oh! I was just looking over the house—I think I'll have this room for myself." How differently the Mississippi Brigade have acted. I don't think any of them have even entered the yard today except Col. Love who came up early this morning and standing at the door with hat off, expressed the greatest sympathy and sorrow and *indignation* for such an order and asked if there was anything he could do to help us. We're going to "Uncle Si Osburnes" cabin, hoping by and by we can somehow get through the lines to Louisville. Pa couldn't get a pass to take us there now. We have sent our books, piano and some furniture over to John Tygert's—couldn't pack the books—just had to dump them in the two horse wagon and I doubt if half will get there for soldiers took a good many out of the wagon—before Uncle

William could get off with them. Oh! what a horrible day it has been! and how bravely dear Ma has borne up. Working so hard—white and trembling with her heart almost breaking, as well I know. The day has been so cold, too; we couldn't keep the door shut. The poor negroes feel this leaving as much nearly as we do and are sort of dazed by it, and the children are all so excited and Henry will be so sassy to the soldiers—bless his brave little heart—I am afraid we will get into some other trouble before we get away.

JANUARY 3RD—

Our last night at dear Mount Air! Tomorrow morning we leave! I can't write! I am tired and cold and heart broken for my brave, helpless father and mother.

❧ CHAPTER FOUR ❧

In late November 1861, a provisional convention composed of 115 delegates from 68 of Kentucky's 110 counties convened at Russellville and proclaimed Bowling Green the Confederate Capital of Kentucky. The convention also selected George W. Johnson of Scott County as the Confederate governor of Kentucky and named William Preston, William C. Simms, and Henry Burnett as commissioners to the Confederate Congress. They named John Burnam of Bowling Green as treasurer for the state's Confederate government. Shortly thereafter, Johnson and his council moved to Bowling Green and the governor established his headquarters in the home of Col. John Grider. With the town firmly under Confederate control, southern sympathizers gained confidence and a few Unionists apparently felt their wrath. The distinction of "capital," however, was a brief honor. Following the South's unsuccessful endeavors in the eastern (Mill Springs) and western (Fort Henry) portions of the state and the advancement of Union forces into central Kentucky, the Confederates decided to pull back to Nashville. Writing to his wife, Johnson grieved that "the time of our severest affliction has now come—our state is about to be abandoned by our armies. . . . I now go with the Army and intend to remain constant in the field." [1]

January 10th

"Uncle Si" Osburne's cabin. Allen County

I must try to take up my sad story where I left off. When Pa came up to find a place for us, he arranged with various farmers around here to take most of the negro men till he could see what was to be done—and Aunt Sis and family and other negro women he also got places for, among the neighbors who are all staunch friends of Pa's and most of them Union men. Aunt Dams—her children and Jake were sent up here the day before we left with the furniture and a few things to make these old cabins as comfortable as they could for us. Col. Rich, of the Missouri Regiment asked Ma to leave her room furnished as he wanted to bring his wife there and he would pay for the furniture. Hurried as we were—no time to pack and properly store anything—as much as Ma hated to part with her furniture, it seemed the best thing to do, so Ma fixed the room as nicely as possible, even leaving the bed made and changes of sheets etc., in the closet and towels on the rack—being glad we would have the extra money for these things—in our uncertain banishment. We could not take every thing with us so left some things we were to send for the next day—when Col. Rich said he would pay for the things he had gotten. We had to leave a good many little things which we stored in a press in the library and locked it, asking Col. Rich—as that was not needed please to let it remain locked—which he said he would do—the next day Uncle Lewis and Henry came down in the wagon to get the things we left and the money from Col. Rich. When Henry asked him for the money, the brute laughed in the dear boy's face and said, "Did your mother think I was going to pay Union people for anything. That's a good joke. This is only a *small confiscation* we call it." Henry said, "I call it a big steal"; but the poor boy was helpless and he and Uncle Lewis had the long ride of 30 miles, 15 down and 15 back, for nothing—returning with the wagon empty as they started and Henry saw that the press we had left locked was already open. It commenced raining the 2nd of January and rained steadily a cold dreary sleety rain for three days. The morning we left Mount Air the rain was colder and worse than ever. Never can I forget the sad procession going down the hill that dreary morning. How can I describe it? The night before we left, the two horse wagon was drawn up as near as possible to the back door and the provisions—we could carry, and with a carpet thrown over them to keep the soldiers from seeing what was there and a few books—were put in, leaving room for our trunks and some bedding. The spring wagon was loaded with meat from our meat house and Aunt Sicily's traps piled on top of that so it looked like a load of "darkey truck." Uncle Lewis and William that night, with all possible secrecy went into the cellar and dug graves for a barrel of Peach brandy, two barrels of our own grape wine and a keg of apple brandy which they carefully buried tramping down the floor again, and this cellar being dark, we hope to find this when we get back—if we ever do. The next morning we started—John driving the wagon, Uncle William and several negro men perched on top of the load. Then two negro boys and Henry on horseback driving two cows, then the spring wagon, Abie driving and Aunt Sis perched on top of the load, a gray blanket around her and all her children with her, like a bunch of half frozen scared crows—and following after, the big old carriage, Uncle Lewis driving, the two bay horses hanging their heads in the wet and cold and humiliation. Dear Ma sat white and tearless, her pride keeping up a dignity and strength wonderful to see; I by her side with little Mary in my lap, Johnny, Marius and "Lady" on the front seat; Martha with her lap full of bundles by the side of the driver. Dear Pa on his beautiful gray horse "Walker" first in front then by our side—helping and directing all—as we went down the hill the road was slippery and the horse in the spring wagon—skittish and nervous—when the wagon slipped against him, he stopped, jumped over the traces and siddled [*sic*] along—Poor Aunt Sis scared! her eyes like new moons—exclaimed, "My Lord! I knowed poor white trash got themselves into fixes—but I never did expect—me and my master to cum to sich a fix as this"—and she expressed the sentiments of all—for it seemed incredible that dear Pa—always a leader and master of circumstances, should be so powerless and helplessly driven from his own home by aliens. When we reached Drakes Creek, there were pickets stationed, which we had not expected.[2] Pa was ahead of the cavalcade then. The pickets halted him and demanded his pass. "Walker" pranced so he could hardly get it out of his pocket and each time he attempted to show it to the picket, "Walker" plunged, knocking the umbrella over his head, finally just as the pickets were about to take it, Walker reared again and the picket said, "All right, I see, go on." Pa put the pass in his pocket—we all forded the creek and came on. Afterward I said to Pa, "I never saw Walker cut up so in my life—I was afraid you would be thrown." Pa replied, "Walker and I understood each other—I had no pass, what I showed the picket was Johnston's order to leave Mount Air." It was night when we reached the cabin, two log rooms with a space [dogtrot] between, open but floored and covered like the cabins with "Clap-boards" held on in many places by rocks instead of nails. Aunt Dams, good faithful servant and friend that she is—had a roaring fire in the big fire-place that extended half across one end of the cabin, had Ma's bed set up and nicely made in one corner and the table set with a white table cloth of her own (ours were not unpacked) and a warm good supper ready for us. When we sat down to the table and Pa asked the blessing, he added, "God bless Damsel for providing us this good supper." A supper strange as it would seem—we ate in more peace than any for some time because there were no rude soldiers prying about us. Poor Ma was completely exhausted and as soon as possible we got her into bed—where she has had to remain most of the time since.

One cabin is, as sitting room, dining room—with Ma and Pa's bed in one corner and a trundle bed under it for the boys, Henry, Marius and Johnny. Little Mary and I sleep in the loft, to which we climb by a ladder and lying in bed we can see the stars through the cracks between the clap-boards—that is, when it isn't raining and snowing. The other cabin is kitchen and quarters for Aunt Dams, Uncle Lewis, Jake and three of their little children. Pa had hoped to get us through the lines to Louisville, going in the carriage through the woods by, by-ways—as the roads and bridges are all picketed and we have no passes—but the rains have flooded the rivers and creeks so they can't be forded, besides dear Ma couldn't stand such a trip in her present condition. What we will do God only knows. The kindness of the people around here is almost pathetic. They are all poor, living on little farms—mostly woods with a few acres poorly cultivated and their house in most cases a log cabin in the midst of a corn field—or close to the road surrounded by a rail fence and chickens. They have always voted for Pa and looked to him as their leader and most of the men who were young—are now—in Mr. Grider's regiment. The older ones come over bringing with them a bag of turnips—or beans—sometimes hickory nuts and hazelnuts—wanting to talk with Pa and have him "*Prophesy*" as they say—what the outcome is to be and indeed it is prophesy for no one knows—but Pa tells them to stand firm for the Union, for this great country must not go to pieces.

JANUARY 15TH—

I am trying to teach the children a little but it is up-hill business—neither they or I can fix our minds with much interest on school books. This cabin is on the high bank of a pretty little stream—a mile or more from any public road—or any neighbor—in the woods—with only a small space cleared around it—and that grown up with briars. There is one blessed thing in the seclusion of the spot, no soldiers to molest us. We haven't seen one since we've been here and yet it is like being buried. We know nothing of what is happening in the world—even in Bowling Green.

January 17th—

"Uncle Si" went to town today and brought us back news and a lot of good letters to gladden our hearts—one from Mr. Western and sister Jupe—who had heard of our being ordered from "Mount Air"—full of sympathy and affection and begging us to come to Memphis and make their house our home. A kind little note from Col. Carrington which I am afraid I am too bitter just now to appreciate and a letter from Aunt Martha and Mr. Norton expressing deep regret that we had to give up our home—but intimating "with great affection" that if we, had been more prudent in our talk it would not have happened and that made us, especially dear Ma, very indignant. The most important part of the letter was that Marius and "Lady Henry" might be sent down to them "with the distinct understanding that this arrangement was only temporary, until conditions were more settled." Under ordinary circumstances Ma would not accept this offer but would keep the children with us—but on every account, their welfare especially, it is best for them to go to Russellville to Aunt Martha. We are so crowded as to be anything but comfortable in this little dilapidated cabin—we want to get away if ever a chance comes; we have very little money—"the children" Lady and Marius—have none and it is better for them to be comfortable with Aunt Martha in their fine settled home which prudence will always preserve—than dragged around where we know not—with us— Uncle Si also brought us some papers.

CHAPTER FOUR

January 20th—

Yesterday morning, Henry and I with Lady and Marius and their trunk—went in the carriage with "Uncle" Lewis—to town—to get them off to Russellville. We took dinner with the Halls and I got the children off in the afternoon train. What dear good friends the Halls are and how dear old Mrs. Hall's eyes flashed when Hugh Gwyn argues with her—the only one he argues with and he does this for fun. We learned of the battle at Mill Springs and of Zollicoffer's death—sad news to bring home and when I told Pa of it—he burst into tears saying, "*I loved the man.*" Oh! how cruel this war is! I had to get a pass to get out of town and Hugh Gwyn drove with me to headquarters—where I met Capt. White and several other officers and astonished them by what no doubt seemed to them unparalleled audacity. Hugh opened the door of the carriage and he and Capt White were both ready to help me out—but I said, "I don't think I will get out if Capt. White will kindly tell Gen. Hardee I should like to see him a moment." The look he and Hugh Gwyn gave each other was funny. Then Capt. said, "Oh, yes, why—certainly," and went to deliver my message. Hugh said, "You may have to wait a while for *possibly* the Gen. is busy." Whether he was or not, he came out in a few minutes smiling and said, "I am glad to see you Miss Underwood, what can I do for you." Then I said, "You are aware General, that my father's family were ordered from their home and had to find shelter elsewhere. There are pickets between town and the cabin where we are staying and I should like an order to your pickets to let my little brother and me, with our carriage, pass them unhindered." "Why, certainly you shall have a pass," said the General. "I don't like to put it that way, General," I said; "heretofore only Negroes had to have *passes.* Couldn't you make it an *order* to *your pickets*"? "Why, certainly," he answered laughing, "any-

147

way to please the ladies you know—you shall have it as you like," and after a few more little pleasantries he went in and sent me out a paper saying, "All pickets on the Scottsville Road are ordered to allow Miss Underwood with her brother, carriage, and driver—to proceed without hindrance, by order of the General commanding—Hardee." Thus, much to the amusement, as well as surprise of Hugh Gwyn and Capt. White, humoring my request and taking no offense at what they thought my audacity. The truth is, I felt it much easier to make a request of a gentleman standing by the carriage, albeit a General, than to go pushing through a crowd of men and soldiers into headquarters *to ask a pass*. I just couldn't humiliate myself that way.[3]

JANUARY 21ST—

Ma is again ill and confined to her bed. If we could only hear from Warner it would do her good—we have only heard once and then he was just getting over Typhoid fever and though sister Fanny was with him & Mr. Baxter like a brother, to take care of him— Ma especially can't help being anxious and uneasy about him.

JANUARY 22ND—

Alas! alas! I am afraid when I was in town the other day the men who are persecuting Pa or putting the powers that be up to doing it, found out his whereabouts through Henry or me. Last night about 11 o'clock somebody knocked at the door and when Pa opened it—who should stand there but old John Burnam to whom Pa has been a life long friend and done many kindnesses. Pa knew at once something important and bad for Pa had brought him so far at that time of night—as indeed was the case. He is one of the biggest and most respectable of the secessionists in town and belongs to the "Council of Ten" who are the citizens who manage and suggest local meanness to the rebels in command. When Mr. B. had come in and got a little warm after the long cold ride—he told Pa that—that afternoon in the Council it was decided to have him arrested and sent South as his attitude encouraged so many to hold out in their Unionism. He said he did all he could to oppose this without avail and no doubt a squad of soldiers would be sent the next day to arrest him. That he left the Council as soon as possible and had ridden hard to warn Pa for, he said—they might call his action what they chose—if they found it out—but he could not see a friend, to whom he owed as much, further persecuted and stand idly by. He said he must get back to town before day, that no one would know of his absence and he did not want to know what Pa would do—but the only chance was for him to leave. Hearing the talking and always fearing the worst, I had crept down stairs and sitting on the bed by Ma we heard it all. They clasped hands, long and silently then Pa saying, "God Bless you, my friend," Mr. B. left us and then the sadness of that hour! Ma sat up in bed begging Pa to order his horse and go at once. Pa sitting by her with his arm around her, saying he could not leave us. Then we looked the situation in the face as calmly as we could and it was plain enough that with Pa arrested and sent South—our situation would be infinitely more helpless and worse and so after much earnest talk and sorrow, Ma, for Pa's sake, bearing up with a bravery and strength—she did not feel, induced him to go and so arousing Jake, Pa ordered his horse and kissing the boys and little Mary as they slept and Ma and me, went out into the darkness and the cold night. Thank God he knows the country well, for he cannot go by public roads—which are all well picketed—but must ford creeks and swim the rivers swollen by the constant rains. I packed a few clothes in his saddle bags and put some biscuit left from supper in, not knowing when he would even be able to get to a place for shelter and food. When Pa was gone, I crept into Ma's bed but there was no sleep for us, and this morning Ma is not nearly so well and has just fallen into the first sleep since Pa left and thank God no soldiers have yet appeared.[4]

JANUARY 23RD—

Yesterday just after dinner as I sat by the little window reading out to Ma who is still in bed—I heard the tramp of horses and looking up, there were six soldiers and a Lieut. at the fence. Oh! how I thanked God Pa was gone! The Lieut. and three soldiers dismounted and came to the cabin, whilst the others held the horses. I waited for him to knock, then went to the door. The Lieut. said: "Is this where Mr. Underwood lives?" I said, "This is where Mrs. Underwood (my mother) and I and the little children are staying." "Isn't your father here," he asked. "No," I said. "Where is he, I wish to see him on business," he asked. I answered, "In Rousseau's camp, I hope—you had better go seek him there, if the business is important." "How long since he left here," he asked. "It might detain you too long if I undertook to count up the time," I answered. He hesitated a little—then said, "We are pretty cold—may we come in and get warm—that big fire looks mighty comfortable." I saw at once that he doubted me and wanted to search in the house. I said "certainly—'though my mother is ill in bed—you can come in to the fire." They came in and took seats around the fire but so they could see everywhere. Henry and John, who had been out hunting rabbits and had seen the soldiers approaching—came bursting into the house—two or three dogs at their heels. Dear Ma sat up in bed with her shawl around her shoulders, asked the boys to drive the dogs out and shut the doors and looked so pale and really ill—that I think the soldiers were touched with pity, but more convincing of our truth—one dog ran under the bed and in getting him out—it was very plain to be seen that nobody was hid under there and the Lieut rising said, "Come, fellows, we will go." The soldiers went out first—then the Lieut. said, "I'm glad your father isn't here, Miss, I don't like this kind of job"—but I noticed that they watched pretty closely as they rode off and stopped quite a while in the woods where they could see the house and fancied themselves unseen. Oh! how thankful we were that Pa was out of their reach and how grateful for Mr. B's warning. What a pity he has so contemptible a fellow as Jim Burnam for a son, dressed in a little brief authority as Capt. in the Rebel army—thinks the only way to show his power and make himself conspicuous is taking every possible opportunity to heap indignities upon Union people.

JANUARY 25TH—

A cold bleak day! Dear Ma is not quite so well. How thankful I am for Aunt Dams to help me so faithfully and for Uncle Lewis who keeps the cabin warm with such splendid great big fires.

JANUARY 27TH—

Ma was very ill last night, for a time we feared she would not live. The hemorrhages are so weakening. It was raining and snowing and no Dr. within 10 miles—but Jake, good faithful boy, got on a horse and through the darkness and cold, fording a swollen creek—he went for Dr. [B. P.] Claypole, who came back with him quicker than I thought possible. Jake said, "he never did see a man ride so fast 'thout [sic] seeing nothing," for the night was black and cold. His friendship and sympathy for Pa spurred him on and Oh! how I thanked God for his coming. Plain country doctor, that he is—he relieved Ma very soon and staid with her till daybreak and through the long night as we sat by the fire talking low whilst Ma slept, the doctor watching and himself giving the necessary medicine. I found his rough exterior hid as tender a heart and chivalrous a nature as is often met with. When Ma said to me, "Josie you had better pay the Dr. now—we may not see him again soon," he said, "My dear Mrs. Underwood please don't mention such a thing. I'd want somebody to shoot me if I made any charge for this visit. *I thank you for sending for me,*" and he spoke in such a way that we could not press the matter but expressed our sincerest appreciation of his kindness.

January 28th—

Ma is sitting up today and very much better every way. Dr. Claypole's medicines seem to be doing her more good than any "City Physic" has ever done her. We haven't heard a word from Pa and can't expect to hear. Our anxiety is dreadful—though we feel wherever he is, he is safer than to have remained here and somehow I feel sure he will get through all right. Answered Tom Grafton's letter—Oh! me!

February 1st—

One dreary month is gone and we are still waiting, "only waiting." Ma and I read and sew. Mary plays with her dolls and says her little lessons to me. The boys hunt rabbits and ride about the neighborhood. Once Henry has been into town but learned no comforting news. He said he crossed through Mount Air without ever a fence to stop him—all gone now. The neighbors come over to see us, and one night two women with a baby came to stay all night, "cause they knowed we must be powerful lonesome so they jes up and come." "Poor white trash" if you will—but I am finding out that it does not need—fine clothes and culture to make kind and loyal hearts and I spend many a pleasant and I may say profitable hour as I stroll with the boys, through the woods, stopping at the cabins for little visits. I told "Uncle Si" I wanted to buy this cabin with a few more acres of woods and name it "Underwood Retreat." He said I might have it now and call it "Osburne's Welcome" which was a very pretty answer, I think. He is a very funny old man. Thinks he is a prophet and talks in Bible language most of the time. Has a long white beard, a bald head except for a fringe of long white hair around the back of his head—wears home-made blue jeans with a vest of sea green, yellow and black striped linsey and is about 6 feet tall, although 70 years old, he is straight and active. Nearly all the younger men in this part of the county are in the Union army—most of them in Mr. Grider's regiment and a few in the confederate army— The old men often come to our cabin, three or four at a time to get Ma to explain moves and measures published in the Bowling Green and Scottsville papers—which some of them go in town for about once a week and which we are more glad to get than they—for poor and unreliable as we think the news—it is all we have and we are thankful, for this is all our connection with any world outside these hills. It is pathetic to see these old men, many of them unable to read intelligently, sitting around Ma, their elbows on their knees and their mouths opening, listening with such absorbed interest as Ma reads and explains the news to them.

FEBRUARY 7TH—

At last we've heard from Pa and he is safe in the Union lines with Warner and Mr. Grider at Columbia. God be thanked! "Old Man" Sanders came over tonight just after supper and sat and *sat*. We wondered why he didn't go; finally when the table was cleared off and the servants and the boys gone to the loft to bed, he pulled a letter out of "his bosom" and handed it to Ma. It was very short but told us most we wanted to know. Pa had gotten through safely, found Warner well over his fever and in camp again, sister Fanny and all well and great hopes of *seeing us soon,* which we know means the hope that the Union troops expect to capture Bowling Green. For Mr. Sanders' sake he could not write too much. The old man had gotten through the lines by all sorts of round-a-bout ways and been in camp to see his two boys. Pa happened to meet him just as he was starting back and had given him that little note for Ma and now we can wait with so much lighter hearts. "Wait! for what? and How long? Only God knows!"

FEBRUARY 10TH—

Our coffee is very nearly gone. The children or I don't drink it any more. Milk is much better for us anyway. It is snowing and very cold today. Snow is better than rain for every time it rains new leaks develop in the roof where the clap-boards rotted and gave way and the other night I was awakened by a sudden downpour of water in my face. We moved the bed and fortunately had a bowl to put under the leaks. There are a few things left to be thankful for. I was glad it came in my face instead of Ma's.

FEBRUARY 12TH—

We are going back to Mount Air! Oh! I am so glad! for even the annoyance of the soldiers overrunning the place and house is better than this exile from all knowledge of anything going on. This afternoon, late, two soldiers, one a Sergeant, rode up to the door and gave Ma a note from Col. Rich saying, "Mr. Underwood—we are about to vacate your premises and advise that you take possession at once lest evil persons destroy the buildings"—so we are to go down as early as possible, in the morning. Ma doubts the sincerity of this note, and thinks it was sent as a trick to draw Pa into a trap. However, we are going— Ma, little Mary, Johnny and I, in the carriage with Uncle Lewis driving— Henry will stay here at the cabin and look after things here and come down with them if we can indeed go back to Mount Air.

Goodbye "Osburne's Welcome" poor little leaky cabin! and all the kind, good, ignorant people of these woods and this journal till I can write again in my own old room at dear Mount Air!

March 1st—Bowling Green, *not "Mount Air"*

Mount Air is in ashes! Our home was left unto us desolate. How can I write the exciting events of the last weeks! Early (in the morning after getting Col. Rich's note), February 13th, Ma and I with Johnny and Mary—started down to town—when we had gotten within a few miles of town we met Mr. Claypole, who stopped us and with sorrow told us our home was burned—the night before—by the soldiers who occupied the place, before they left. That a great many of the troops had left the town and all from our home. We hurried on, our hearts heavy with this news. When we got to the turn of the pike, we saw the gable end of the house. Ma was leaning back, her eyes closed—but I saw and cried "O Ma look! Mr. Claypole was mistaken, the house is there"—so we told Uncle Lewis to drive on fast and cut across the fields. There were no fences left to hinder us. We had not gone very far through the fields before we saw that the trees around the house were all charred and burned and that only the gable end of the house was standing, a smoldering smoke rising about it and as we drove up through the garden—all trodden down like an old common—the last standing wall fell in with a crash and we arrived only in time to witness this final catastrophe and standing there helplessly watched the smoldering ruins of our once beautiful and happy home. Both orchards were cut down—the avenue of big trees leading toward town were all gone—not a fence left on the entire 1000 acres and only the barn and two cabins left of all the buildings. Ruin, devastation and desolation everywhere! With sad hearts, we went on to town to our friend, Mrs. Hall's. It had commenced to snow a cold wet snow. At Mrs. Halls we met with a warm welcome and heart-felt sympathy. They told us how early the night before they saw the light in the East and looking saw dear old Mount Air all in a blaze and sorrowfully watched it's burning. The bridges across the river had also been burned that night. We had a good hot dinner there and learned that it was very apparent that the Rebels were sending their troops south. Whether Bowling Green was to be entirely evacuated we did not then know. After dinner Ma left me with Mary, to stay all night with the Halls, and she with Johnny drove to Mr. John Tygert's where most of our furniture, the piano and books were—to stay all night there, saying she would come for me the next morning when there seemed nothing for us to do but to go back to the cabins. All that night buildings in the town were being burned and little sleep was there for anybody in the town. Hugh Gwyn came up to see us, expressed the greatest condemnation of the burning of our home, and as much sorrow for it as the kindest friend could feel. He was not in uniform but told us he had joined the 23rd Tenn. with the rank of Capt. I knew he had been intimate with the officers of that regiment all along and once had said he would join when they needed him. He stayed late and we talked of everything—but if he knew he did not tell us Bowling Green was being evacuated though it was plain to see there were not half so many troops there as a few weeks before. The next morning, February 14, will I ever forget it! Ma had come in for me. The carriage was at the door—it was about 11 o'clock and dear old Mrs. Hall had insisted that we have some hot coffee and lunch before starting on our long cold ride—back to the cabins—so we were sitting at the table—when we heard the boom of the cannon—another and then another— Mrs. Hall's home is on one side of the open space in the center of which the Depot and Roundhouse were and also there was an immense long building that had been temporarily put up by the Rebels as a storehouse for food supplies, and this was full of corn, ham and meat and other things. The shells were being thrown from Union cannon—on Bakers Hill we learned—and thrown around this square to save the Depot, Roundhouse and supplies—if possible. How rejoiced we were to learn that a Union army was just across the river and how we longed to know if—our friends—Mr. Grider's regiment and John Ward's and Col. Hawkins were with them. Faster and faster the cannon and shells came till we learned to distinguish the shells from the balls as they shrieked through the air and "juked" [*sic*] into the slush and snow. One shell crashed through the corner of Mrs. Hall's kitchen and a piece of metal fell in the biscuit dough Aunt Sallie was kneading—she rushed into the house where we were, all spattered with flour—saying—"Bless de Lord—A Union shell in my biscuit dough."[5] The biscuit making, needless to say, was abandoned. Pandemonium reigned supreme. Soldiers were rushing wildly through the streets—cavalry and infantry—horses were being taken anywhere and everywhere found—citizens, men, women, and children, white and black, were fleeing over the hills to get out of reach of danger—whilst the steady Boom—

swish—shriek and *bang*—of cannon shot and shell went on—most of the balls and shells falling with wonderful accuracy in the space around the Depot and the snow and slush preventing many of them bursting. In Mrs. Hall's house—Mike Hall had quickly ordered Uncle Lewis to put the horses in his barn and the carriage in the yard behind the house. He had a fine horse there and in a little while Hugh Gwyn came tearing up on his fine iron gray horse—which was also put in the stable. He said he knew the house was full of women and children and more exposed than any other and only one man (Mike Hall) there, so he came to stay with him till all danger was over. The stable door was locked, but time and again soldiers jumped over the fence and tried to get at the horses, and but that Mike and Hugh with pistols in hand, constantly watched and threatened to shoot any man breaking in the stable door, all the horses would have been taken. There were at Mrs. Hall's, Mrs. Hall who is old and very feeble—Mrs. Hodge and her two boys, the oldest one with consumption and at that time sick in bed, Nannie Smith, Mrs. Hall's adopted child, Ma, myself, little Mary and Johnny and every woman in the crowd excited and wanting to do some impossible thing. Ma wanted to get in our carriage and "*fly.*" Mrs. Hodge wanted to "go over the Hill, for we will all be killed here." If we had attempted to "*fly,*" the horses would have been immediately taken, and to go over the hills, with poor sick Ed Hodge and Mrs. Hall in such weather, would have meant death to them, if not for Ma too. This was before Hugh Gwyn came. Poor Mike was so beset he didn't know what to do and once exclaimed, "Great God, what will I do with all these women!" I remembered Pa had told us if ever we were in a house in range of shot to go into the cellar—so I told Mike that and he said, "That's the place"—so we snatched the blankets and comforts from the bed (just here Hugh came) and taking Mrs. Hall in his strong arms, carried her and we all got into the cellar—the only entrance to which was an outside one with doors that lifted up on the side of the house toward the Depot—so we could see what was going on there—leaving the doors open as we did. Mike and Hugh got a few chairs into the cellar—but boxes and barrels did well enough for seats. Mrs. Hall was calm, only her set mouth and flashing eyes—showing her excitement. Mike, always thoughtful of his mother, had given her a drink of brandy—insisting that Ma and Mrs. Hodge also take a little— Ma sat rocking her body and praying, "Good Lord save us—Lord have mercy on us." Mrs. Hodge had a nervous chill—her teeth clattering like castanets. Hugh Gwyn kept up everybody's spirits with all sorts of ridiculous speeches and putting an extra blanket round Mrs. Hodge and one hand on her head and the other under her chin—said, "I must save your teeth some way, for old Daugherty (the town dentist) is half way to Tennessee by now." The people and soldiers were still flying by and every now and then some one seeing the open cellar door—got into the cellar as speedily as possible—till we have a heterogeneous crowd—among them the Catholic Priest—Father DeVries—who was a great assistant for keeping up the spirits of the crowd and his remarks were very funny—as feet would suddenly appear in the descent into the cellar. Hugh had on his new uniform of Gray Jeans—with a velvet collar with the gold braid insignia—but as he had rushed up to Mrs. Hall's he had stopped at the Tailor's to get the coat which was not quite finished, the lining of the collar being loose and hanging. As the hours in the cellar wore on, the cannon keeping up the steady boom, everybody felt a little safer in the situation. I noticed his collar and offered to sew it for him—so he and I rushed out of the cellar into the house where I got Mrs. Hall's basket and sewed it on, whilst he foraged in the Pantry and we took back into the cellar, cold beat biscuit—half a ham and a jar of pickle, just as we were at the cellar door a

ball whizzed right in front of my face and if Hugh hadn't
jerked me back, I think it would have taken my head off—for
it buried itself in the ground not 6 feet from us. After a while,
it was growing dark and the booming grew slower and
ceased—the soldiers seemed gone and the rushing of officers with their fierce commands—to fleeing men was ended.
(We learned afterward that several citizens, Dr. Porter, a
prominent Union man, chief among them, had gone with a
flag of truce to the river and told the Union troops that the
soldiers were all gone. (They had "*Skedaddled*" good fashion)
and the firing only endangered the lives of citizens—so the
firing was discontinued. We were all in the sitting room again
and Hugh said—I think all danger is over and I must leave
you now, to join my regiment (If I can find it). Ma said, "Why
must you go, Hugh—now is a good time for you to give up
such thoughts—for you have never taken any oath of allegiance to the confederacy." All his gravity was gone in a moment as with a solemnity of look and manner, I had never
seen before in him—standing there in the midst of his best
friends—all Union people—he raised his right hand as in
taking an oath and said, "Never before Madam, but before
God I now do!" Then, kissing Mrs. Hall, who was in bed, and
shaking Ma's hand and telling the little children good-bye—
the rest of us went into the other room with him—where
Mike said to him, "Hugh you have only a small pistol, mine is
better, you had better take mine." It was growing very cold
and Hugh said he could keep warm enough except his feet.
I told him I heard red pepper pods would keep one's feet
warm—so Nannie and I got from the large strings on the
back porch some pods and crumbled them up. He took off
his socks and put it in them, next to his feet, then after he put
his boots on Mike insisted on his pulling a pair of his heavy
yarn socks over his boots and so equipped after again telling
us all good-bye—Mike, Nannie and I followed him to the

160

gate where mounting his beautiful gray horse—he rode off
in the dusk—kissing his hand to us as he turned the corner
out of our sight—rode into the darkness and to what God
only knows. When Nannie and I told Mrs. Hall about the
pepper she said, "it should not have been put next [to] the
feet—that now the poor fellow's feet would be all blistered
and Nannie and I were heartbroken at the mistake. The dusk
and darkness came on illuminated in a fearful way by burning buildings all over the town—which the Rebels had fired
before leaving. The biggest fire being half the stores on the
square one of which belongs to Pa. When all was quiet, at
least no more firing—as Nannie and I stood at the window
towards the depot—we saw five Texas Rangers ride furiously
up to the depot—jump off their horses—light torches they
had in their hands and rushing in and out the depot, roundhouse and the building of stores—set fire here and there,
they mounted their horses, waited a little while till the flames
were seen bursting out in various places and then galloped
off. In a very little while, the whole place was a mass of
flames—which could not be checked and a fearful and grand
sight it was. In the midst of all this horror as we watched the
fire—one thing amused us—Old "Gen" [Samuel] Blackburn—whose attitude and talk was of little consequence to
anyone, was a secessionist—without much influence of any
kind—but the poor old man was evidently in great conster-
nation—as to the consequences of his secession talk after his
friends, the Rebels were gone—so whilst the depot and buildings were burning—all through the night we could see him
flitting around in the fire light with an old fashioned, long
barrel shotgun under his arm—*reversed—at trail arms*—I believe it is called. Mike Hall said he wanted to show his abject
surrender. He was pathetically funny. The bridges across the
river were all burned and the river was very high, way out of
it's banks—the Rebels destroyed every possible way they

could of getting across—but somehow by earliest dawn, the next morning, Feb. 15th, some Union soldiers were over. I think they found some skiffs miles down the river. We had watched all night, Nannie and I especially jumping up from our pallets in the parlor, having given her room to Ma and the children, to look out. Nannie saying she was so glad the Union soldiers were coming—she expected to embrace the first *blue* coat she saw and Oh! how we hoped to see some of our own loyal friends—but alas what a disappointment we had. About day, we saw a squad of Union blue-clothed men about the burning depot and throwing up the window waved out handkerchiefs frantically. They came over and Mike Hall went out and asked in a lot of hungry coarse *Dutchmen*! for Turchin's Brigade was in advance and the first to enter Bowling Green. Than which nothing could have been more unfortunate for the Union cause in this town and section. We gave these men breakfast and others and others came and the servants and all of us cooked, and fed them till 12 o'clock, that day and still they poured into the town, going to various houses *demanding* food and in one or two instances treating Union women with a great deal of rudeness, calling them "dam [*sic*] Rebels" and ordering them to get them something to eat "D—quick" and some of them went into Mr. Younglove's cellar (Mr. Y is a druggist and *one* of the strongest and best Union men in the town) and filled their canteens with Copalsamish [*sic*] taking it for molasses.[6] This I heard and don't know the truth of it, though I do know they did a great deal of damage—there and that they destroyed in a few days more Union sentiment than the Rebels had—been able to do in six months. It was a great mistake not to have Rousseau, Crittenden and our own loyal *Americans* in the advance to take the place of the "Southern Chivalry" instead of these foreign Dutchmen with their broken English. It has almost compensated the secessionists for the way their friends left the town, in a regular skedaddle—after proclaiming Bowling Green the "Gibraltar of the Confederacy," and I have been asked several times—"If I were studying Dutch" etc. All sorts of funny things happened—during the evacuation of the town—funny afterwards, though serious enough at the time—I wonder how Hugh Gwyn enjoyed hearing of the one in which Mattie Cook figured. I use to think she was engaged to Hugh—till his friend Calvin Ready came on the scene. The morning the town was bombarded, Mattie had started out to make some calls, arrayed in a blue silk dress—a black velvet cape and a white velvet bonnet with white Marabeau plumes on it. When she was down at Bell Donaldsons—the bombardment commenced—so, rushing home as fast as she could—when she got there—she found all the family gone and somebody told her they had gone on "Vinegar Hill"—so jerking up a worsted dress that lay on the bed and a little "bonnet trunk" in which were some treasures, among them, Adjutant Ready's letters—with the trunk in hand and the dress under her arm she started to follow the family over the hill, trudging along through the snow and mud as best she could.[7] Charlie Porter overtook her—he had a pair of cavalry boots over his arm and kindly offered to carry Mattie's trunk and she take his boots. They hadn't gone very far before Adjutant Ready overtook them—having even in his haste—gone by Mattie's home for a last hurried adieu—and then followed her flight. He hurriedly took her up behind him—boots and all—forgetting poor Charlie trudging on with the heavier load—so they galloped on till 5 miles on the other side of town—he came upon as much of his regiment as had managed to get together. They hollered, "Keep on to Tennessee, Adjutant—now you've got her"—"Hurrah for the girl you've *got behind you*" and etc.—finally putting her down at a farm house—whilst he went on with his regiment—and I understand poor Mattie hasn't heard from Charlie Porter or her trunk and love letters though she still has the cavalry boots. We learned that Mr. Grider's regiment wasn't with the Union army on the other side of the river, so making arrangements with Mr. Shewer, who had sister Fanny's house, to take it and knowing how uneasy dear Henry would be about us—late the afternoon of the 15th of February, we went back to the cabins—to bring our things down to town and take sister Fanny's house and *wait*. When we got there poor Henry was nearly beside himself with anxiety. He had heard the cannon and thought a big battle had been fought and didn't know what had happened—yet with all his eagerness to know—to get on his pony and haste to town, like Casibianca—he faithfully stayed at his post.[8] It did not take us long to pack up our few belongings and come back to town. The day after we got there, Pa came and oh! what a joy to see him. The next day Mr. Baxter appeared. He was so overcome with—relief he said, at finding us well and safe again—that he could hardly speak—when we met and in spite of myself, I found my own eyes—overflowing—which was the very worst thing they could have done—under the circumstances—. A few days later Mr. Grider's regiment did come and although they were stationed across the river for all the time they were here, before marching on south— Mr. Grider stayed at home. when sister Fanny and boys arrived, and Warner was with us as much as possible. Warner, only 15, looking so handsome in his Lieutenant's uniform. Dear Ma is so proud of him though it nearly broke our hearts when with the regiment—he marched through town on the way South—perhaps to battle and death, though I hope to glory and victory. We got leave for the officers, Capt. Wheat, Capt. Forman, Major Bodine and others, with Warner to come over almost every evening and often went out to camp to see them. One afternoon I rode out with Mr. Grider on horseback and when we returned they were making some change in the Pontoon bridge and had only a plank across where a boat had been moored. I rode my horse across the plank—which was very easy to do and no other way of getting across and was no little embarrassed—when some soldiers shouted, "Hurrah for the lady on horseback."

The Union troops are steadily pouring in—but not to stay, most of them marching on South. Mr. Grider generously wants us to keep his house with sister Fanny, till the war is over—and a letter came from Mr. McCann sending Pa or saying he had sent Pa $1000 in gold—as having some ready money might be most needed. Pa was almost overcome by such generosity from his sons-in-law—who could not be kinder were they own sons. Sister Jupe is coming up soon as she can to stay with us—as Mr. Western is away in the Confederate Army and it is best for her to be with us here—since she cannot be with him. So we are all very thankful to be together once more—even with the sorrow of having our dear old home left us in ruins—and one great comfort is that we can now hear often from Warner and Mr. Grider. It almost, in fact *does,* make me sorry for the Rebels—when I see how much better clad and equipped every way the Union army is than were they, though I think the gray uniform especially that of the officers with so much gold lace—is much prettier than that blue of our army—but no flag is so beautiful as the Stars and Stripes and I never knew how I loved it till I saw it go up again, where it had been pulled down and another unknown banner put in its' place.

❧ *CHAPTER FIVE* ❧

The pathways through Bowling Green led thousands of Union troops to the South's bloody battlefields. Josie and her friends expressed pride in the fine-looking troops—a Wisconsin regiment was "more stalwart and healthier looking" than all others—and horror at the fate that awaited many of them in the days to come. However, as regiment after regiment moved through the commonwealth, many residents of the Bluegrass State began to distinguish between Kentucky unionists and those from other states. Quickly, the destructive nature of the invading armies became associated with troops from north of the Ohio River.

A captain from Hopkinsville stationed in Bowling Green and Russellville during most of the Federal occupation compared the invaders and the damage and havoc they created to a five-mile-wide plague of locust and frequently referred to them as "Yankee rascals." In a letter to his daughters, he undoubtedly expressed a view shared with many residents of the Bluegrass State: "These Yankees are great rascals. They are abolitionists of the worst kind. . . . I wish the rebels were whipped. I wish the cursed Yankees were out of the country, no good feeling has grown out of their occupation of our state, but a dissimilarity of the most striking is manifest, in the way we feel and think about everything, and I must say I greatly prefer our own way. I don't know what will come of it. I fear the worst for our future peace and harmony."[1]

MARCH 10TH—

Today I saw a perfect impersonation of war, as Gen. Lovell H. Rousseau, on an immense black charger, with his full staff—all in full uniform wearing soft felt hats with black plumes—galloped by—at full speed. Gen. Rousseau is six feet, four inches tall, large but not *fat* and carries himself superbly. He might well make Mars envious.

MARCH 12TH—

Regiment after regiment of Cavalry passed by today, we do little but watch the passing of troops. "Jinney" bemoans the horses and today her lament for them was indeed touching—as watching them she said—"Poor dum beasts! ef humans ain't got no more sense than to go to war and kill theyselves—that's they own lookout—but 'taint fair to take poor dum horses—that can't hep—theyselves and git'um killed." *No t'aint.*"

MARCH 16TH—

"The pride, pomp, and circumstance of glorious war." Fine sounding, delusive phrase—banishing the thought of the sick, wounded and weary men who follow so surely and blot out the glory from many hearts and homes. There are three or four hospitals already in town and all more than full. Dear Ma, sister Fanny and some other ladies, notably Mrs. Hodge and Miss Jones—visit them daily, carrying soup and various dainties. Ma keeps "Aunt" Emily busy most of the time making broths and other things for the poor sick fellows. Every regiment marching through Bowling Green leaves its quota of sick men behind—and the "soldiers grave-yard"—is the most pitiful thing in all the war.

MARCH 26TH—

Sister Fanny's home where we now are—being on the street leading to the Nashville Pike, all the troops going south pass by our door; Cavalry—Infantry—Artillery. The tramp, tramp of men and horses—the jingling of trappings, the rattling of artillery—passing day after day often night after night—has become the pervading sound of our days—frequently the regimental bands playing as they march along—always some gay inspiring tune, to which the soldiers keep step with a buoyant happy air, as though they were on some holiday parade instead of going to battle and death—for there is fighting at the front and any day the terrible battle may be fought—in which Mr. Grider's regiment and dear brother Warner in it, would surely be—as they must be below Nashville by now. Mr. Western is with Gen. Forrest and most of our friends and relatives in the confederate army are somewhere round about Ft. Donelson and Henry. Somebody from Hopkinsville told us Cousin Robert Henry had been killed. Poor Aunt Cornelia!

MARCH 29TH—

A Wisconsin regiment marched by this afternoon and I think I never saw such a fine looking body of men. All of our troops look splendidly—so well equipped and comfortably clothed but it seems to me the Wisconsin men are larger—more stalwart and healthy looking than any. Poor "Confeds!" My heart goes out to them in pity. Though all wrong from my standpoint—there is something grand and heroic in the reckless daring that could ever induce them to put themselves against this strong government, with its inexhaustible supply of men and money—and they don't seem for a minute to realize the self sacrifice they are making and are absolutely confident of winning out—even when they were hungry and cold. Better for them that the war be in the South for half the soldiers have no overcoats. How I would love to get a few of these great comfortable overcoats, through the lines to a few

poor fellows I know. Treason! treason! Maybe so, I acknowl-
edge my weakness—alas!

April 1st—

No funny fooling today—it is raining. The streets are in
horrible condition—yet on and on go more troops marching
south, through the slush and mud. The hospitals are full to
overflowing. Last night Ma came home from one and told
me I would have to give up my room—as she had gotten permission to bring a "poor boy" home, who would die if left
in the crowded ward in the hospital—as she said, he had no
business in the army, so young and needed a mother's care.
I had to hurry to get my things out, as the poor fellow was
then being lifted from the carriage at the door. He has fever. I have taken up my quarters on the parlor sofa at night
and my clothes are anywhere. The sick Lieut. is so grateful
and so much better even today that I wish I had another
room to give up to some sick soldier. It is a curious thing
how war and gaiety go together. The sound of "revelry by
night"—bright lights shining "over fair women and brave
men"—might have recalled Waterloo to some, last night at
the pretty hop—given by the officers at headquarters. The
former parlors of the old Green River hotel looked quite
fine with flags festooned around the walls. Though the
lights were only coal oil lamps, and some of these a little
smoky, the music was fine; there were plenty "brave men"
and I for one had a very pleasant time. A number of the
Rebel girls were there—and I could but wonder if they were
not wiser than I had been. Only Lizzie Wright has taken
the stand toward the Union officers—that I did toward the
Rebels—I would not have felt it loyal to my father, or to my
country to have done other than I did and I respect Lizzie
for the attitude she takes. The very man she might have

danced with last night—may next week—kill her lover—to whom she is engaged. Dear Lizzie, she is happier to stay away. The very man with whom I danced with last night, might kill Tom Grafton too. Oh! it is hard, hard every way and I am the weakest of girls![2]

APRIL 3RD—

Rode with Pa out to Mount Air. The negroes are gathered back in the cabins that were not burned and are making an effort (doubtful as to results) to put in the crops. We find that Union soldiers are not much more regardful for personal property than were the Rebels—only now Pa has some chance of getting his rights redressed and that too, without insult. The Union troops are occupying camps on the Hill—but not so many of them as there were Rebels and are more temporary. Besides it is getting warm now—so the fences put up last a *little* longer—but the dear old place is "left unto us desolate"—though nature is making a beautiful effort to cover up some of the ruins. The trees near the house that were more or less burned are putting out straggling bunches of leaves. Pa told some of the soldiers (whose camp is in the yard) of the barrels of peach and apple brandy and home-made wine buried in the cellar before we left Mount Air and now deep covered under the bricks and debris of the ruins and promised to divide with them if they cared to dig it out. The rush for picks and shovels—was very amusing. 4th Lieut. Mason hasn't been so well today. His father is coming to take him home. I hope the poor fellow will be able to go. It does not look so now. I have a poor chance to keep up this journal—having no especial room just now—but it is like a little talk with a friend and so I keep it up as best I can.

APRIL 5TH—

This morning I was lazy and did not "take up my bed and walk" as soon as I should have done and was no little mortified when Capt. Clay called to ask me to go riding with him—I was at breakfast. "Jinney" asked him in the parlor—when I went in—the most conspicuous object was the sofa with pillow, blanket and sheets—though he kindly took a seat with his back to it—I had some difficulty in also seeming unconscious of the untidiness. Pa and Ma went out to Mount Air to see the result of the excavation for brandy, etc. Poor soldiers! Their disappointment was great—all the barrels had burst—except one small keg of peach brandy. The hoops on this were still hot and the soldiers said the brandy was just like the richest cordial—had thickened by the heat. The small quantity left for Pa to taste verified their statement. They said they determined that Pa should have the *big* barrel and they would just take the *little* keg and they felt very sorry that *Pa's barrel* had bursted. Pa was very willing they should divide it that way.

APRIL 6TH—

We are horribly uneasy. There were rumors today of a big battle. If there was, all those we love on both sides must have been in it. God have mercy and stop this cruel war—I pray—

APRIL 15TH—

The rumor was true! A terrible battle, lasting two days, has been fought at Pittsburg Landing or Shiloh. Oh! the horror of it! Every soul I know on either side was in that battle. Brother Warner was wounded. Shot through the arm whilst waving his sword aloft to cheer on the men. His captain was killed and he being 1st Lieut—boy though he was, had to take command then and there in the midst of the battle and bravely he did his duty. Col. Grider had two horses shot under him and a bullet went through the crown of his hat. John Ward was slightly wounded. Fred Price was struck by a spent cannon ball and knocked senseless for some time and Oh! so many were killed. We haven't yet seen a list of "killed and wounded" on the Rebel side and dear sister Jupe who is here with us—is almost beside herself to hear from Mr. Western—who is with Forrest! Oh! the sadness of our position! Rejoicing over the victory of the Union forces and excepting dear Warner and Mr. Grider and a few near friends grieving most over the dead and wounded in the Rebel army—where so many men and dear to us are fighting—estranged as we are now—the old time love is still warm in our hearts. Pa was in Louisville when the first news of Battle came and was appointed, with others, to go down on a boat to look after Kentucky's wounded. He telegraphed for Ma and she barely got to Louisville in time to catch the boat. Ma writes when they reached Pittsburg Landing the sight of wounded and dying men was heartbreaking. At one place surgeons were amputating arms and legs in a little cabin and throwing them, in a pile out the window. She was hunting for Warner among the wounded on a boat. Asking one of the attendants if he knew anything of Lieut. Underwood, he said—"Yes madam, he had that cot there by you—he died this morning and has just been taken out." "In god's name—where have they taken him," exclaimed Ma as she sank upon the cot. Just then, Pa came up with the news that Col. Hawkins of the 11th Kentucky had taken Warner home with him on a boat that had already gone. The poor dead Lieut. was another Underwood and dear Ma's grief for his mother's sorrow was measured by what her own was for the moment. Warner got home several days ago. Pa and Ma haven't yet come. When Warner came he looked white and exhausted, his right arm in a sling—the coat sleeve split up to the shoulder. The bandages around his arm were dirty and stiff though the dear boy had tied a clean rag on the outside. I got some nice soft linen cloths and warm water to cleanse and dress his wound. When I unwound the dirty bandages—*maggots* fell out and the wound itself was full of them and stunk so—it nearly knocked me down. I had hard work to keep from fainting. Poor Warner. The sight, more than the pain made him sick, too and instead of pitying himself what did the brave, blessed boy say—but, "God pity the poor fellows who are wounded so much worse and couldn't come home."[3]

April 20th—

Ma has returned. Pa can't return for some time yet. Her meeting with Warner overcame us all. She had not known till then just how badly he was wounded, having missed all letters. Joy, sorrow and pride all mingled. Sister Jupe was comforted by the assurance that Pa would leave nothing undone to get news of and help to Mr. Western, if wounded. Ma says the indignation felt against Gen. Grant was outspoken and great. The first day's fight went against our forces *because* Grant instead of being on the field or where he should have been was on a boat *drunk*—and but for Buell's army reaching there by forced marches—the result of the battle would have been a terrible defeat for the Union army instead of the glorious victory it turned out to be. I asked Warner if he did not feel frightened as they were drawn up—waiting to be ordered in to the fight. He said his heart "got *mighty still* for a little while" and then he hated to step on dead bodies when the fight got thick but sometimes couldn't always step over them. He told us whilst they were drawn up in line waiting—a rabbit sprang

174

up from some where—running as fast as it could—down in front of the line towards the woods. A great big fellow near him sang out, "Run Mollie Cottontail run! I wish to God I was a rabbit so I could run, too." The feeling between the rebel and Union people gets bitterer and bitterer as the war goes on— Lizzie Wright sits on her porch across the street and I on ours and merely the coldest bows and never a visit now.[4]

APRIL 25TH—

We have gotten news of the Rebel wounded and killed. Mr. Western was unhurt. But alas! alas! Jack Henry was killed; his brothers, Tom and Gus, were unhurt. Jack the noblest of all, *killed,* shot through the body. Hugh Gwyn found him leaning (sitting) against a tree. He said, "Hugh—I am done for—can you find Gus?" Hugh fortunately had just seen Gus and galloping for him told him of Jack's condition and whereabouts. Gus just got there to see him die. A nobler, sweeter soul never entered Heaven—no matter how wrong the cause for which he died, he believed in it—to him it was sacred. Oh! the *crime* of the men on both sides. Fanatics North and South who brought about this cruel war.

MAY 9TH—

Lieut. Mason has gone home much better—fairly on the road to recovery but I still must occupy my sofa in the parlor—for sleeping, as sister Jupe—who is far from well must have my room. The days are so beautiful now—but the poor little town looks distressingly dilapidated. The buildings burned when the rebels left, have never been rebuilt. The streets are in dreadful condition, ever so many hospitals, full of sick soldiers—and poor convalescent men—pale, *weak*— *homesick* looking fellows sitting and straggling around in the sunny places. Deserted camping grounds—in various suburbs of the town—with all sorts of cast-off things, scattered around. The soldier's "graveyard" getting bigger—every day nearly, a few more new boards at the head and foot of mounds of fresh earth, maybe a name on the boards—maybe just a number. The other side—there are quite a number of pleasant officers—stationed here in command of the comparatively few troops garrisoning the town. They have "hops" at headquarters—visit the girls. They are often up here to call—take tea and I ride quite often with several of them—as today I rode with Lieut. Harris out around dear "Mount Air." Beautiful even in its desolation, but the sweet spring day, Lieut Harris' wit nor the exhilaration of horseback riding could banish the sadness this war is bringing into my life and if into mine how much more—into thousands of other lives—not so blessed as mine. I haven't heard a word from Tom Grafton since the confederates left Bowling Green. At first I thought it well since by other means I could not find it in my heart to forbid his writing. Today I would give anything for one of his letters. What a weak foolish girl I am!

MAY 20TH—

Col. Hawkins is going to New Port Ky. to visit his brother (who is Mayor of that city) before returning to join his regiment at the front. Annie is going with her father and they beg me to go with her. I am a little afraid to go—for I am afraid—John [Hunt] Morgan might make one of his daring raids and tear up the railroad tracks and something happen that I couldn't get back home. There is too much of interest going on in this part of the world for me to want to be away from here and the dangers to those I love.[5]

June 12th—

I was over-persuaded and went to NewPort, Ky. with Annie. Her uncle and Aunt are delightful people and would not let us come home at the end of a week as we had intended—but made us stay till yesterday. Fortunately we had prepared for unexpected contingencies so had all our good clothes with us. Everything was done for our pleasure and we did have a good time in a way. Met a lot of young gentlemen, I would have considered very entertaining—in times gone by—but who could care for strong healthy *young* men—who stay at home to amuse themselves—or to make money when their country is in such need of their services. If they are in sympathy with the rebels, as some of these Newport men are—the Confederacy needs them far more. I expressed my views on this subject rather mildly to one of them—when he said—"Ah, Miss Underwood—I fear you are too *intense.*" Maybe I am—but I like men whose principles are decided and not those who are making money out of what brave fellows are dying for.

June 14th—

We are all so delighted. Mr. Grider's father who is our Congressman has given brother Warner the appointment to West Point. The dear boy wanted to go back to the front to rejoin his regiment—but Pa's judgment over-ruled and though his wound is not yet healed and he must still keep his arm in a sling—he will leave in a few days to learn the theories of war, after having had such experiences of its realities. Pa pointed out to him how much better service he could render his country by becoming an educated man and soldier—than—he could hope to do if he stopped his education, boy that he is—only 16—and ruined his health, by the exposure of war, hard for even mature men to stand. So he goes to West Point.

JUNE 15TH—

Ma has been appointed—receiver and distributor of sanitary stores, sent by various societies throughout the north. The first consignment came today and never in all my life did I see so many good and thoughtful things provided for poor sick and wounded soldiers. Boxes and boxes of everything on earth good to eat—breads—jellies—dried fruits—canned, preserved, wines, cordials, many of the wine demijohns were labeled "for *sick soldiers, not for* nurses and surgeons." Then there are all sorts of nice warm double comforters and shirts for wounded soldiers buttoned up in such ways that they could be put on comfortably no matter in what condition the man might be—bandages of all kinds—boxes of linen lint and even cases for wounded fingers. Ma had had a room on the back porch cleared for them—but it would not hold half—so they are piled up on the porch and a soldier has been detailed to guard them. The Doctors of the different hospitals are fast making requisitions for what they need and many poor sick fellows call down God's blessing on the good women who have added so much to their comfort and indeed to their recovery. A right funny thing happened today. Two soldiers were opening the boxes for Ma and five or six others were waiting to take things to the hospitals. A box of quilts was opened—on one was pinned a paper—with these lines written on it.[6]

> "Mary Jackson is my name
> Single is my station
> Happy will be the soldier boy—
> Who makes the alteration."

All the soldiers there—clamored for it, declaring their desperate lack of covers. Ma told them to stand in a row and draw straws for it. When the man who got the shortest straw was about to take possession of the quilt—the others protested saying he was a married man. So Ma put it by, saying she would give it to some "soldier boy" who proved himself worthy of the industrious and patriotic Mary Jackson. Dear Ma is wearing herself out—in the constant work at the hospital and for sick soldiers, and the constant excitements, anxieties and unavoidable irregularities and confusions in this crowded household are trying, in the extreme to her in her overwrought nervous condition. Means of living is getting to be a serious question too. The negroes on the farm hardly make enough for their own support. The houses Pa rented were all burned as well as our home. His law practice is all broken up. Mr. Grider in the Union army—Mr. Western in the rebel army—sister Fanny with her three little children and sister Jupe in her trying [pregnant] condition—made far more so by not knowing whether Mr. Western is alive or dead and being unable to hear from him, with Marius and "Lady" besides his own family to look after—makes his burdens heavy enough—and any ending of the war seems farther off than ever—and the hatred between the Union people and secessionists gets more and more intense, and spiteful speeches and deeds of more and more frequent occurrence. Yesterday a common "secesh" woman met Ma as she was going to the hospital with some good things in her arms and said, "I expect you live very high at your house since *your northern friends* have sent so many good things for their soldiers." Ma replied as she walked on, "We live very well, thank you—but not nearly so well as you would—under the same circumstances." But what good is there in hitting back. So scrupulous is she about giving these sanitary supplies to the soldiers in the hospitals for whom they were sent—that she wouldn't let Lettie Hamlet and me have a *small* box of most delicious dried cherries, which we wanted to share with brother Warner—a *wounded soldier.* She laughed at lugging brother Warner in—but we did not get the cherries, [and] neither did Warner.

JUNE 18TH—

Warner left today. God bless the dear brave boy! Mr. Grider, (Col. of the 9th Ky) gave such splendid service at Shiloh and ever since the war began that he was recommended for promotion to Brigadier General. He commanded a brigade at Shiloh—but the appointment was not confirmed—alas! alas! he has the same failing that *Grant* has and as much as I love him—just as if he were my own brother instead of brother-in-law, I can but think it a great wrong to put the lives of so many brave men in the hands of a man that drinks.

JUNE 22ND—

Got a letter today from Willis Green—who is a prisoner at Columbus, O. He was in a Mississippi regiment and captured at Shiloh. Oh! I wonder if he knows Tom Grafton. When Pa was first in Congress—when I was only 14—he took sister Lute and me with him to Washington—put me in school—sister Lute was in society there and Mr. Green was one of her frequent visitors. When I went down to the Hotel to spend Sundays with Pa and Lute—I often met Mr. Green—but never dreamed he remembered me. I am going to send him a lot of books if I can get permission. The other day I was going out to see Belle Skiles. Whilst I was waiting for my train—the train came from the South—there were two *cattle cars,* attached—crowded with poor confederate soldiers; prisoners dirty, half clad—unwashed—uncombed, yet trying to be jolly as people were cruelly staring at them—maybe not *cruelly*—for I too was eagerly scanning the crowded *pens* to see if perchance I might recognize a face— They were trying to buy apples and pies from an old woman and boys with stamps and confederate "shin-plasters"—very few of them had even a dime. It nearly broke my heart to see the poor fellows. Thank the Good Lord I happened to have five dollars in good U.S. money. I bought the whole basket of pies and apples for them and did not go to see Belle for I had no more money. Today I was mad enough to knock a little upstart of an officer down. He came up to me with a smirk and said, "Miss Underwood—I heard of the incident at the depot in which you figured and *as a friend* I would advise you to be careful of giving aid and comfort to Rebels." I replied in a flash— "When I wish advice I will seek it of *my friends.* Pardon me for not thanking you for yours." Aid and comfort to rebels indeed—poor hungry prisoners! Oh! consistency thou art a jewel! This man spends time and money on a girl the most arrant rebel in the town.[7]

JUNE 25TH—

We are all in quite an excitement. Pa had a letter from Senator Crittenden and also one from old Col. Grider—saying in substance they had talked with Lincoln of Pa's loyalty and sacrifices and advising him to come on to Washington—just the import of it all I don't know—but Pa is going and is going to take me with him. Pa was a Bell and Everett elector and did all in his power to defeat Lincoln and is not in sympathy at all with him. We are all indignant the way [General George B.] McClellan is being treated. So Pa can't expect any favors from Lincoln.

JUNE 26TH—

Busy getting my things in order and packing for Washington. We leave in the morning. Mr. Baxter came down from Louisville and will go back with us tomorrow. He had to give up joining the army when the Queen ordered all English subjects to remain neutral. Has lived in Louisville since.

JULY 20TH—

Nearly a month since I left you old Journal. Well, here am I again to record, my unimportant doings in the midst of all important happenings. Pa has been appointed Consul to Glasgow—Scotland! and there is not much doubt of his appointment being confirmed. When we reached Washington we went at once to the National Hotel, where most of the Kentucky delegation stop—as well as a good many other distinguished Senators and Congressmen and also Vice President [Hannibal] Hamlin. The first evening we were there what a brilliant set of men were assembled in one of the parlors! Senator Crittenden, Attorney General Joseph Holt, Col. Henry Grider and Robert Mallory, Congressman; Emerson Etheridge of Tenn., Clerk of the House of Representatives; Generals Lovell H. Rousseau and Green Clay Smith; (the last has the prettiest eyes I ever saw) and by no means least in brilliancy, my own dear father. Mr. Mallory had that day had an interview with [Edwin] Stanton, Secretary of War—who had not treated him with the courtesy he had reason to expect from any gentleman. Mr. Mallory was so angry and his account of the interview so very funny that the others roared with laughter though Mr. Mallory, in his righteous indignation, failed to see any occasion for laughter which made it all the funnier to the others. This was but one incident of the evening. I sat with ears (if not mouth) open, listening with delight—to the men talking—whose speeches I had read with such interest. Finally Senator Crittenden took me into his private parlor to spend the rest of the evening with his wife, who had long been one of the most prominent leaders in Washington society—but this season is not going out much—on account of *severe* rheumatism in her arm, as she informed me—but as I learned afterwards was in reality a slight stroke of paralysis. However, she is the gracious elegant lady and I should be very happy if I could ever attain to manners like hers. Mr. Etheridge brought his sister-in-law—Miss Bell of Tenn. to see me the next morning. She and I went up to the Capitol with Mr. Etheridge—whilst Pa was attending to his own affairs. The rooms of the "Clerk of the House" at the Capitol were elegant—and Mr. Etheridge said Miss Bell and I could have the reception room for our own if we wouldn't intrude into his office. We promised and for that morning and many others had pleasant times there. Mr. Etheridge introducing us to many pleasant people and once or twice when we were there ordering up refreshments. But the best thing he did for our pleasure—was to give us his Box at Ford's Theatre. I think it had been presented to him for the season. He rarely went—but my! what lots of pleasure it gave us. We invited a lovely lady, a Mrs. Wadsworth, to be our chaperon. (Mrs. Crittenden graciously took me under her care at the Hotel, but could not go out with us) and so almost every evening during my stay enjoyed a feast, theatrical as [Edwin] Forrest and [John] McCullough were giving fine plays which neither "Jackie" Bell or I had ever before had a chance to see. I never shall forget McCullough's, Adrien De Maupier in Richelieu. McCullough boarded at the "National" too and as I had never seen a real actor off the stage—I was quite interested in seeing him in his every day clothes, like any other man, though it destroyed somewhat the illusion of the stage performance. Pa had met Mr. Lincoln before this trip and knew Mrs. Lincoln well—when she was Miss [Mary] Todd and Pa a young man in the Kentucky Legislature. The President and family were staying at the Soldiers Home. The day after we reached Washington, Pa had called on Mr. Lincoln at the White House—but a few days after—in the afternoon—he got a carriage and invited Mr. Etheridge and Miss Bell with me—to dine with him to pay our respects to Mrs. Lincoln. I was most agreeably surprised when I met her. Instead of seeing the coarse, loud, common woman the papers had made her out to be—she was really a handsome gentle woman dressed in deep mourning (for her little boy—not long dead) her conversation was agreeable.[8] Her manner gentle—Mr. Etheridge thought—this owing to the sadness which was very apparent though she did not intrude it upon us—only responding to Pa's very appropriate expressions of sympathy and then tactfully passing on to other subjects. However, it was—I think it a great shame to so misrepresent a president's wife or any other woman. Mr. Lincoln was not there when we called. As we returned to the city, about sun down, there were no other people in sight on the road except a lone horseman we were meeting. He was on a long-tailed black pony (the horse looked so small) galloping along—a high silk hat on his head—black cloth suit on, the long coat tails flying—behind him. Pa called our attention to him—saying "some farmer—who has been in the hot city all day and is now eager to get home to supper and his family." So Miss Bell and I thought the man and he looked it. As we met, Pa had the carriage stop. The man did the same and Pa introduced us to Mr. *Lincoln*. He leaned over, shook hands with us, then slouched down on one side of the saddle—as any old farmer would do, as he talked for ten or 15 minutes with us. Pa and Mr. Etheridge thought it very imprudent and unwise risk for him in such a time of warfare and especial hatred of Mr. Lincoln himself for him to be riding unattended, unguarded out a lonely country road—and called his attention to the dangers—Mr. Lincoln's smile—expressed kindliness to all men and fear of none—as he said—he "did not think anybody would hurt him *that* way"—shaking hands again with us—he galloped on, neither did we meet anybody else for quite a little way so it was very evident there were no guards—following him. Pa and Mr. Etheridge thought this *very* wrong. Lincoln in appearance certainly falls far short (though he is so long) of my idea of how a President should look. In fact a very common-looking man he is—but I must confess there was a kindliness in his face—that does not fit the tyrant—unfair man I have been thinking him. I wonder if it can be his fault that McClellan is being so unjustly treated. Thinking of his kind, troubled face I can't believe it is. He named an hour for Pa to call on him next day. Pa called. In the interview he told Mr. Lincoln he must state a few facts which might change his kindly intentions towards him. That he had been a Bell and Everett elector and worked hard to prevent Mr. Lincoln's election and since, had not been in sympathy with his administration or war policies—though no man could more earnestly desire the restoration of the Union than he or would sacrifice more to bring this about, etc. Mr. Lincoln said, "that was no consequence and he knew it all before. That he wanted a man for Consul at Glasgow, Scotland and Pa *"fitted the place."* He said he wanted a good lawyer—a *strong Presbyterian* and a Southern Union man; and "Pa filled the bill" if he would accept the place. Dear Pa! It comes like a God-send in the gloomy outlook. Things getting worse around us all the time. Business all broken up and worst of all dear Ma's health surely breaking down under the many nervous strains she has to bear. Though from the Capitol, we could see the Rebel flag flying far on the heights, across the Potomac, the war did not seem so real and near as it does here in Kentucky—though the City was full of soldiers, and officers from Gener-

als to Lieutenants were everywhere—it was not just the same.
Gen. Rousseau was awfully nice to me. I thanked him for the
help his patriotic speeches had given me in my early arguments with my secession friends in Memphis and he was no
little amused when I quoted several of his finest perora-
tions—which he said he did not himself remember. One day
I was greatly flattered when he brought Mrs. Don Carlos
Buell and her daughter to call on me—for who am I that the
wives of my heroes should call on me! I think Mrs. Buell one
of the prettiest women I ever saw—when I returned her call
it was a hot afternoon, her parlor with its white matting, linen
covered furniture, lace curtains and a great vase of sweet
scented honeysuckle was refreshingly cool. When Mrs. Buell
came in, in a soft white nainsook dress—open at the neck
and "angel" sleeves. Her dark wavy hair drawn loosely back
from her forehead—her manner so gracious—yet dignified,
I was sure I had never seen a lovelier woman. At the "National" was Prince and Princess Salam Salam (*Slam Slam,* Col.
[J.J.] Polk called him) and two other Prussian officers to
whom we were introduced. They are already in—or seeking
service in our army.[9] One night such a funny thing happened.
The Princess had just returned from a ride shortly before
dinner and in her riding habit was standing hear the Parlor
doors. Col. Polk coming up in the shadows of the dim yet
unlighted hall—took her for a young lady in the hotel whom
he knew very well—and who often rode horseback—with the
freedom of an old friend (old in years as well as acquaintance) he put this arm lightly around her shoulder saying
"been having a ride Julia?" The Princess gave a little scream
and was up the steps before the Colonel could finish his apol-
ogy and explanation. After dinner, Pa and I with the usual
crowd—that assembled in one of the parlors every evening—
were startled by the Prince—rushing in from one of the other
parlors where he had been flying around like something cra-

zy. A revolver in his hand—a one-eye glass by a string, which fell off his eye as fast as he put it on. "What's the matter with the Prince?" General Rousseau who saw him first exclaimed. We were not long in doubt. Rushing up to our group, he asked of nobody, "Where ish—de *Col. Poky*"? Fortunately, "de Col." was not there. General Rousseau and Pa soon asked the trouble. "He haf insult my wife." They went out with the excited little fellow and learned the facts—above. Mr. Etheridge going to find Col. Polk and keep him out of the way till the Prince could be quieted down. Of course Col. Polk was very glad to make all necessary apologies. The other two young officers were very agreeable—one of them I wish I could remember his name—I never could pronounce it— played beautifully on the "Zither"—his room was on the same floor as ours—and opened onto—the balcony which extended under our windows also— Often in the soft summer night—he came out near our windows and played for hours— such exquisite—music as I never heard before—as never before had I heard the Zither—somehow there is a pathos in its tones, no other instrument has. It seemed to speak to me of all those I love—in the danger of battle—the sadness of broken friendships—the eternal partings and all heart-breaking things—till I could not control my feelings—one night. I sobbed so, Pa, from his adjoining room heard me. when I told him it was the music, he said "He would go right out and stop the fellow," but I didn't want it stopped—for in all my life I never heard anything so exquisitely sweet. "So sad! so sweet!" The whole time we were in Washington was just filled with splendid new experiences for me. Coming home, we stayed over night at the Galt House;[10] Mr. Baxter called—for the first time in our acquaintance—he made me very angry. He had himself led me to telling him of my Washington experiences. Growing foolishly enthusiastic in my expressions of admiration for one gentlemen I met—whom it seems Mr.

Baxter knew—he said, "I am surprised that *your father* permitted you to meet such a man; he must know his reputation." I answered "*all know his reputation,* as being one of the bravest, most competent officers in our army as well as the most gentlemanly agreeable man and I must beg that you do not presume to criticize *my father.*" He then got quite excited, saying, "I must insist that you drop his acquaintance and never see him again. He is not a fit man for you to know." I replied, "I cannot admit your right, Mr. Baxter, to dictate to me as to whom I shall or shall not know." I was dying to know what he knew of the man, but wouldn't have asked for the world. I don't really care anything for the man—but didn't like Mr. Baxter's assuming—people *he* did not like *I* must not know. We were fast verging on a real quarrel when Pa and Gen. Alec. [Alexander] McD. McCook came in and Mr. Baxter left. Gen. McCook, came down next day on the same train with us, going on to join his command, and was as jolly as a boy—and looks like a boy with his fair ruddy complexion and fine blue eyes. Mr. Baxter was at the train to say good-bye—neither of us referred to the evening before—for we could not be really angry with each other, if we tried. We are at home again, anxiously waiting the confirmation of Pa's appointment. All my life, I have longed to go to Europe. *Now,* Oh! how I will hate to go so far away.

July 22nd—

Dear Ma is not so well as when we left—and worst of all Aunt Martha Norton writes she has had indirect news that Uncle Winston has been wounded in a battle near Richmond. He is with [Thomas "Stonewall"] Jackson. Ma does not speak of it—or mention his name—and has not, since he resigned from the U.S. Army and joined the Confederates. She grieved then as if he were dead to her and she said he was. But *he is not*—her heart is too tender for that and she loved him, her only brother, too well—now though she does not mention him—she is white and the tears often in her eyes—and every day since the letter came she shuts herself alone in her room for a long time. I know she is praying for the brother of whom she will not speak. God grant her prayer for I love Uncle Wint. like a brother.

July 23rd—

The secessionists look happier someway and I hear they have a hope that the Rebels may again get possession of Bowling Green. I hope not, goodness knows.

July 24th—

Mr. Grider writes that he may be back, up this way with his regiment. That looks queer. We don't understand it. Maybe the Rebels are trying to get back—that would be the only reason for the Union troops coming, back this way, it seems to me.

July 25th—

Warner writes he is very glad to be at West Point, though the old cadets are pretty hard on "new comers." One morning he helped himself to *hash* and dished out a mouse which had been put in it for his benefit.

July 26th—

An awful embarrassing but such a funny thing happened this evening. Henry, Mary G. and I were driving—overtaking Capt. Wolson, he asked to go with us—when we got out on the Scottsville pike, there were some pretty wild flowers near the road in the woods, we decided to get out to pick them. Henry was driving—Capt. W. got out first, I, next—when Mary went to get out, Henry turned the front seat of the rockaway over to make room and what was the foot or support of the seat one way—made a little arm which stuck up when turned over. Capt W. taking Mary's hand to help her out—she jumped *very sprily* [*sic*] and fell on the Captain's bosom! for horror of horrors! her hoop which she had not managed as she should have done—caught on the upturned foot—jerking down tight between it and the front of the carriage—so holding Mary—neither on the ground or in the carriage—her pretty little feet dangling between the two, Captain W. supporting her as best he could, he tried to raise her so the hoop would come out. Henry tried to jerk it out. No go—it was tight fastened. Capt. said "*Cut it.*" Mary's "*Please do*" was pathetic. Henry whipped out his knife and sawed away, it seemed to me an interminable time—an eternity to poor Mary—though it was only a minute or so I reckon. I could only stand by in embarrassment and be thankful the little feet and exposed underclothing were so neat and pretty, since so unexpectedly on exhibition. At last it was cut and Mary on her feet—with face much redder than any roses, we were going to gather and the rest of us no less so— Henry drove on a little ways— Capt. W. managing somehow to go with him—leaving me to help Mary— I asked of course—"Mary are your hurt?" "No, I ain't hurt," she said—"but I am *awful pestered.*" She is a dear modest little country girl—who—when on rare occasions she comes to town—spends the night with us—she says she "aint coming any more till Henry and Capt. W. have had time to forget." I hope she won't put it off that long.

July 27th—

Received a beautiful copy of Scott's Novels from Gen. Rousseau and a letter from Mr. Campbell (a Scotchman I met in Washington) telling me of various beautiful places worth visiting in Scotland. It certainly was kind of him to write it, for it will be better than a guide book.

July 29th—

The most pitiful things in war are not told in history. This evening as I came from Miss Jones about sun-down, I saw across the field in an abandoned camp what I at first took to be a big dog—then discovered it to be a poor bent old woman—going over to her I found she was gathering up all sorts of trash, rags of cast-off soldier clothing—canteens—a few beans in an old can she had. Talking with her I learned she had managed to get here from New Albany, Indiana—hoping to find her son who was in an Indiana regiment—and she heard was sick. She "never writ him she was coming, but jess up and come." When she got here, the regiment had gone on south; somebody told her her boy was dead"; she couldn't get back—her money was all gone—she had taken possession of an old abandoned shanty on the edge of the Camp ground—eking out her miserable life with the help of the little food some charitable negroes near by gave her. I brought her home with me after a good deal of reluctance on her part, to leave the trash she had gathered in an old broken basket; she brought the basket along—which sister Fanny filled with all sorts of good things to eat and comfortable clothes. The poor old soul was in faded calico rags. We must get her back where she says "she knows most everybody but never had nobody *belonging to her but jess Jim.*" Poor old mother!

July 30th—

Busy all day sewing trying to get our clothes in order. Made little Mary quite a pretty dress out of my old blue check. Dear Ma was in bed all day with sick headache. We have heard nothing more from Uncle Winston. The main cause no doubt of Ma's breakdown—though she does not mention him. Everything is so hard! God help us!

July 31st—

Mr. Geddes promises me transportation for poor old Mrs. Jacobs. A number of officers have made up quite a good little purse for her and ladies have given clothing. I will have the new dress a merchant gave me for her finished tomorrow and she goes the next day. When I asked her how she wanted it made—with sacque or cape—the poor old soul said: "Jiss which ever is *the fashion.*" Oh! the woman dwells in the velvet gown; And *the woman* still lingers in rags.

August 1st—

We are continually hearing of mean remarks made by secessionists about Pa's appointment. There is always some *kind* (?) friend to report. Today a spiteful woman said, "Oh! it is but fair the Yankees should *pay* him for his services, but I call Consul to Glasgow—might small pay—for going—against his own people." I'll be so glad when we get away—and yet—I wonder why Willis Green does not write again. He must have gotten the books.

August 2nd—

There was the greatest excitement in town today. Soldiers dashing about at a great rate. Morgan is reported—making raids pretty close by—some say to cut the L. and N. road— some say to get horses—all sorts of rumors are floating in the air and we don't know the truth of any and if the officers do they won't tell—but something unusual has certainly happened.

AUGUST 3RD—

Got old Mrs. Jacobs off this morning. Sent her *by Express*. The express messenger promising to make her comfortable on the way and see her safely landed in New Albany.

AUGUST 4TH—

Last night went to a pretty party at Mr. Hobson's—most of the gentlemen were officers. Infantry, Cavalry and Artillery were all represented. Their uniforms with red—yellow and blue trimmings and brass buttons made it a very brilliant assemblage—with so many pretty girls in fleecy summer things. There were, few, if any gentlemen out of uniform—and no home boys—all these are either in the Rebel army or at the Front in the Union army. I had a very pleasant evening and made some agreeable new acquaintances—but the officers we meet now are mostly—on their way to or from their regiments and only here for a little while and few have I ever met or heard of before—so there is no background of association to give ease or interest to meeting them. Nevertheless every man offering his life in defence of the Union and our Flag is a hero in my eyes. But last night all thought of war and its sorrows were apparently banished and everybody had a good time.

AUGUST 5TH—

More good things for the soldiers came. Poor fellows—the hospitals are full and they need the delicacies, this hot weather. When a box of the nicest home[made] bread I ever saw—was opened, one loaf had a very small hole at one end. I was taking the bread out, Lettie Hamlet helping me—as I handed it to her, we heard a queer little squeak—we dropped the bread, the loaf with the hole in it broke open—it was only the outside crust, and inside a nest of young mice. A mouse had gotten in, made her nest and she and her little ones fared sumptuously and could have nourished many generations on the good things in the box. Needless to say—there was no more unpacking for Lettie and me till the soldiers, opening the boxes, had caught mother mouse and disposed of the little ones.

AUGUST 6TH—

Mr. Grider came today. His regiment is in Camp about 10 miles south of town. He will camp with the regiment—but can come home often. I hope Capt. Wheat and some others can come in, too—but Mr. G. says not. They may be there only a little while. I am so glad for dear sister Fanny—Little "Judgy" Grider sits on the gate post and when soldiers march by—shouts as loud as his baby voice will let him: "Hurrah for the Union, the Constitution and the 'forcement of the Law." Today when he did this a company going by halted and gave "Three cheers for the little boy on the gate post"; Judgy received the honor with the sedateness of his name-sake.

AUGUST 7TH—

Pa is very busy trying to put his affairs in a condition to leave—very difficult to do with any satisfaction with everything so disorganized. He is trying to hire out as many of the negroes as he can to good people where they will have good homes and be cared for till he gets back. Those left on the farm will do the best they can with "Uncles" William and

Lewis to boss things and report to sister Fanny, who will have general supervision. If they make enough to eat they will do well—with soldiers prowling around, so much and they or trifling people stealing everything they can carry off from watermelons to chickens and pigs.

AUGUST 8TH—

A letter from Aunt Martha says—they have had news—that Uncle Winston's wound was not as bad as first reported and he is able to join his command. (He is on Stonewall Jackson's staff we heard). Thank God! Though Ma said "better be dead than fighting against his country." She thinks she feels that—but I don't believe she does way down in her tender heart.

AUGUST 12TH—

All sorts of exciting things have been happening. Rumors of Morgan raids here, there and everywhere. Organizing the old men and Young boys (Union citizens of the town) into sort of home guards—for the garrison of soldiers is small—to help defend the town in case of attack. Almost every night the long roll is sounded; Pa, Henry and Marius rush down in town with other enrolled citizens. Ma and Mrs. Smith meet at the front gate in night gowns, and wrappers, questioning every solder that gallops by—as to news. There is no sleep for anybody for hours. Pa and the boys come back. Morgan hasn't come *this time* and we quiet down to wait in anxious expectation for the next excitement as George Todd used to say "expecting every moment to *be our next.*" One night when Ma and Mrs. Smith called to a hurrying soldier for news, he said as he galloped on, "Sorry I can't stop for a moonlight tete-a-tete ladies—some other time—delighted."

August 15th—

This war is too heartbreaking and there seems no end to it. Mr. Grider's regiment was ordered to go after confederates who were reported trying to tear up the railroad track down near Franklin.[11] They met the Rebels had a brisk little fight, drove the Rebels back. They did not make much resistance and after it was all over, Mr. Grider and several officers went into Sandy Arnold's farm house—for breakfast. The table was all set—but in disorder. Mr. Arnold said to Mr. Grider—"Yes, you can have breakfast, just sit right down here Grider (indicating a chair) and finish the coffee your brother-in-law, Will Western began." Mr. Western is Captain of an independent company of Cavalry in Forrest's command and it was his company with which Mr. Grider had had the skirmish. He told sister Jupe if he had known it was Will Western—he would not have stopped till he had caught him and brought him back to her. How thankful we all were that neither were hurt or killed—it would have been too terrible—a few men were wounded—but none killed in Mr. G's regiment and he thought not in Mr. Western's company.

August 16th—

Got letters from Mr. Baxter and Johnny Ward and Ma one from sister Lute. Dear sister Lute—way out in California—a month or more for a letter to reach her; she is so anxious about us all. I am awfully tired tonight and wish I had a private room to sleep in instead of waiting till I can go to bed *on my sofa* in the parlor.

August 18th—

Yesterday sister Jupe's little baby was born. A dear little boy—she came near dying and is still very ill.[12]

CHAPTER FIVE

AUGUST 21ST—

Sister is a little better and her baby is a beautiful little fellow. She has named him William Wallace Western for his father—whom he may never see. Sister, as sick as she is, has already begun to talk about getting through the lines. Pa promised he would, through Gen. Rousseau get a letter through to Will Western telling him of the birth of his little son. He will be so proud and so miserable, too.

AUGUST 25TH—

More and more troops are coming back into Kentucky. People think the confederates are making a desperate effort to get to Louisville. Goodness knows I hope they won't succeed and God forbid they ever take Bowling Green again. The secessionists would come down with double vengeance upon the Union people. Something is in the air to make the Rebels here more hopeful, that is very evident. I hope we won't have to go till whatever it is happens. Last night Annie Hawkins came up and we went over to Mrs. Smith's to sit awhile. There we met Capt. Forman—on his way to the Front—A friend of the Smith's. He talked so beautifully of the condition of the country, Kentucky's position, etc. that I was sorry when the time came for Annie and me to leave. He walked home with us. Most men are so confident of their bravery. He said—he had never yet been in battle and was awfully afraid he would run— he hoped he would not—but would be mighty glad when he had been in a fight and found he could stand and be shot at—*if* he found that he could—but he was doubtful about it.

AUGUST 27TH—

Capt. Forman did not go away yesterday. Called last night with Mrs. Smith. Is as handsome as he is pleasant. I don't believe there is much danger of his running. He knows all my friends in the army.

AUGUST 28TH—

Hot! Hot! How dreadful for poor wounded men. There is a great deal of fever in the hospitals. Ma is turning over her sanitary work to sister Fanny and Mrs. Hodge. If she don't get away soon she will break completely down, I am afraid. I went up to Mrs. Hall's last night to tea. I feel so sorry for Mike Hall. His sisters with their children and his dear feeble old mother to take care of—he must stay at home doing common-place work—without honor—without glory and even sometimes unappreciated—whilst his whole soul is in the Union cause and he is almost sick with desire to join the army and have the action and glory—(maybe death too, alas!) that men no more brave and not half so patriotic are winning. The men like him who must sacrifice ambition for duty, are really the bravest of all. Sister Jupe is fast growing strong again—the dear little Willy baby is lovely. There is no telling when the poor little fellow will see his father. How proud Mr. Western will be—married six years and this is the first baby. May he live to see him!

AUGUST 30TH—

More and more raids by John Morgan—bridges burned, tracks torn up—troops sent out from town—reports of skirmishes with Rebels. All sorts of excitement and the only thing I know for certain is that we citizens don't know any thing at all about what is really going on in the armies.

AUGUST 31ST—

I cannot go away without saying good-bye to Lizzie

Wright. I believe I have been the ungenerous one. I am on the victorious side; our troops hold the town. The man she loves and is engaged to she cannot hear from except on rare and dangerous chances. How sad she must be! I *will go* see her this very night!

September 1st—

I went to see Lizzie! I was sitting on our porch in the moon-light just after supper. Lizzie all alone on hers—across the street. I seemed to feel her loneliness—so, bracing myself to meet a snub, if she gave it (as I felt she would not) I went over. I blurted out—"Lizzie I am going away and I can't go without saying good-bye to you"—"I am glad you can't," she said (as she held out her hand—which I still held as I sat down by her) "and I was just sitting here wishing you would come over." We did not let go hands till her brother Web came out and I arose to shake hands with him. We did not talk at all of the war—which was most in our thoughts but of my going away to Scotland—of the interest it would be to visit the scenes of Scott's Novels and Poems, etc. Lizzie only saying, "But I shouldn't like to go so far away *now.*" "Neither do I," said I—"but I must," and God knows how truly I spoke. I stayed quite a while—she and Web going to the gate with me, I shook hands with Web, kissed Lizzie good-night and went home with a much lighter heart than when I came over. Sister Fanny being on the porch said, "You surely have not been over to the Wrights!" "Yes," said I, "I did not want to go away estranged from Lizzie." "Well! you surely are the biggest *simpleton* I ever knew," remarked my good sister. Maybe I am—anyway I feel better for going.

September 2nd—

Trying to gather up my things and the childrens to pack. In the evening drove with Pa out to dear old Mount Air. He too, feels sad to go away so far with everything so uncertain— but it is the only thing to do—and he can do good service for our country—in stopping the building of privateers on the Clyde [River]. That is the important reason for his going. His *main business,* Mr. Lincoln said.

September 3rd—

Tom Grafton dead! Killed! At Fair Oaks near Richmond. A bursting shell—oh! it is too horrible to write. Poor fellow! poor fellow! how, I wish I had loved him! Mr. Green wrote "no nobler man or braver soldier than Major Grafton ever gave his life for a cause he loved." Alas! how sadly my heart assents to that. Is any cause worth two such lives? Tom Grafton's and Jack Henry's and the thousands of others as dear to some poor heart as these to me. All my patriotism is gone tonight— "No one in all the world to grieve if I should die," he said. Ah! Tom Grafton—how mistaken you were. Who next—God help us!

> "Bloom sweetly around him, ye pale drooping roses,
> Breathe softly ye winds o're his cold narrow bed!
> Fall gently, ye dews where *this* soldier reposes,
> And hallow the wild flowers that bloom o'er his head."

Oh! me! Oh! me![13]

CHAPTER FIVE

SEPTEMBER 6TH—

We are going sooner than we had intended, for fear Morgan will tear up the tracks between here and Louisville, so we can't get away at all.

SEPTEMBER 7TH—

It is harder than I thought to go. All our friends have been coming today to say good-bye and who knows when or how we will meet again.

SEPTEMBER 8TH—

Morgan has burned the bridge across Salt River.[14] We leave in the morning. How I wish we could wait a few days longer. John Ward's regiment, Rousseau's command and so many I want to see once more—are marching this way and may any day now reach Bowling Green. It has been a sad day though there is much to look forward to—there is so much to dread for those we leave behind. Pa, Ma, the children, sister Fanny and I went out to Mount Air to tell the negroes good-bye, white and black we all cried. Pa told them sister Fanny would look after everything so they would not have any difficulty—if they got into any sort of trouble just to go to her. Still, to have "Mars Warner, Miss Lucy and the *chillen* go across the *Ocean*" seems terrible to them. And now, good-bye, poor war dilapidated little Bowling Green with friends—associations and estrangments, good-bye. "Mount Air" dear old home, "even in thy desolation what is like to thee. Thy wreck a glory and thy ruin graced with an immaculate charm which cannot be effaced." And thou old Journal, safe, silent confidant, good-bye, till we meet on the other side [of] the Atlantic![15]

❧ *EDITOR'S POSTSCRIPT* ❧

In the autumn of 1862, the Warren County Circuit Court drew up indictments against many of the Confederate "Philistines" as well as about 150 area residents who supported the South's cause and had befriended the interlopers. The indictments included accusations of usurpation of office, grand larceny, unlawful conspiracy, and various misdemeanors and malfeasance in office. The court issued indictments for treason against more than three dozen men who had "levied war" against the Commonwealth and made "War on the citizens thereof." Since many of those named in the indictments had left the state, only locals could be served with bench warrants. A few paid fines or served a short time in jail until they could furnish bond. None, however, were brought to trial. Nevertheless, the indictments were not withdrawn, and the accused, including future governor Simon Bolivar Buckner, Chief Justice of the Kentucky Court of Appeals Thomas Henry Hines, president of the American Medical Association David Yandell, and many others, remained under the indictments for the rest of their lives.

Shelved and forgotten, the indictments were found ninety-five years later during the renovation of the Warren County Court House. The circuit court dismissed the accusations in 1958.

⊰ APPENDIX ⊱

Who's Who in Josie's Journal

Underwood Family

Warner Underwood (1808–1872), son of John and Frances Rogers Underwood, was a native of Goochland County, Virginia, studied law at the University of Virginia, and practiced his profession in Bowling Green. In the late 1830s he and his wife Lucy purchased Mount Air, a farm of about six hundred acres on the northeastern edge of Bowling Green (current site of Mt. Ayr Estates). In addition to his law practice, Underwood represented Warren County in the state legislature from 1848 to 1853 and the 3rd district in the U.S. Congress from 1855 to 1859. He served as a Bell elector in 1860 and, following Lincoln's election, campaigned to hold Kentucky in the Union. In 1862 President Lincoln appointed Underwood as consul to Glasgow, Scotland, a position in which he served less than two years. Warner's twin sister, Jane Underwood Wilson, died in 1830.

Warner's Siblings

Joseph Rogers Underwood (1791–1876) enjoyed a lengthy political career. He served in the state legislature during the 1820s, on the state court of appeals from 1828

205

to 1835, in numerous sessions of the Kentucky legislature, and as a Whig in the U.S. House of Representatives from 1835 to 1843. In 1847 he was elected to the U.S. Senate, served one term, and retired to "civilian life." A staunch Unionist, Joseph joined the state legislature in 1860 to fight the secession movement; when all danger of Kentucky's joining the Confederacy was over, he returned to his law practice and farm. Joseph and his second wife, **Elizabeth (Aunt Liz)** lived northwest of town on a thousand-acre farm they called "Ironwood." In 1841, Elizabeth's frequently unemployed brother **Bob Cox** married Joseph's eldest daughter, Julia. The couple lived for many years with the Joseph Underwoods and apparently depended on their largess. Two of Elizabeth and Joseph's children, John and Robert, are also mentioned in the diary. Shortly after **John** (1840–1913) graduated from New York's Rensselaer Polytechnical Institute, he joined the Confederate Army and served as a military engineer in Virginia and Tennessee. In the postwar years he was elected mayor of Bowling Green, and lieutenant governor of Kentucky (1875–1879). **Robert** (1844–1907) practiced law in Bowling Green. Two other Rogers cousins are also mentioned in the diary. **Jane Rogers** (1830–1907) was the daughter of Warner's brother Joseph and his first wife. Jane married a distant cousin, **George C. Rogers** (1826–1870), the grandson of Warner and Joseph's uncle, Edmund Rogers.

Henry Underwood (1794–1863), Warner's bachelor brother, was the only one of the Underwood siblings living in Virginia in 1860. His brother Joseph once commented, but did not explain, that "intemperate ways" had led to insolvency for both Henry and their father.

Lucy Ann Underwood (1799–1884) married William Hamilton Skiles (1799–1881). The couple had several children, including **Henry,** a Harvard graduate who purchased the *Bowling Green Gazette* in 1860, and his younger sister **Isabelle,** who was about the same age as Josie. The Skiles family lived at Three Springs, a few miles to the south of Bowling Green.

Louisa Underwood (b. 1802) married Franklin Gorin of Barren County. The couple had two daughters, Malvina and Maria Louise. The latter married William Bell, owner of Bell's Tavern, a famous hotel near Mammoth Cave. Bell's Tavern burned in the late 1850s.

Malvina Underwood (1805–1889) married John Todd of Russellville. Their son **John** (1830–1878) graduated from West Point and was second in command at the U.S. armory at Baton Rouge when it was surrendered. Young Todd later resigned his commission and joined the Confederate Army. The couple had two other sons and a daughter, Joseph, George, and **Jane Harrison**.

Lucy Craig Henry Underwood (1815–1893), daughter of Mathis (sometimes written as Matthews; however the Underwood Family Bible and a biographical sketch written by a cousin both list him as Mathis) Winston Henry (1790–1838) and Juliette Pitts Henry (1797–1845). Lucy was one of twelve children. Unfortunately, little is known about her beyond what is in Josie's diary.

Lucy's Siblings

> **Gustavus Henry** (1804–1880) graduated from Transylvania, read law with John Boyle (chief justice of Kentucky's

court of appeals), and in the 1830s moved to Tennessee, where he practiced law and was elected to the Tennessee legislature. During the war he served in the Confederate Congress; his sons **Jack** and **Patrick** practiced law in Memphis before the war and fought for the Confederacy. Jack was among the casualties at Shiloh.

Martha Henry Norton (1824–1878) lived in Russellville, where her husband **George Norton** (1814–1884) was a successful businessman and banker. The couple had seven children. During her school days in Russellville, Josie visited frequently with the Nortons. George's much younger brother **Eckstein** was one of Josie's beaus.

Eliza (Hassie) Henry (b. 1835) lived in Missouri.

Matthew (Mathis?) Winston Henry (b. 1838), Lucy's much younger brother, who went by the nickname of Wint, resigned his commission several months after graduating from West Point in 1861. On hearing that he had enrolled in the Confederate Army, Lucy proclaimed that she would rather he had died serving his country than for him to fight as a traitor. After the war, Wint lived in Mexico, then California.

William Henry, father of Corrine, Marius and Gabrielle, died in the mid-1850s and the Warner Underwood family raised his three children. Gabrielle married in 1854, but Corrine (**"Lady"**) and **Marius** lived with Josie's family at the outbreak of the Civil War. Josie's sister and brother-in-law, Frances and Benjamin Grider, served as the children's legal guardians.

Robert Henry joined the 9th Kentucky Cavalry and

fought at Perryville. After the war he owned several lumber enterprises in Chicago and Duluth.

Warner and Lucy's Children

Frances (Fanny) (1833–1901) married Bowling Green attorney **Benjamin Grider** (1826–1874), the son of area judge Henry Grider. In the late 1850s, Benjamin Grider invested in land in Kansas, but eventually he decided to remain in Bowling Green. A staunch Unionist, in 1861 he organized the 9th Kentucky Regiment. He fought at Shiloh, rose in rank to brigadier general, and resigned his commission after the Battle of Stones River. Their son, Judge Loving Grider (called Judgie), was named "Judge" after Warren County attorney William Voltaire Loving, who *was* a judge.

Juliette (Jupe) (1835–1909) attended Visitation Convent School in Washington, D.C., and in 1856 married **William Western** (d. 1870), a Hopkinsville native. In the spring of 1861 the Westerns lived in Memphis, where he practiced law with Jacob Torian. A strong secessionist, Western volunteered in the Southern army shortly after Tennessee joined the Confederacy. In the autumn of 1862 he accepted an appointment as emissary to Great Britain. The Confederate government hoped that as the son-in-law of Warner Underwood, then Lincoln's consul to Glasgow, he would not be intercepted while running the Union's blockade. However, Grider reportedly learned of his plans and caused Western's arrest. Captured in Canadian waters, Western was tried for violating Canadian neutrality and was sentenced to a long term in prison. He escaped and, on his return to the United States, rejoined the Southern army. Following Western's death, Jupe married Ferdinand Long. (See *Kansas City Journal,* June 14, 1915, and *Louisville Courier-Journal,* November 18, 1940.)

Lucy (Lute) (1838–1915), married Baltimore native **Ferdinand McCann**. During the early years of their marriage the McCanns lived in California and Kansas. Following a visit to Kentucky in the spring of 1861, they and their children returned to California.

Warner (1845–1874) studied law and practiced briefly in Bowling Green.

Henry (1848–1925) became a Bowling Green businessman and banker.

John (1854–1930). No information available.

Mary (1857–1920) married John Poyntz and later Bowling Green businessman Malcolm H. Crump.

Corrine (Lady) and **Marius Henry,** the orphaned children of Mrs. Underwood's brother, also lived with Warner, Lucy, and their children. In 1870, Lady and Josie married in a double wedding for which Marius served as a witness.

OTHERS

Anderson, Robert (1805–1871), is remembered as the Union commander who surrendered Fort Sumter. A veteran of the Seminole and Mexican wars, he had been sent to Charleston following South Carolina's secession to direct and protect Forts Moultrie and Sumter. On April 11, when Confederate forces learned that a shipload of provisions was en route to

Sumter, they began to bombard the fort; thirty-six hours later Anderson surrendered to General P. G. T. Beauregard. Anderson later commanded Union troops in Kentucky, but his poor health forced an early retirement.

Baker, Larkin (1822–1873), and **Polly** (1822–1884) lived on the hilltop across the river from Bowling Green. Because its location provided an excellent view of anything coming toward the town by river, road, or rail, the Confederates constructed a small fort behind the Bakers' home. Forts were also constructed on the other hilltops surrounding Bowling Green.

Baxter, Edwin, was an Englishman visiting in Bowling Green during the early months of the war. Despite his pro-Union sentiments, Baxter followed Queen Victoria's dictates that British subjects should remain neutral during the American conflict.

Beauregard, Pierre Gustave Toutant (1818–1893), a native of Louisiana and veteran of the Mexican War, directed the bombardment of Fort Sumter. After Albert Sidney Johnston's death at Shiloh, Beauregard assumed command of Johnston's army. (See Thomas H. Williams, *P. G. T. Beauregard: Napoleon in Gray* [Baton Rouge: Louisiana State Univ. Press, 1955].)

Bell, John (1797–1869), practiced law in Nashville and enjoyed a lengthy political career as a Whig member of the U.S. House of Representative and Senate and as President William H. Harrison's secretary of state. In 1860, he and Edward Everett of Massachusetts ran for president and vice president on the Constitutional Union Party ticket. Composed of old-line Whigs, Know-Nothings, and dissident Democrats, the party took no stand on slavery and recognized no political principle other than "the constitution, the union of states, and the enforcement of the laws." Kentucky was one of three states that supported the Bell-Everett ticket. Following Lincoln's call for troops, Bell became convinced that the Republicans intended to impose a military dictatorship on the South and reluctantly endorsed Tennessee's secession.

Blackburn, Samuel Daviess (1807–1868), a Bowling Green attorney who acquired the rank of "general" during the Mexican War. He made his spacious home (no longer standing) at 10th and Adams available to Albert Sidney Johnston for his headquarters.

Bragg, Braxton (1817–1876), a North Carolina native, commanded a corps at Shiloh and in the autumn of 1862 succeeded General P. G. T. Beauregard as commander of the Army of Tennessee. Following his bold advance across eastern Tennessee and into central Kentucky, Bragg met Union forces at Perryville. Unwilling to fight to a decision, Bragg withdrew, for which he was severely criticized. He also led troops at the Battle of Stones River, at Chickamauga, and at Chattanooga. (See Grady McWhitney, *Braxton Bragg and Confederate Defeat* [New York: Columbia Univ. Press, 1969; reprint, Tuscaloosa: Univ. of Alabama Press, 1991].)

Breckinridge, John C. (1821–1875), enjoyed a lengthy and successful political career as a Kentucky legislator, U.S. congressman, U.S. senator, vice president of the United States, and Confederate secretary of war. His only political defeat was his 1860 bid for president of the United States. During the war Breckinridge served in the Confederate Army and led troops at Shiloh, Murfreesboro, Chickamauga, Chattanooga, and New Market. (See Frank H. Heck, *Proud Kentuckian: John C. Breckinridge* [Lexington: Univ. Press of Kentucky, 1976].)

Breckinridge, William Campbell Preston (1837–1904), unlike several members of his immediate family, supported the
Confederacy and served in the 9th Kentucky Cavalry. In the
postwar years he edited a Lexington newspaper, enjoyed a
political career, and earned a reputation as a silver-tongued
orator. However, a sensational 1893 breach of promise trial
ended his political career. (See James C. Klotter, *The Breckinridges of Kentucky: 1760–1981* [Lexington: Univ. Press of Kentucky, 1986].)

Bristow, Benjamin Helm (1832–1896), a Hopkinsville attorney and ardent Unionist, helped recruit the 25th Kentucky
Infantry Regiment, served with Federal forces during the
early months of the war and in the Kentucky Senate during
the last two years of the conflict. As U.S. attorney for postwar
Kentucky, he coped with Klan violence. In 1870, President
Grant appointed Bristow solicitor general and four years later secretary of the treasury. In the latter position he helped
expose and prosecute the "whiskey ring." Following his unsuccessful quest for the Republican presidential nomination
in 1876, Bristow practiced law in New York City.

Buckner, Simon Bolivar (1823–1914), graduated from the
U.S. Military Academy, served with Winfield Scott during
the Mexican War, and in 1860 accepted an appointment
as inspector general of the state militia. When all efforts to
preserve Kentucky's neutrality failed, he joined the Confederate Army and led troops into Bowling Green in September
1861. Transferred to the western part of the state later that
autumn, he surrendered Fort Donelson to General Ulysses
S. Grant in February 1862. Following a prisoner exchange,
he commanded troops in the western and trans-Mississippi
theaters. After the war, Buckner worked briefly as a journalist
in New Orleans and returned to Kentucky in 1868. Following

his noteworthy term as governor of Kentucky (1887–1891), he retired to his native Hart County. (See Arndt Stickle, *Simon Bolivar Buckner: Borderland Knight* [Chapel Hill: Univ. of North Carolina Press, 1940].)

Buell, Don Carlos (1818–1898), assumed command of the Department of Ohio (which included Kentucky) in November of 1861. In February of 1862 he took control of Bowling Green and that autumn saw action against Braxton Bragg at Perryville. Shortly thereafter he was relieved of command for failing to prevent the escape of Bragg and his army after that battle. (See Stephen D. Engle, *Don Carlos Buell: Most Promising of All* [Chapel Hill: Univ. of North Carolina Press, 1999].)

Crittenden, John Jordan (1786–1863), enjoyed a long political career peppered with elections, appointments, resignations, and partially served terms in the U.S. Senate, as governor of Kentucky, and as U.S. attorney general. As the sectional crisis worsened in the months preceding the outbreak of war, Crittenden introduced a compromise designed to preserve the Union, but it, as well as the border state convention over which he presided, failed to prevent war. (See Albert D. Kirwan, *John J. Crittenden: The Struggle for the Union* [Lexington: Univ. of Kentucky Press, 1962].)

Davis, Jefferson (1808–1889), a Todd County, Kentucky, native raised in Mississippi, graduated from the U.S. Military Academy at West Point and served in the Mexican War. Appointed secretary of war by Franklin Pierce, Davis was elected to the U. S. Senate in 1847 and 1857. He was a leading supporter of states' rights and served as the only president of the Confederate States of America. (See William J. Cooper Jr., *Jefferson Davis, American* [New York: Knopf, 2000]; Steven E.

Woodworth, *Jefferson Davis and His Generals* [Lawrence: Univ. Press of Kansas, 1990].)

Douglas, Stephen A. (1813–1861), was a veteran politician from Illinois, the principal architect of the controversial 1854 Kansas-Nebraska bill, and a leading supporter of "popular sovereignty." His debates with Abraham Lincoln for the U.S. Senate in 1858 marked a high point in stump speaking and propelled Lincoln to the rank of a national figure. In 1860, Douglas ran as the Northern Democrat candidate for president and, following his defeat, gave his full support to Lincoln. He worked tirelessly in the Senate to preserve the Union. (See Robert Johannsen, *The Frontier, the Union and Stephen A. Douglas* [Urbana: Univ. of Illinois Press, 1989].)

Dulaney, William L. (1838–1904), read law with Judge William V. Loving and during the war rode with John Hunt Morgan. In the postwar decades he served two terms as judge of Warren County's common pleas court and a single term as judge of the circuit court.

Etheridge, Henry Emerson (1811–1902), a West Tennessee Unionist, served in the Tennessee House of Representatives, three terms in the U.S. House, and was clerk for the House from 1861 to 1863. In the postwar years he ran unsuccessfully for governor, pushed for the restoration of voting rights for former Confederates, and helped the movement that overthrew Radical Reconstruction in Tennessee.

Foote, Henry Stuart (1804–1880), studied law at Washington College and served in the U.S. Senate from 1847 to 1852, and as governor of Mississippi from 1852 to 1854. He moved to California in 1854, but returned to Mississippi in 1858 and shortly thereafter moved to Tennessee and represented the Volunteer State in the Confederate Congress. President Hayes appointed the postwar Republican as superintendent of the mint at New Orleans.

Forrest, Nathan Bedford (1821–1877), is best known as one of the finest of the Confederacy's military leaders. Prior to the war he acquired a substantial fortune as a planter and slave dealer, and in the postwar years the Tennessean was instrumental in the formation of the KKK. (See John A. Wyeth, *Life of General Nathan Bedford Forrest* [1898; reprinted as *That Devil Forrest* (New York: Harper, 1959)].)

Freeman, Terah M., enlisted at Camp Boone in July 1861. Following the evacuation of Bowling Green, he went to Fort Donelson. Taken prisoner when Donelson was surrendered, Freeman later escaped from Camp Morton and joined John Hunt Morgan's cavalry, serving as a lieutenant and as adjutant of the 4th Kentucky Cavalry Regiment.

Grafton, Thomas (d. 1862), a Mississippi attorney practicing in Memphis during the winter of 1860–1861, joined the Shelby Grays but later resigned, enrolled in a Mississippi regiment, and achieved the rank of major. Grafton died at the Battle of Fair Oaks, Virginia.

Grant, Ulysses S. (1822–1885), was a graduate of the U.S. Military Academy. The Ohio native saw action in the Mexican War, and on the eve of the Civil War he helped organize companies of Illinois volunteers. In May of 1861 Lincoln appointed Grant to command the 21st Illinois. A few days after assuming his command, he led his troops into Paducah, and six months later moved against Fort Donelson and Fort Henry. When Buckner asked for his terms, Grant answered "unconditional surrender," thus earning his nickname. Grant also saw action at Shiloh and Vicksburg. Following Grant's success in eastern Tennessee, Lincoln appointed him as the commander of all the armies of the United States. On April 9, 1865, Lee surrendered to Grant at Appomattox. Three years later the grateful nation elected Grant to be the eighteenth president of the United States. (See Michael Korda, *Ulysses S. Grant: The Unlikely Hero* [New York: HarperCollins, 2004].)

Grider, Henry (1796–1866), practiced law in Bowling Green. A Whig, then Democrat, Grider served four terms in the state legislature and was elected to five terms in the U.S. Congress (1843–1866). His son **Benjamin** (1826–1874) married Josie's sister, Frances (Fanny), and his daughter **Jane** (1829–1913) served as Josie's companion and chaperone during the trip to Memphis.

Grider, Tobias (1824–1882), was the grandson of one of Bowling Green's founders, Robert Moore. Shortly after their marriage he and his wife built a fine home that still stands. In recent years it has been known as the Deemer home

Gwin, William (1805–1885), was a graduate of the Medical Department at Transylvania and served as a representative from Mississippi in the 27th Congress. On moving to California, he was reelected to the Senate, where he served from 1850 to 1861. Gwin joined the Confederate Army and later served as one of the spokesmen between the Confederacy and Maximilian's Mexican Imperial Government.

Gwyn, Hugh (b. 1836), is listed on the 1860 census as a railroad engineer. In the autumn of 1861 he joined a Confederate regiment and left the state.

Hall, Mike (1827–1866), was a Bowling Green merchant and the son of Edmund (1785–1837) and **Nancy Burnam Hall** (1800–1865). At the outbreak of the war he lived with his mother and widowed sister, Mary Ann Hodge (1821–1886), in a small brick house near the railroad depot, where Warner and Lucy Underwood lived during the early years of their marriage. The structure still stands and in recent years has served as a Standard Oil gas station and a tire shop.

Hardee, William J. (1815–1873), a graduate of West Point and an able tactician, served in the Mexican War and a few years later prepared a tactics manual for the Army. The manual was used by both Union and Confederate officers during the Civil War. In the early days of 1861 Hardee resigned his commission and joined the Confederate forces. He led attacks at Shiloh, Perryville, and Murfreesboro and saw action in eastern Tennessee and Georgia. At the war's end Hardee and his men were in North Carolina. (See Nathaniel Cheairs Hughes, *General William J. Hardee: Old Reliable* [Baton Rouge: Louisiana State Univ. Press, 1965].)

Hobson, Atwood G. (1815–1898), began building a fine Italianate home on the eastern edge of Bowling Green before the war's onset. Realizing the strategic importance of his hilltop building site, Hobson, then in the Union army, sent a message to General Simon Bolivar Buckner asking that his unfinished home not be destroyed. Buckner agreed, and the Confederates merely used it for the storage of arms and constructed a fort nearby. Hobson's lovely Italianate home, Riverview at Hobson Grove, was completed in 1872. Today it is a history museum and is open to the public.

Holt, Joseph (1804–1894), from Breckinridge County, worked on behalf of the 1856 candidacy of James Buchanan and under

Buchanan served as commissioner of patents, postmaster general, and secretary of war. A staunch Unionist, Holt strove diligently to hold Kentucky in the Union and in 1864 was named to head the new Bureau of Military Justice; in the latter position he played a conspicuous role in numerous courts-martial and in the trial of Lincoln's assassins. In lieu of a biography of Judge Holt, see Edward Steers Jr., *Blood on the Moon: The Assassination of Abraham Lincoln* (Lexington: Univ. Press of Kentucky, 2001), and Henry Burnett, *Some Incidents in the Trial of President Lincoln's Assassins: The Controversy between President Johnson and Judge Holt* (New York: D. Appleton, 1891).

Johnson, George W. (1811–1862), supported John C. Breckinridge in 1860 but denied that Lincoln's election justified secession. However, when Kentucky's neutrality ended, the Scott County native became a volunteer aide for General Buckner. A key figure in the Russellville conventions, he accepted the position of the Confederate governor of Kentucky. His jurisdiction, however, extended only to the area under C.S.A. control, and when the Confederates abandoned Kentucky in February of 1862, he followed the army southward. At Shiloh he joined the 4th Kentucky Infantry, was wounded during the battle, and died the following day. (See Lowell H. Harrison, "George W. Johnson and Richard Hawes: The Governors of Confederate Kentucky," *Register of the Kentucky Historical Society* 79 [winter 1981]: 3–39.)

Johnston, Albert Sidney (1803–1862), served as the Director of the Army of the West, a Confederate military line that stretched from the Appalachian Mountains across south central Kentucky to the Mississippi River. The Mason County native established his headquarters in Bowling Green. Unfortunately, defeats at Fort Donelson and Fort Henry forced him to pull his army back to northern Mississippi. Late on the first day of battle at Shiloh, as he and his medical director inspected the field, Johnston asked the latter to remain and care for a group of Union prisoners. Shortly thereafter a bullet tore open the artery in the back of Johnston's knee and he bled to death. (See Charles P. Roland, *Albert Sidney Johnston: Soldier of Three Republics* [Austin: Univ. of Texas Press, 1964; reprint, Lexington: Univ. Press of Kentucky, 2001].)

Loving, William Voltaire (1803–1896), a Warren County judge and businessman, served several terms in the state legislature and was appointed commonwealth attorney and then circuit judge for the Sixth District. Nominated for governor in 1855, he was forced by ill health to withdraw his name; the nomination went to Charles S. Morehead, who became Kentucky's nineteenth governor. Josie's nephew, "Judgie," was named for Judge Loving.

Magoffin, Beriah (1815–1885), believed in the right of secession but hoped to prevent it. At the onset of war Governor Magoffin rejected both U.S.A. and C.S.A. requests for troops, and when the legislature voted for neutrality he proclaimed the state's policy on May 20, 1861. By late February 1862, the Union army controlled the state, yet Unionists distrusted Magoffin. In August of that year he indicated he would resign if replaced by a conservative. His lieutenant governor, Linn Boyd, had died shortly after the election, and Magoffin refused to accept the Speaker of the House, John Fisk, as governor. When Fisk resigned and was replaced by moderate James Robinson, Magoffin bowed out in favor of Robinson and returned to his law practice. (See Lowell H. Harrison, "Governor Magoffin and the Secession Crisis," *Register of the Kentucky Historical Society* 72 [April 1974]: 91–110.)

Mallory, Robert (1815–1885), an attorney from New Castle and a Union Democrat, served as a representative from Kentucky in the U.S. House from 1859 to 1865.

McClellan, George B. (1826–1885), became one of the more controversial figures of the war. A West Point graduate, he saw action in the Mexican War, served as instructor at his alma mater, worked as chief engineer of the Illinois Central Railroad, and became president of the Ohio and Mississippi Railroad. Three weeks after he joined the Ohio Volunteers, Lincoln appointed him major general, outranked only by Winfield Scott. McClellan succeeded Scott on the latter's resignation in November 1861. Despite great promise, McClellan overestimated the enemy and time after time seemed unable to win; he was replaced in late 1862 by Ambrose Burnside, and then by Joe Hooker a few months later. In 1864 McClellan unsuccessfully ran for president, carrying only three states. In the postwar era he served a single term as governor of New Jersey. (See Stephen W. Sears, *George B. McClellan: The Young Napoleon* [New York: Tichnor and Fields, 1988].)

McCook, Alexander (1831–1902), was the highest ranking of the fourteen "fighting McCooks" who saw Civil War service. A former instructor of tactics at West Point, he commanded a brigade in Kentucky, and later the 2nd Division of the Army of Ohio at the capture of Nashville, the Battle of Shiloh, and the siege of Corinth. He also directed a corps at the battles and campaigns of Perryville, Murfreesboro, Tullahoma, and Chickamauga.

Morgan, John Hunt (1825–1864), conducted guerrilla warfare along the Green River during the fall of 1861 and became well known for his effective raids behind enemy lines, cutting communications and supply lines and spreading fear. His most strategic raid resulted in the burning of the L&N

tunnels near Gallatin, Tennessee, in the fall of 1862, thus disrupting the supply line for the Army of the Ohio. On September 4, 1864, he was killed at Greeneville, Tennessee. (See James A. Ramage, *Rebel Raider: The Life of General John Hunt Morgan* [Lexington: Univ. Press of Kentucky, 1986].)

Norton, George (1814–1889), a prominent Logan County banker and businessman, married Lucy Underwood's sister **Martha Henry**. During her school days in Russellville, Josie visited frequently with her aunt and uncle and their children, **Juliette** and **Earnest**. During the Confederate occupation of south central Kentucky, Norton, then president of the Southern Bank of Kentucky, expressed concern about the bank's funds, lest they be confiscated by the Southern forces. When the Confederate provisional government showed interest in the bank's money, George and the cashier, Marmaduke Morton, removed the bank's funds to a safe place, returning them after the Confederate evacuation. George was one of six boys; his youngest brother, Eckstein, was the beau mentioned in the diary sometimes as E, Ed, and Ex.

Prentice, George Dennison (1802–1870), one of the state's leading journalists, possessed a talent for writing short paragraphs filled with wit, humor, and sarcasm. While editor of the *Louisville Journal,* his paper became a popular newssheet throughout the state and Ohio Valley and became an important voice for the Whig and later the Constitutional Union parties. Despite his strong Union sentiments, both of Prentice's sons fought for the Confederacy. (See Betty Carolyn Congleton, "George D. Prentice: Nineteenth Century Southern Editor," *Register of the Kentucky Historical Society* 65 [April 1967]: 94–119.)

Rodes, Clifford (1839–1930), son of staunch Unionist Robert Rodes of Bowling Green, served in the postwar years as president of Citizens National Bank of Louisville.

Rousseau, Lovell Harrison (1818–1869), fought in the Mexican War, practiced criminal law in Louisville, and in 1860 was elected to the Kentucky House of Representatives. At the war's outbreak the Lincoln County native helped raise troops for the Union, joined the army, and by October 1861 had been promoted to brigadier general. Rousseau saw action at Shiloh, Perryville, Chickamauga, Nashville, and in Alabama, Mississippi, and western Tennessee.

Rutherford, Tom, served briefly as tutor to the Underwood children. Shortly after the war began he returned to Virginia.

Salm-Salm, Felix von (1828–1870), the younger son of a reigning minor German monarch, came to the United States in 1861, joined the Union Army, and commanded a New York regiment in Virginia and Tennessee. His wife, a Vermont native, traveled with him during the war and helped care for the sick and injured. At the war's end the prince joined Maximilian's army in Mexico. He was captured by the Mexican forces, unsuccessfully appealed to Benito Juárez for the life of the emperor, and, following Maximilian's execution, returned to Europe. He died in battle during the Franco-Prussian War. (See Agnes Salm-Salm, *Ten Years of My Life* [New York: R. Worthington, 1876].)

Sigel, Franz (1824–1902), a German immigrant and commander of the 3rd Missouri Volunteers, saw action in Missouri, Arkansas, and Virginia and was defeated by Kentuckian John C. Breckinridge at the Battle of New Market. An inept commander, Sigel nevertheless excelled in recruiting and motivating German immigrants who spoke little English beyond "I fights mit Sigel."

Skiles, Henry Hamilton (1832–1889), Josie's first cousin, received a law degree from Harvard in 1856 and a few years later purchased and became editor of the *Bowling Green Gazette*. Following a fire that destroyed his printing office, the staunch Unionist served four years as county attorney. After the war Skiles reestablished his newspaper. During the 1880s he served four years in the state legislature and made a fortune from investments in western lands.

Smith, Green Clay (1826–1895), enjoyed an eclectic career. The nephew of emancipationist Cassius Marcellus Clay, Smith fought in the Mexican War, practiced law with his father, served briefly in the state legislature, joined the 4th Kentucky Cavalry in March 1862, and by that summer had risen to the position of brigadier general. He resigned his commission in 1863 and in 1866 accepted the position of territorial governor of Montana. Ordained in 1869, he became pastor of a Frankfort, Kentucky, church, was a candidate of the National Prohibition Party in 1876, and spent the last five years of his life as pastor of a Baptist church in the nation's capital.

Talleyrand, Charles-Maurice de (1754–1838), was a French statesman and diplomat noted for his capacity for political survival. Talleyrand held high positions in the French government during the French Revolution, under Napoleon, and at the restoration of the Bourbons. His American contemporaries perhaps knew him best as the instigator of the XYZ affair.

Torian, Jacob (b. 1805), was a Memphis attorney and the

partner of Josie's brother-in-law William Western. Torian and his wife, Casiah, were strong Unionists.

Todd, John, son of Warner's sister Malvina (Aunt Mal), graduated from West Point and was stationed at the Baton Rouge Arsenal when it fell to Louisiana state troops. Todd later resigned his commission and joined the Confederate Army.

Turchin, John Basil (1822–1901), Ivan Vasilovitch Turchinoff, trained at Russia's Imperial Military School in St. Petersburg, immigrated to the United States, and worked for the engineering department of the Illinois Central Railroad. He received a commission in the Union Army in the summer of 1861. Because he supported the European idea that to the victor belonged the spoils, his regiment was known for its disregard for civilians and their property. Courtmartialed (but pardoned) for his actions, he resigned his commission in 1863. (See Stephen Chicoine, *John Basil Turchin and the Fight to Free the Slaves* [Westport, Conn.: Praeger, 2003].)

Ward, John H., read law with Warner Underwood. A strong Unionist, the Green County native's name appeared on a May 1861 note to President Lincoln as one of a half-dozen Kentuckians recommended to supervise the distribution of arms across the commonwealth. The day after the Confederates arrived in Bowling Green, Ward enrolled in the 27th Volunteer Infantry Regiment (U.S.A.). He served as a lieutenant colonel and colonel in the Federal army.

Williams, John Stuart (1818–1898), served in the Mexican War and won his nickname, Cerro Gordo, which Josie misspelled, at the Battle of Cerro Gordo. Opposed to secession, the Bourbon County native nevertheless joined the Confederacy, rose to the rank of brigadier general, and during the postwar years enjoyed a prominent career in politics.

Wright, Ann Elizabeth (Lizzie) (1842–1931), daughter of Dr. Thomas Briggs Wright and Andromache Loving Wright, lived in a home on the current site of the State Street Methodist Church. She and Josie had been close friends since early childhood, but the pro-Confederate sentiments of Lizzie and her brothers **Cooper** and **Webb** jeopardized their relationship. In January 1866, Lizzie married Richard C. Thomas, a graduate of the Nashville Medical College, who had served in the Confederate medical service throughout the war. Their three sons became a local judge, minister, and physician. Lizzie's brothers also achieved prominence. Webb practiced law; Cooper became a physician.

Yandell, Lunsford, Jr. (1838–1884), a member of a prominent Louisville medical family, graduated from the Medical Department of the University of Louisville, practiced briefly in Louisville, and in the summer of 1860 accepted an appointment on the faculty of the faltering Memphis Medical College. In the spring of 1861 Yandell joined a Tennessee cavalry unit and spent the autumn and winter of 1861–1862 at Columbus, Kentucky. After the evacuation of Columbus, Yandell went to Nashville, then Corinth, and helped care for the wounded at Shiloh. He served with General William J. Hardee's army for the remainder of the war. Returning to Louisville, he joined the faculty at the University of Louisville. (See Nancy D. Baird, "A Kentucky Physician Examines Memphis," *Tennessee Historical Quarterly* 37 [summer 1978]: 190–202; and Nancy D. Baird, "There Is No Sunday in the Army," *Filson Club History Quarterly* 53 [October 1979]: 317–27.)

Yandell, David (1826–1898), Lunsford's older brother, studied medicine at the Medical Department of the University of Louisville as well as in England and France, and accepted a position on the U of L medical faculty in the late 1850s. During the war he served as Medical Director of the Army of the West, and following Johnston's death as medical director and physician for the armies of Braxton Bragg, Joe E. Johnston, and Edmund Kirby-Smith. When asked later about his wartime medical experiences, he indicated that the war had been a "great, though terrible school" for learning surgical techniques. In 1866, Yandell rejoined the faculty of the University of Louisville and taught surgery for about twenty-five years. In 1872 his fellow physicians elected him president of the American Medical Association. (See Nancy Disher Baird, *David Wendel Yandell: Physician of Old Louisville* [Lexington: Univ. Press of Kentucky, 1978].)

Zollicoffer, Felix (1812–1862), served in the Tennessee legislature and in the U.S. Congress prior to the war. A strong states' rights advocate, he supported John Bell in 1860 and was a member of the 1861 Washington Peace Conference. However, in July 1861 he accepted a commission in the Confederate Army and was sent to eastern Tennessee. He led troops into Kentucky that autumn and in January 1862 engaged Union forces at Mill Springs. During the Mill Springs confrontation, the near-sighted Zollicoffer rode into a Federal unit and was shot, the first Confederate general officer killed during the war. (See Raymond Myers, *The Zollie Tree* [Louisville: The Filson Club, 1964].)

❧ NOTES ❧

INTRODUCTION

1. J. E. Carnes to Josie Underwood, January 28, 1860 (Henry Underwood Collection, Kentucky Library, Western Kentucky University). Russellville is about thirty miles south of Bowling Green.

2. Journal of Agatha Rochester Strange (Strange Collection, Kentucky Library), typescript, 60–61.

3. Diary of Warner Underwood, February 11, 1849; Aug. 17, 1864 (Underwood Collection, Kentucky Library, Western Kentucky University); *Speech of Mr. Warner L. Underwood, Delivered in the House of Representatives, August 5, 1856* (Washington, D.C.: n.p., 1856), 2. The Know Nothing Party was a strong outgrowth of the nativist political movement, which culminated in the Bloody Monday election-day riot in Louisville. See Wallace B. Turner, "The Know Nothing Movement in Kentucky," *Filson Club History Quarterly* 28 (July 1954): 266–83; Agnes G. McCann, *Nativism in Kentucky to 1860* (Washington, D.C.: Catholic University of America, 1944). The 1850–1851 letters of Elizabeth Underwood (Underwood Collection) contain considerable information about preparing a family of slaves for their trip to Liberia.

4. *Speech of Hon. W. L. Underwood of Kentucky Against the Admission of Kansas as a State Under the LeCompton Constitution: Delivered in the House of Representatives, March 30, 1858* (Washington, D.C.: n.p., 1858), 10. The sectional tensions that alarmed the Underwoods had haunted the nation since its beginning and accelerated after Missouri requested statehood in 1820. Despite the Missouri Com-

promise, the issue continued to fester; it exploded again in 1850 when California asked to be admitted as a free state. Thereafter, radical hotheads in and out of Congress made the slavery question an issue that overshadowed all else, as they argued about its morality, constitutionality, and economics. Fearing that a majority in Congress might outlaw the institution, many southerners quoted from the Kentucky and Virginia Resolutions of 1798–1799. The documents stated that free and independent states had created the national government and had delegated to it "certain and definite powers." If federal law violated the constitution or the rights of individual states, they could declare such laws null and void. Carried to its extreme, separation from the union was a viable, legal alternative. Numerous published studies address the states' rights issue, including: Don E. Fehrenbacher, *The South and Three Sectional Crises* (Baton Rouge: Louisiana State Univ. Press, 1980); Michael F. Holt, *Political Crisis of the 1850s* (New York: Wiley Publishers, 1978); Robert V. Remini, *Henry Clay: Statesman for the Union* (New York: Norton, 1991); William J. Watkins Jr., *Reclaiming the American Revolution: The Kentucky and Virginia Resolutions and Their Legacy* (New York: Palgrave Macmillan, 2004); John C. Waugh, *On the Brink of Civil War: The Compromise of 1850 and How It Changed the Course of American History* (Wilmington, Del.: Scholarly Resources, 2003).

5. Diary of Lemuel C. Porter, January 1, 1861 (The Filson Historical Society, Louisville, Kentucky). In the 1860 election, Kentuckians gave Bell 66,051 votes; Breckinridge 53,143; Douglas 25,638; and Lincoln 1,364 (only forty-two of which came from the seven counties of south central Kentucky—five in Butler, five in Warren, three in Logan, fourteen in Barren; fifteen in Edmonson and none in Allen and Simpson).

6. Abraham Lincoln to Orville H. Browning, September 22, 1861, in Roy P. Basler, ed., *The Collected Works of Abraham Lincoln,* 9 vols. (New Brunswick, N.J.: Rutgers Univ. Press, 1953–55), 4:539. The often repeated statement that Lincoln hoped God was on his side but that he had to have Kentucky can be found in E. Merton Coulter, *The Civil War and Readjustment in Kentucky* (Chapel Hill: Univ. of North Carolina Press, 1926), 53.

7. Beriah Magoffin to Simon Cameron, April 15, 1861, in *The*

War of the Rebellion: A Compilation of the Official Records of the Union and Confederate Armies, 128 vols. (Washington D.C.: Government Printing Office, 1880–1901), series III, vol. 1, 79 (hereafter cited as *O.R.*). In mid-summer the Union began recruiting soldiers in eastern Kentucky and in August established Camp Dick Robinson in Garrard County, thus further violating the state's neutrality. For additional information on Kentucky's role in the crisis and conflict, see Lowell H. Harrison, *The Civil War in Kentucky* (Lexington: Univ. Press of Kentucky, 1975); Coulter, *The Civil War and Readjustment in Kentucky*; biographies of various Kentuckians, regimental histories, and studies of battles fought in Kentucky and in which Kentuckians participated.

8. Mary Julia Neal, *The Journal of Eldress Nancy: Kept at the South Union, Kentucky, Shaker Colony, August 15, 1861–September 4, 1864* (Nashville: Parthenon Press, 1963), 9. Camp Boone was near Guthrie (about fifty miles southwest of Bowling Green) on the Kentucky-Tennessee border. The settlement at South Union (about fifteen miles south of Bowling Green) suffered greatly during the war, for both armies expected the Shakers to supply food, horses, and medical care for their troops.

9. "Reminiscences of Elizabeth Gaines" (SC 999, Kentucky Library, Western Kentucky University), 8.

10. John Hill to his sister, November 24, 1861 (SC 811, Kentucky Library, Western Kentucky University); James McWhirter to sister Zellora, January 18, 1862 (SC 181, Kentucky Library, Western Kentucky University).

11.Charles R. Mott Jr., ed., "War Journal of a Confederate Officer," *Tennessee Historical Quarterly,* 5 (September 1946): 238; R. F. Bunting to editors, January 19, 1862, in *San Antonio Herald,* February 15, 1862 (Robert Franklin Bunting Papers, University of Texas-Austin).

12. Mott, "War Journal of a Confederate Officer," 237–38.

13. The small rural communities of Oakland and Dripping Springs are about ten miles northeast and twenty miles north, respectively, from Bowling Green.

14. David W. Yandell to W. W. Mackall, November 23, 1861 (Papers Relating to David W. Yandell, General and Staff Officers' File,

Old Army Section, National Archives, Washington, D.C.). Concerned about the large number of bodies buried in shallow graves, in the spring of 1862 Joseph Underwood requested that the legislature order that a "sanitary survey" be conducted of the Bowling Green area; his request apparently was ignored. Less concerned about sanitation than aroma, on March 8, 1862, the pro-Union *Louisville Daily Journal* quipped that live Confederates smelled bad but dead ones smelled even worse!

15. J. Fraise Richard, ed., *The Florence Nightingale of the Southern Army: Experiences of Mrs. Ella K. Newsom, Confederate Nurse in the Great War of 1861–1865* (New York: Broadway Publishers, 1914), 17–18.

16. Simon B. Buckner to Warner L. Underwood, October 4, 1861, *O.R.*, ser. II, vol. 3, 725.

17. The Federal victory on January 19 at Mill Springs and the surrender of Fort Henry on February 6 destroyed both ends of the Confederate defensive line across southern Kentucky and made possible Union penetration into the Confederacy through Cumberland Gap and the Tennessee River. Thus Albert Sidney Johnston decided to pull back and establish his line at Nashville; after the fall of Fort Donelson on the Cumberland River in mid-February, he began to move his army farther south. The Confederate defeat at Mill Springs harmed the Southern cause, but the fall of the western Kentucky forts was a catastrophe for the South and a great morale boost for the North. See Benjamin F. Cooling, *Forts Henry and Donelson: The Key to the Confederate Heartland* (Knoxville: Univ. of Tennessee Press, 1987); David Dalton, "Zollicoffer, Crittenden and the Mill Springs Campaign," *Filson Club History Quarterly* 60 (October 1986): 463–71; "Reminiscences of Elizabeth Gaines," 12.

18. Paul G. Ashdown, "Samuel Ringgold: An Episcopal Clergyman in Kentucky and Tennessee during the Civil War," *Filson Club History Quarterly* 53 (July 1979): 235; John Atkinson to Agnes Frier, May 10, 1866 (SC 715, Kentucky Library, Western Kentucky University); John Beatty, *Memoirs of a Volunteer* (New York: Norton, 1946), 85; Frank Moore, *The Rebellion Record: A Diary of American Events. . . . ,* 11 vols. (New York: Putnam, 1862–1868), 4:136. A literary work published by the young ladies at Potter College in Bowling Green also relates Ringgold's activities, as well as the arrival of

Union troops and their bombardment of the town. See "A History of Bowling Green," *The Green and Gold* 1 (March 1903): 4. In his official report of February 15, Brigadier General Ormsby Mitchell confirmed the damage to town buildings and the railroad and the abundance of abandoned supplies. He planned to distribute the flour and beef to area civilians; his army would use the shoes, tents, saddles, and other military supplies (*O.R.*, ser. I, vol. 7, 419–20).

19. Josephine Covington to Judge Wells, March 2, 1862 (SC 236, Kentucky Library, Western Kentucky University; the original letter belongs to the Filson Historical Society, Louisville); Atkinson to Frier, May 10, 1866 (SC 715).

20. Diary of Mary E. Van Meter, March 1, 1863 (typescript, Kentucky Library, Western Kentucky University); Obadiah Knapp to "Friend William," April 9, July 17, 1864 (Knapp Collection, University of Texas-Austin).

21. Diary of Henry Underwood, January 6, July 20, 1863 (Underwood Collection, Kentucky Library, Western Kentucky University). Young boys, then as now, apparently found the macabre fascinating. David Rizzio, the supposed lover of Mary Queen of Scots, was murdered in her bedroom in March 1566.

22. Underwood kept a close eye on the shipyard constructing the screw steamer *Pampero* and searched for evidence to prove the ship violated Britain's neutrality agreement. Eventually, he hired several spies and obtained the proof he sought. In December 1863, Scotland officials ordered the ship taken into custody. For an overview of Warner Underwood's activities in Scotland, see Neill Fred Sanders, "Lincoln's Consuls in the British Isles, 1861–1865" (Ph.D. diss., University of Missouri, 1971). Many of Warner Underwood's letters written during his two years in Scotland can be found in the Thomas Dudley Collection (Huntington Library, San Marino, California) and in the State Department Records: Consular Dispatches (Library of Congress, Washington, D.C.).

23. Henry Underwood to Warner Underwood, June 7, 1866; Josie to Henry Underwood, March 12, 1882 (Henry Underwood Collection, Kentucky Library, Western Kentucky University). Today, the Mt. Ayr subdivision contains some of the community's finest homes. Its earliest owners had spelled the farm's name "Mt.

Ayr"; however, Warner Underwood thought "Ayr" was pretentious and changed the spelling after he purchased the land.

24. Josie Nazro to Henry Underwood, October 8, 1882, March 12, 1889 (Henry Underwood Collection, Kentucky Library, Western Kentucky University); Underwood Family Bible (Kentucky Library, Western Kentucky University).

25. [Bowling Green] *Park City Daily News,* November 14, 16, 1923; Last Will and Testament of Josie Underwood Nazro, November 1923 (Warren County Clerk's Office, Bowling Green).

CHAPTER ONE

1. Josie's traveling companion and chaperone, Jane, was the sister of her brother-in-law Benjamin Grider.

2. "The Lady of Lyon" was a popular play written by the English politician-poet-novelist Edward Bulwer-Lytton (1803–1873).

3. Josie's quote of Ellen Douglas is from "Lady in the Lake," by Sir Walter Scott.

4. Eckstein (Ex) Norton, a friend and suitor during her school days in Russellville, was the much younger brother of her uncle George Norton.

5. Josie seems a bit mixed up. She "promoted" her cousin to major; he was a lieutenant. She also wrote of the surrender of the arsenal four days before the event. On January 11 the armory's commander, Brevet General J. A. Haskin informed U.S. Adjutant General C. Cooper that he had surrendered the Baton Rouge Arsenal the previous evening at about five o'clock. In a dispatch addressed to Colonel H. K. Craig, Chief of Ordinance Department, U.S. Army, and dated January 10, 1861, Lieutenant John W. Todd, U.S. Ordnance Department, wired the Chief of Ordnance Department, "The arsenal was surrendered this evening to the Governor of Louisiana. . . . Please give me instructions where to proceed with the detachment under my command" (*O.R.,* ser. I, vol. 1, 490–91). Neither Baton Rouge nor New Orleans newspaper accounts of the surrender mention Aunt Mal's (Malvina Todd) majestic retreat from the fort. Nor has it apparently appeared in the eyewitness accounts of other participants at the surrender.

6. A popular five-act play, *Ingomar, the Barbarian* addressed the power of female love and virtue over rude barbarian strength.

7. Tennessee law neither forbade nor declared legal the marriages between slaves. See R. J. Meigs and William F. Cooper, eds., *The Code of Tennessee* (Nashville: E. G. Eastman, 1858), 480–88.

8. Brown's Lock, a few miles down river from Bowling Green, was one of four locks constructed on the Barren River by the federal government during the 1830s.

9. The Shelby Grays were a pro-southern military group in Memphis.

10. One of the addresses by Charles-Maurice de Talleyrand-Perigord (1754–1838) contained the line: "Speech was given to man to disguise his thoughts." A prominent statesman of the French Revolution, Napoleonic era, and restoration period, Talleyrand perhaps is best remembered by Americans for his part in the XYZ affair.

CHAPTER TWO

1. The origin of the nickname "dark and bloody ground" is unknown. Historians surmised that after the extermination of the Allegewi (early inhabitants of Kentucky) in the fifteenth and sixteenth centuries, the area immediately south of the Ohio River became known in Indian lore as "dark and bloody." At the signing of the Treaty of Sycamore Shoals (1775), Cherokee Chief Dragging Canoe is said to have tried to discourage settlement by warning Richard Henderson and others that the land beyond the Kentucky River was a "bloody ground" that would be "dark and difficult to settle."

2. The Buckner State Guard was the state militia. Although Kentucky was officially neutral and remained in the Union, many members of the state militia went with Buckner when he joined the Confederacy.

3. The Underwood Bible, now housed in the Kentucky Library at Western Kentucky University, contains a list of family slaves and their birthdates. Phillis, born in 1775, was the mother of nine children.

4. "Maude Muller" was one of John Greenleaf Whittier's best-known poems. The 1839 play *Richelieu,* by Edward Bulwer-Lytton, concerned a plot against Louis XIII's famous statesman Cardinal de Richelieu. The Chavalier de Mauprat was one of the conspirators. The play's second act contains the often quoted lines:

Beneath the rule of men entirely great
The pen is mightier than the sword.

5. George D. Prentice (1802–1870), editor of the *Louisville Journal,* favored Bell and the Constitutional Union Party and, following Lincoln's election, worked to keep the commonwealth in the Union. Despite his strong pro-Union sentiments, both of Prentice's sons joined the Confederate Army. See Betty Carolyn Congleton, "George D. Prentice: Nineteenth Century Southern Editor," *Register of the Kentucky Historical Society* 65 (April 1967): 94–119.

6. A French military group composed of Algerians, the Zouaves gained fame for their colorful, non-standard uniforms. During the Civil War a number of "Zouaves groups" formed in Kentucky and elsewhere.

7. Owen Lovejoy (1811–1864), a Republican congressman from Illinois, was an outspoken opponent of slavery and bitterly denounced it and the South in Congress. He also strongly supported Lincoln and Lincoln's reconstruction plan.

8. Cerro Gordo was a nickname for John Stuart Williams (1818–1898), an attorney from Paris, Kentucky, who served with distinction at the Battle of Cerro Gordo during the Mexican War. Williams fought in the Confederate Army and in the postwar years served in the state legislature. In 1875 he lost his bid for governor by a narrow margin.

Russellville's Bethel College boasted an attractive campus of about thirty acres and provided fine educations for the young men of south central Kentucky and elsewhere. Its first class graduated in 1857, and its last class left in the mid-1930s. The Union army used the school's main building as a hospital from 1862 to 1864.

Roderick Dhu, a famed Scottish chieftain, was one of the principle characters in Sir Walter Scott's "Lady of the Lake." The play concerns Dhu's fight against James V of Scotland and Dhu's love for his cousin Ellen, daughter of the outlaw Douglas.

9. Maximilien-François Robespierre (1758–1794) led the radical element during the French Revolution's Reign of Terror. In the closing days of the revolution, he met the same fate visited on many of his "enemies": he was guillotined before a cheering mob.

10. Born in the German state of Baden, Franz Sigel (1824–1902) immigrated to the United States in 1852. At the outbreak of war he organized the 3rd Missouri Volunteers, and distinguished himself in campaigns in Missouri, Arkansas, and western Virginia, but was defeated by General Breckinridge at New Market. Sigel spoke with a thick accent, which many found humorous and mocked.

11. The quote is from Lord George Gordon Byron's *Childe Harold's Pilgrimage*. John Todd eventually resigned his commission and joined the Confederate Army.

CHAPTER THREE

1. "Reminiscences of Elizabeth Gaines" (SC 999, Kentucky Library, Western Kentucky University).

2. The sentences beginning " Heavens! how I felt . . ." through "terrible grip, that will prevent its ever beating free again" were not part of the typescript but were handwritten on a separate page that appears to be either a photocopy of a page in the original or something that was to be added. When compared to letters Josie wrote during the 1880s, the addition appears to be in her handwriting. The editor has inserted it in Josie's description of and reaction to the Confederates' arrival in Bowling Green.

3. Muldraugh's Hill is a long, steep ridge about forty miles south of Louisville that rises five hundred feet above the Rolling Fork River. The ridge posed an obstacle to early transportation, and in the late 1850s the Louisville and Nashville Railroad constructed a series of tunnels and trestles to enable the train's passage. During the Civil War, the railroad (and its tunnels and trestles) was strategically important for carrying supplies to the Union army stationed in Nashville and at other points south. Today, the major north-south artery (Interstate 65) is so well banked that traffic

traverses the ridge with ease, and the traveler barely realizes the sharp elevation.

A regiment from the Lone Star State led by Benjamin Franklin Terry patrolled the road and railroad between Bowling Green and the Green River Bridge at Woodsonville. Terry was killed during a mid-December skirmish (not in September, as Josie wrote) with an Indiana regiment. Shortly thereafter, his colleagues began to call themselves "Terry's Rangers."

4. Those members of the State Guard who followed Buckner into the Confederacy did so of their own free will. They were not forced, as Josie suggests.

5. Horehound is an aromatic Eurasian plant. An extract from its bitter leaves is used as a cough remedy. The hospital to which Mrs. Underwood took the syrup and soup probably was the tent facility dubbed "Camp Recovery," located in the flat area now part of Bowling Green's Fairview Cemetery.

6. The lines are from "To October" by poet Hugh Macdonald.

7. Ewing's Ford, a few miles southeast of and up river from Bowling Green, was a shallow crossing on the Barren River; today the interstate bridge crosses the river at about Ewing's Ford. Columbia, some sixty miles east of Bowling Green, was the location of the Union's Camp Boyle.

8. The transcriber surely mistyped the number, which probably should have been "3,000." The combined Confederate forces stationed in the Bowling Green/south central Kentucky area have been estimated at between twenty thousand and twenty-five thousand. It is doubtful that all of them participated in the same drill and sham battle.

9. The Underwood home at Mount Air sat near the top of a hill overlooking the river, road, and rails through Bowling Green. Thus, it and other hilltops surrounding the town were strategically important and both armies built and manned forts on these high spots.

10. "Choirester Boys" refers to the young male members of a cathedral choir.

11. The lines are from "The Rainy Day," by Henry Wadsworth Longfellow.

CHAPTER FOUR

1. "Letters from George W. Johnson, Provisional Governor of Kentucky under the Confederates," *Register of the Kentucky Historical Society* 40 (October 1942): 353. Johnson was killed at Shiloh. See also Lowell H. Harrison, "George W. Johnson and Richard Hawes: The Governors of Confederate Kentucky," *Register of the Kentucky Historical Society* 79 (winter 1981).

2. Josiah Osburne resided in Warren County, but the cabin he loaned to the Underwoods was located in neighboring Allen County. Drakes Creek flows north from Simpson through Warren County and into the Barren River.

3. A Union victory, the Battle of Mill Springs (January 19, 1862) was the first in a series that destroyed the Confederate line of defense across southern Kentucky. Confederate casualties (125 killed, 309 wounded) included General Felix K. Zollicoffer; the Union forces, under Brigadier General George Thomas, suffered 39 killed and 207 wounded.

4. A group of self-appointed Confederate sympathizers probably composed the Council of Ten, but nothing in the town or county records mentions such a group.

5. Extant records do not indicate how long the town was shelled. Very shortly after the shelling began, several residents crossed the river and informed the Union forces that the enemy had evacuated the town; the bombardment then ceased.

In addition to torching the roundhouse and railroad depot and destroying the wooden footbridge and the railroad bridge across the Barren River, a fire destroyed about half of the north side of the square; sources differ concerning who set the fire. General William J. Hardee undoubtedly saved much of the town when he issued a warning that anyone caught torching a building would be shot without trial. Mount Air may have been the only residence destroyed by the retreating forces.

6. Josie probably meant copal Amish, a resinous substance used in making varnish and printing ink.

7. The "hill" Josie referred to is the one south of town, known to area residents as Vinegar Hill. The Confederates constructed

forts on all the hilltops surrounding the town—at Baker's Hill, home of Larkin and Polly Baker on the north side of the river (recently "topped" by the highway department); at Fort Webb, on the western edge of town, overlooking the river and adjacent to the current grounds of the Bowling Green Country Club; at the site of Riverview, the Italianate home built by Atwood Hobson after the war; on Vinegar Hill, on the south side of town and now part of the campus of Western Kentucky University; on College Hill, the current location of a commanding red, white, and blue water tower; and on the rise behind the Underwood home at Mount Air. Union forces strengthened and expanded all of the forts, especially the one on Vinegar Hill. Today, during the winter when the trees are leafless, one can stand near the water tower or look out the second story windows of WKU's Van Meter Hall and view the other hilltops and the approaches to Bowling Green. Portions of Fort Webb and the fort on Vinegar Hill (named Fort Lytle by the Union) have been preserved.

8. "Casabianca," written by Felicia Dorothea Hemans (1793–1835), concerns a young lad who:

> Stood on the burning deck
> Whence all but he had fled.
> The flame that lit the battle's wreck
> Shone round him o'er the dead.

CHAPTER FIVE

1. Samuel Starling to his daughters, March 7, 1863, Lewis-Starling Collection, Kentucky Library, Western Kentucky University.

2. Bowling Green's Green River Hotel stood on the southeast corner of the town square. Built in the 1830s and partially remodeled during the early twentieth century, the three-story structure remained in use until after World War II.

3. The April 6–7 battle at Shiloh Church (near Pittsburg Landing on the Tennessee River) in southwest Tennessee involved about sixty-five thousand Federal troops and about forty-five thousand Confederates. Each side suffered about 1,750 deaths; among the fa-

talities was General Albert Sidney Johnston, C.S.A. Pittsburg Landing is the Tennessee River boat landing near the Shiloh Church.

4. On the typescript someone wrote "not true" above the sentence indicating Grant was drunk. Although historians refute the explanation that his delay was due to inebriation, Ulysses S. Grant did have the reputation of enjoying his liquor. A rumor, probably untrue, later circulated that when Lincoln appointed Grant as commander of the Union Army, someone objected, pointing out that the general drank too much, to which Lincoln supposedly answered that he wanted to know Grant's brand so he could give it to all of his commanders!

5. Although the cry, "Morgan is coming" created fear, Morgan apparently bypassed the Bowling Green area on each of his raids into Kentucky.

6. The Sanitary Commission, founded in the early days of 1861, began as a civilian auxiliary to the Union Army's medical department. Its volunteers tended the wounded and ministered to the morale and comfort of the Union Army.

7. Camp Chase was a Union prison at Columbus, Ohio. A shinplaster was paper money issued by a private concern (and thus of questionable value), so named because of its similar appearance to the paper used in plasters for sore legs. The U.S. government began issuing paper money (greenbacks) during the Civil War.

8. Mary Todd Lincoln suffered a nervous breakdown following the February 1862 death of Willie, the Lincolns' eleven-year-old son, who died of typhoid fever.

9. Don Carlos and Margaret Buell had two daughters, Elizabeth and Emma. Prince Felix von Salm-Salm (1828–1870), the younger son of a minor German monarch, commanded a New York regiment.

10. Throughout most of the antebellum years, the Galt House was Louisville's best-known hotel. During his brief visit to Louisville in 1842, Charles Dickens stayed at the Galt House and proclaimed the hotel a "splendid" one where he and his fellow travelers were "as handsomely lodged as though we had been in Paris."

11. Franklin is a small town in Simpson County, about twenty miles south of Bowling Green.

12. Because of the high incidence of hemorrhaging and "child bed fever" (infection), childbirth was a major cause of death among young women in the nineteenth century.

13. During the May 31–June 1 Battle of Fair Oaks, Virginia (also known as Seven Pines), the Confederates suffered more than six thousand casualties. The stanza is from "Lament for the Ettrick Shepherd," by James Murray.

14. The Salt River flows through the central portion of Kentucky and some of the state's most fertile land, then empties into the Ohio near the small town of West Point.

15. The following two poems appear at the end of the diary typescript. The provenance of the first is unknown. The second is from "Adieu," by Thomas Carlyle. Both poems are reproduced here exactly as they appear in the typescript:

Mourn not for the Past; 'Tis a dream that has fled,
Its sunshine has vanished; its garlands are dead;
Deep, deep in its shadows bright hopes are laid low,
O call them not back to the land whence they go.
They have passed, but a voice lingers now on my ear
In accents which fall from some higher sphere;
Mourn not, child of earth, for the hopes that have set
Yield not to sorrow, for life's darkest day,
Gives many a sunbeam to brighten thy way;
But glean from the Past, from each blessing that flies
A gem to illumine thy crown in the skies.
The future is o'er thee! The present is thine,
To shroud it in sadness, or make it divine,
To sink in life's ocean, or find on its wave
A halo that lights e'en the gloom of the grave.

*   *   *

A long road full of pain, of pain,
  A long road full of pain
One soul, one heart, no more to part
  Tho' we ne'er meet again

My dear ——
Tho' we ne'er meet again.

The saddest tears must fall, must fall,
　　The saddest tears must fall
In weal or woe in this world below
　　I'll love thee ever and all
　　　My dear
I will love thee ever and all.

⤬ *SELECTED BIBLIOGRAPHY* ⤬

Because of the topic's fascination to both amateur and professional historians, research libraries contain hundreds of fine works about every aspect of the Civil War. Most of those selected for this bibliography are recent publications that relate to the war in Kentucky, most especially in South Central Kentucky.

MANUSCRIPT COLLECTIONS

Alexander Collection, Kentucky Library, Western Kentucky University.

Atkinson Collection, Kentucky Library, Western Kentucky University.

Robert Franklin Bunting Papers, University of Texas-Austin.

Josephine Wells Covington Letter, The Filson Historical Society, Louisville.

Diary of William P. Davis, Typescript, Kentucky Library, Western Kentucky University.

Recollections of Elizabeth Gaines, Typescript, Kentucky Library, Western Kentucky University.

Reminiscence of Martha W. Jackson, Typescript, Kentucky Library, Western Kentucky University.

Obadiah Knapp Collection, University of Texas-Austin.

Lewis-Starling Collection, Kentucky Library, Western Kentucky University.

Lemuel C. Porter Diary, The Filson Historical Society, Louisville.

Shaker Records, Kentucky Library, Western Kentucky University.

Strange Collection, Kentucky Library, Western Kentucky University.

SELECTED BIBLIOGRAPHY

Underwood Collection, Kentucky Library, Western Kentucky University.

Yandell Family Papers, The Filson Historical Society, Louisville.

BOOKS AND ARTICLES

Adams, George Worthington. *Doctors in Blue: The Medical History of the Union Army in the Civil War* (New York: Collier Books, 1952).

Attie, Jeanie. *Patriotic Toil: Northern Women and the American Civil War* (Ithaca, N.Y.: Cornell Univ. Press, 1998).

Baird, Nancy Disher. *David Wendel Yandell: Physician of Old Louisville* (Lexington: Univ. Press of Kentucky, 1978).

Baird, Nancy Disher, and Carol Crowe Carraco. *Bowling Green and Warren County: A Bicentennial History* (Bowling Green: Bicentennial Committee, 1999).

Berry, Mary Clay. *Voices from the Century Before: The Odyssey of a 19th Century Kentucky Family* (New York: Arcadia, 1997).

Bollet, Alfred Jay. *Civil War Medicine: Challenges and Triumphs* (Tucson, Ariz.: Galen Press, 2002).

Brown, Kent Masterson, ed. *Civil War in Kentucky: Battle for the Bluegrass State* (Mason City, Iowa: Savas Publishing, 2000).

Channing, Steven A. *Confederate Ordeal: The Southern Home Front* (Alexandria, Va.: Time-Life Books, 1984).

Clinton, Catherine, and Nina Silber. *Divided Houses: Gender and the Civil War* (New York: Oxford Univ. Press, 1992).

Connelly, Thomas Lawrence. *Army of the Heartland: The Army of Tennessee, 1861–1862* (Baton Rouge: Louisiana State Univ. Press, 1967).

Cooling, Benjamin Franklin. *Fort Donelson's Legacy: War and Society in Kentucky and Tennessee* (Knoxville: Univ. of Tennessee Press, 1997).

———. *Forts Henry and Donelson: The Key to the Confederate Heartland* (Knoxville: Univ. of Tennessee Press, 1987).

Copeland, James E. "Where Were the Kentucky Unionists and Secessionists?" *Register of the Kentucky Historical Society* 71 (October 1973): 344–363.

Crocker, Helen Bartter. "A War Divides Green River Country." *Register of the Kentucky Historical Society* 70 (October 1972): 295–311.

Crofts, Daniel W. *Reluctant Confederates: Upper South Unionists in the Secession Crisis* (Chapel Hill: Univ. of North Carolina Press, 1989).

Crenshaw, Ollinger. *The Slave States in the Presidential Election of 1860* (Gloucester, Mass.: Peter Smith, 1969).

Cunningham, Horace Herndon. *Doctors in Gray: The Confederate Medical Service* (Baton Rouge: Louisiana State Univ. Press, 1958).

Daniel, Larry J. *Shiloh: The Battle That Changed the Civil War* (Baton Rouge: Louisiana State Univ. Press, 2004).

Daniel, Larry J., and Lynn N. Bock. *Island No. 10: Struggle for the Mississippi Valley* (Tuscaloosa: Univ. of Alabama Press, 1996).

Davis, William C. *Brother against Brother: The War Begins* (Alexandria, Va.: Time-Life Books, 1983).

———. *Breckinridge: Statesman, Soldier, Symbol* (Baton Rouge: Louisiana State Univ. Press, 1974).

———. *Jefferson Davis: The Man and His Hour* (New York: Harper-Collins, 1991).

Davis, William C., and Meredith L. Swentor. *Bluegrass Confederate: The Headquarters Diary of Edward O. Guerrant* (Baton Rouge: Louisiana State Univ. Press, 1999).

Dew, Aloma W. "'Between the Hawk and the Buzzard': Owensboro during the Civil War." *Register of the Kentucky Historical Society* 77 (winter 1979): 1–14.

Flannery, Michael A. *Civil War Pharmacy: A History of Drugs, Drug Supply and Provision and Therapeutics for the Union and Confederacy* (Binghamton, N.Y.: Haworth Press, 2004).

Freehling, William W. *Road to Disunion* (New York: Oxford Univ. Press, 1990).

———. *The South vs. the South: How Anti-Confederate Southerners Shaped the Course of the Civil War* (New York: Oxford Univ. Press, 2001).

Gardner, Sarah E. *Blood and Iron: Southern White Women's Narratives of the Civil War, 1861–1937* (Chapel Hill: Univ. of North Carolina Press, 2004).

Goodwin, Doris Kearns. *Team of Rivals: The Political Genius of Abraham Lincoln* (New York: Simon and Schuster, 2005).

Gorin, Betty J. *"Morgan Is Coming!": Confederate Raiders in the Heartland of Kentucky* (Louisville: Harmony House, 2006).

Hafendorfer, Kenneth A. *Perryville: Battle for Kentucky* (Owensboro, Ky.: McDowell Publishing, 1981).

Harrison, Lowell H. *The Antislavery Movement in Kentucky* (Lexington: Univ. Press of Kentucky, 1978).

————. *The Civil War in Kentucky* (Lexington: Univ. Press of Kentucky, 1975).

————. "Civil War in Kentucky: Some Persistent Questions." *Register of the Kentucky Historical Society* 76 (January 1978): 1–21.

————. "The Civil War in South Central Kentucky." *South Central Kentucky Historical Quarterly* 2 (April, July 1974): 1–4.

————. "A Confederate View of Southern Kentucky, 1861." *Register of the Kentucky Historical Society* 70 (July 1972): 163–78.

————. "George W. Johnson and Richard Hawes: The Governors of Confederate Kentucky." *Register of the Kentucky Historical Society* 79 (winter 1981): 3–39.

————. "Governor Magoffin and the Secession Crisis." *Register of the Kentucky Historical Society* 72 (April 1974): 91–110.

————. *Lincoln of Kentucky* (Lexington: Univ. Press of Kentucky, 2000).

Heck, Frank H. *Proud Kentuckian: John C. Breckinridge, 1821–1875* (Lexington: Univ. Press of Kentucky, 1976).

Heidler, David S. *Pulling the Temple Down: The Fire-Eaters and the Destruction of the Union* (Mechanicsburg, Pa.: Stackpole, 1994).

Hughes, Nathaniel Cheairs. *General William J. Hardee: Old Reliable* (Baton Rouge: Louisiana State Univ. Press, 1965).

Johannsen, Robert. *The Frontier, the Union and Stephen A. Douglas* (Urbana: Univ. of Illinois Press, 1989).

Johnson, Kenneth, ed. "The Early Civil War in Southern Kentucky as Experienced by Confederate Sympathizers." *Register of the Kentucky Historical Society* 68 (April 1970): 176–79.

Klotter, James C. *The Breckinridges of Kentucky, 1760–1981* (Lexington: Univ. Press of Kentucky, 1986).

Kirwan, Albert D. *John J. Crittenden: The Struggle for the Union* (Lexington: Univ. of Kentucky Press, 1962).

Korda, Michael. *Ulysses S. Grant: The Unlikely Hero* (New York: HarperCollins, 2004).

Lucas, Marion. *A History of Blacks in Kentucky: From Slavery to Segregation, 1760–1891* (Frankfort: Kentucky Historical Society, 1992).

Matthews, Gary Robert. *Basil Wilson Duke: The Right Man in the Right Place* (Lexington: Univ. Press of Kentucky, 2005).

McKnight, Brian D. *Contested Borderland: The Civil War in Appalachian Kentucky and Virginia* (Lexington: Univ. Press of Kentucky, 2006).

Moore, Frank, ed. *The Rebellion Record: A Diary of American Events with Documents, Narratives, Illustrative Incidents, Poetry, Etc.*, 11 vols. (New York: Putnam, 1862–1868).

Mott, Charles R., Jr., ed. "War Journal of a Confederate Officer." *Tennessee Historical Quarterly* 5 (September 1946): 234–48.

Myers, Raymond. *The Zollie Tree* (Louisville: The Filson Club, 1964).

Neal, Mary Julia. *The Journal of Eldress Nancy: Kept at the South Union, Kentucky, Shaker Colony, August 15, 1861–September 4, 1964* (Nashville: Parthenon Press, 1963).

Noe, Kenneth W. *Perryville: This Grand Havoc of Battle* (Lexington: Univ. Press of Kentucky, 2001).

Ramage, James A. *Rebel Raider: The Life of General John Hunt Morgan* (Lexington: Univ. Press of Kentucky, 1986).

Randall, James Garfield. *Lincoln and the South* (Baton Rouge: Louisiana State Univ. Press, 1946).

Reinhart, Joseph, and Peter S. Carmichael. *Two Germans in the Civil War: The Diary of John Daeuble and the Letters of Gottfried Rentschler, 6th Kentucky Volunteer Infantry* (Knoxville: Univ. of Tennessee Press, 2004).

Roland, Charles P. *Albert Sidney Johnston: Soldier of Three Republics* (Austin: University of Texas Press, 1964; reprint, Lexington: Univ. Press of Kentucky, 2001).

———. *An American Iliad: The Story of the Civil War* (Lexington: Univ. Press of Kentucky, 1991).

Schroeder-Lein, Glanda R. *Confederate Hospitals on the Move: Samuel H. Stout and the Army of Tennessee* (Columbia: Univ. of South Carolina Press, 1994).

Sehlinger, Peter J. *Kentucky's Last Cavalier: General William Preston, 1816–1887* (Frankfort: Kentucky Historical Society, 2004).

Smith, John David, and William Cooper Jr. *A Union Woman in Civil War Kentucky* (Lexington: Univ. Press of Kentucky, 2000).

Smith, Krista. "Slaveholders vs. Slaveholders: Divided Kentuckians on the Secession Crises." *Register of the Kentucky Historical Society* 97 (autumn 1999): 375–401.

Stampp, Kenneth M. *And the War Came: The North and the Secession Crisis, 1860–1861* (Baton Rouge: Louisiana State Univ. Press, 1950).

———. *The Causes of the Civil War* (Englewood Cliffs, N.J.: Prentice Hall, 1965).

Stickles, Arndt. *Simon Bolivar Buckner: Borderland Knight* (Chapel Hill: Univ. of North Carolina Press, 1940).

Stowe, Steven M. *Doctoring the South: Southern Physicians and Everyday Medicine in the Mid-Nineteenth Century* (Chapel Hill: Univ. of North Carolina Press, 2004).

Taylor, Amy Murrell. *The Divided Family in Civil War America* (Chapel Hill: Univ. of North Carolina Press, 2005).

Troutman, Richard, ed. *The Heavens Are Weeping: The Diaries of George Richard Browder, 1852–1886* (Grand Rapids, Mich.: Zondervan Publishing House, 1987).

Volo, Dorothy Denneen, and James M. Volo, *Daily Life in Civil War America* (Westport, Conn.: Greenwood Press, 1998).

Warner, Ezra J. *Generals in Blue: Lives of the Union Commanders* (Baton Rouge: Louisiana State Univ. Press, 1964).

Warner, Ezra J. *Generals in Gray: Lives of the Confederate Commanders* (Baton Rouge: Louisiana State Univ. Press, 1959).

The War of the Rebellion: A Compilation of the Official Records of the Union and Confederate Armies, 128 vols. (Washington, D.C.: Government Printing Office, 1880–1901).

Welcher, Frank J. *The Union Army, 1861–1865.* Volume 2: *The Western Theater.* (Bloomington: Indiana Univ. Press, 1993).

Wiley, Bell Irvin. *Confederate Women* (Westport, Conn.: Greenwood Press, 1975).

———. *Life of Billy Yank, the Common Soldier of the Union* (Baton Rouge: Louisiana State Univ. Press, 1978).

————. *The Life of Johnny Reb: The Common Soldier of the Confederacy* (New York: Bobbs-Merrill, 1943).

Winston, Norma Dix. "George D. Prentice and Secession in Kentucky" (Master's thesis, University of Chicago, 1930).

Wyeth, John A. *Life of General Nathan Bedford Forrest* (New York, 1898); reprinted as *That Devil Forrest: Life of General Nathan Bedford Forrest* (New York: Harper, 1959).

❦ *INDEX* ❧